Wolf Warriors V
Wolves in Time

Edited By
Sendokidu Adomi

A Thurston Howl Publications Book

WOLF WARRIORS V: WOLVES IN TIME

Copyright © 2019

First Edition, 2019. All rights reserved.

A Thurston Howl Publications Book
Published by Thurston Howl Publications
thurstonhowlpublications.com
Lansing, MI

Edited by Sendokidu Adomi

Printed in the United States of America
10 9 8 7 6 5 4 3 2 1

CONTENTS

The Saboteur
Rose LaCroix   1
When Balance is Lost, Who Truly Wins the Game of Life
Ann Crystal   26
Wolves and a Kohkum Spirit
Ann Crystal   27
A Life Best Lived
Fenrir Black   33
Where is Mama
HJ Pang   70
The Wolf of Gubbio
Dana Sonnenschein   71
Wolves
Virginia Romero   74
Song for a Desert Hollow
Shannon Barnsley   75
Mexican Wolf Meditation
Dana Sonnenschein   79
We'll Never Have Paris
Hermal Rana   80
The Howling Temeraire
Jonathan W. Thurston   84
New Year's Adventure: A Peter Gray Tale
Nathan Hopp   85
Petit Mal
Dana Sonnenschein   94
Wolf's Song for a Fallen Snow Cat
Ivic Wolfe   95
Instinct
HJ Pang   96
Tasmanian Wolf
SL Westerfield   132
Rocky Mountain Rose
J. Daniel Phillips   133
The Wolf's Reign
Sherayah Witcher   176

The Wolves of Eternal Return: Of Lupine Cosmology and Time
  Paulina Angela Szymonek   177
Why
  Patricia Lehtola   190
We Were Warriors...
  Sam Dutton   191
From Darkness, She Arises
  Hemal Rana   192
The Corn Wolf's Tithe
  Shannon Barnsley   196
Wisdom Keepers
  Virginia Romero   222
Wolf Speaks
  Michael Bodin   223
Wolf Watcher
  Dana Sonnenschein   227
The Wolf of Roma
  HJ Pang   229
The Ratcatchers
  Chris Albert   231
Embrace
  SL Westerfield   241
Moonlight Howl
  Travis Kane   243
Remembering the Forgotten
  HJ Pang   244
Wolf Ring
  Monique Box   251
The Red Covenant
  Dana Sonnenschein   252
Companions Across the Timeline
  Patricia Lehtola   255
Ceren
  Sorren Redpelt   256
Crossing the Line
  Virginia Romero   260
Legends
  T.F. Webb   261

WOLF WARRIORS V

THE SABOTEUR
Rose LaCroix

A pair of hawkish eyes trained on the German line from high above Chapelle D'Armentieres.

One small area on a farm just a short distance beyond the line had Cpl. Charlie Green's attention. It was scarcely twenty yards long and well-hidden behind a screen of burlap, and it looked like it should be some sort of artillery battery.

Except...it wasn't.

"Still no sign of them," the stoat grumbled to his companion, Cpl. Jim Stanwick, a dour-looking stag with a trace of a Norfolk accent. "Nothing but more bloody barrels and crates. Not a single gun in sight."

"How about them? Any luck?" Jim asked, gesturing to another balloon further down the line.

Charlie sighed. "So far as I know, they didn't see anything."

All at once, the balloon shuddered and shook. Both creatures were knocked to the floor of the basket.

The stoat scrambled to his feet first, peering apprehensively over the edge of the basket. He shrieked in terror as he saw the ground moving rapidly away, the mighty tether cable that had held the balloon in place reduced to a pitiful tassel.

"Crikey, Jim! We broke loose!" he cried, grabbing a parachute and strapping it on with shaking hands.

Jim followed suit, checking the rip cord, fumbling with his straps, hastily knotting them around his waist. He slung his legs over the edge of the basket, holding for dear life onto the rope that held the basket to the envelope. "On three!" he cried. "One, two, three!"

The stag and stoat jumped, opening their chutes just in time to see the balloon soar high over no creature's land toward the German line.

On the ground, the artillery crew ran to meet them as they drifted downward. The stoat breathed a sigh of relief as he wafted toward terra firma, his booted feet planting comfortably in the soft French mud, still comfortably behind the British line.

"You alright Charlie?" asked a fox with a scar from where a bullet had grazed his cheek and taken a piece of his ear.

"None the worse for wear," the stoat declared, affecting cool detachment.

"Charlie! Come look!"

The stoat ran across the fields, his chute still dragging behind him. Jim stood near the balloon winch, holding the severed end of the tether.

"What is it?" Charlie asked.

"Look at this!" the stag declared, holding the cable right under the stoat's nose.

Charlie grabbed the cable, turning it over in his hands, carefully examining it. The strands looked like they had broken in an odd way; the fraying looked a little too even.

His breath caught in his throat. "Must have been shrapnel," he muttered.

Jim narrowed his eyes, tossing his head and dragging a hoof along the ground in agitation. "No, mate, there's no shrapnel this far from the line. That's sabotage."

Pte. David Belmont of the King's Shropshire Light Infantry kicked down a narrow-cobbled street in Armentieres.

The creatures in this town weren't so bad. Sometimes, they were a bit rude, but they were always willing to sell whatever they had. A bit of bully beef or some sweets went a long way. The shops were still open, but feeding an army had left them bare, and their few remaining items were priced accordingly. The last deck of cards David bought had cost one and six when he could get a very good deck at home for a sixpence.

His latest acquisition, the brown paper-wrapped bundle he jealously clutched under his arm, had been dear, but it was certain to make the lads smile.

Billets were in a building that, before the war, had been called "L'hotel Constitution," set back from the claustrophobic Rue de Constitution with a forecourt behind a gilded iron gate about ten yards deep and wide.

There were most of the usual crew, under an old acacia tree playing cards. Richard "Towser" Townsend, a mongrel canine, was fighting to stay expressionless. He'd hidden his infectious smile well enough, but his twitching eyebrow gave his hand away. Allen "Chumsy" Blythe, a weasel of few words and a surly Old Contemptible, wasn't concerned. Albert "Alby" Carrick, a wolf, had his eyes on his cards, entirely focused on the game for its own sake.

Conspicuously absent was Alby's brother, Willy. It wasn't like him to run off at this hour.

Chumsy played his hand. "Nineteen," he said.

Towser slapped a straight flush on the table and stopped trying to hide his silly grin.

There was a round of subdued grumbling. Alby folded quietly. Chumsy reached into his pocket and payed Towser four shillings and the remains of an assortment of sweets from home he'd been saving.

"Hullo lads," David said, setting the big, heavy bundle on the table. "I got something for you!"

The genet untied the twine and brown paper to reveal a wooden box. Wrapped inside, fresh from the churn, was about a pound of real butter formed into daintily-pressed pats with the sun, moon, and fleur de lys of the town's coat of arms.

"Crikey! Is that real butter?" Towser yelped.

"I watched them churn it!" David purred. "Only cost me three tins of bully beef."

There was a commotion in the forecourt as every creature crowded in to look. Not a single one of them had seen fresh butter since they arrived in France, much less eaten any.

"I'm going to put this away for now, somewhere cool," the genet said. "Say, you lads haven't seen our Willy, have you?"

"Took too much stomach tonic last night," Chumsy said, pulling a half-crushed woodbine from his coat pocket and lighting the tortured end of it. "He was stumbling about when they called him for sentry duty. Sarge gave him Number One,"

David gasped. "Number one? That's a bit harsh!"

Alby's ears splayed. "Sarge reckons he picked up too many vices in India. Says he needs to be whipped into shape to be a real soldier again. Had to make an example, you know."

"Do make him comfortable if you see him before I do," David said, rewrapping the butter.

"Of course," Towser murmured. "Can't envy him."

"You're a Christian, aren't you, sir? Don't you reckon one chap being crucified for my sins is enough?"

Pte. William Arthur Carrick watched Sergeant Enstone's scowl turn to a bitter grimace and braced himself in the all-too-brief moments before the otter's dirty palm gave the wolf's chops a proper crumping.

"If I were in your position," the sergeant huffed, "I wouldn't patronize an officer with so much blasphemous cheek!"

And what a position poor Willy was in! Field Punishment Number One was supposed to be done with one's feet firmly on the ground and the arms close behind; instead, Willy was on his toes with his arms bearing most of the weight, spread wide to either side.

"It's not blasphemy if it's true, sir," the wolf muttered under his breath.

The sergeant narrowed his beady eyes. "What did you say?" he hissed.

The otter grabbed his muzzle roughly and held an empty bottle of Humphrey's Tonic—a tincture of fennel, hyssop, and cannabis indica the wolf swore by—a few inches from his nose. "You had a really cushy post in India, did you!?" he screamed. "Thought you'd pick up a few local vices, did you!? You're a regular Balzac, you are! This isn't the blasted Hashish Eater's Club, sonny! This is the army! I'm going to lick you into proper shape, and it's going to hurt as much as I can get away with!"

The Sergeant stomped the wolf's toes. Willy didn't dare scream. He knew this trick already; he'd been the company whipping boy long enough. If he screamed, it would be worse.

Willy bit his lip, shutting his eyes tight. But he did not scream. He held it.

Disgusted at Willy's lack of reaction, Sgt. Enstone stormed away, his thick tail swaying behind him.

Peace and quiet at last. The fence Willy was tied to, on the edge of a field near the river Lys, was just far enough behind the lines that stray shells and bullets were rare but not unheard of. Scarcely a few yards to his right was a shell hole and a gap in the fence where a coalbox exploded about a week before. Two hours was certainly plenty of time to be hit by an errant shell or two.

He listened for that dread sound of a hurtling shell, but nothing came; the birds whistled, and a gentle breeze made the poppies dance.

About half an hour passed. Willy's wrists went numb. If he turned his head and eyes as far as both would go, he could make out his hands, starting to turn purple and bloat alarmingly.

It stopped hurting after a while. Something within began to kill the pain, and the wolf found himself back in his childhood home again. The portrait of Queen Victoria, Mother's old clock, the slight bubbling in the blue paint on the parlor walls that always reminded him of a bear wearing a chef's hat...

"Wake up, you stupid cur!"

He felt the sharp kick to his back and came back to his senses on the ground, groaning.

"The bear in the hat..." he muttered, only half aware of the meaning of his words.

"What the devil are you talking about?" the sergeant demanded.

A fox medic stepped forward, putting his hand on Willy's forehead. "It's not good, sir! He's gone barmy from the strain," he said. "You had him in a bad position. That's not how Number One's supposed to be!"

Sergeant Enstone sneered. "I'll be the judge of how to punish my men! I know this one. He's tough as an ox, he can take it. I don't see why he can't go another hour."

"You'll kill him, sir," the medic said, checking Willy's pulse. "I can't allow that on my watch, can I? The colonel'd have my nuts for breakfast on a jam tart!"

"He'll have 'em anyway. I'll see to that," the Sergeant growled. "Take him if you want, but you'll have to answer for it."

Two stretcher bearers, both of them red deer, came

forward and picked him up, placing him on a stretcher as the medic knelt over him. "You'll be right as rain in a bit," he said, patting Willy's cheek as the stretcher bearers lifted him up and carried him a tortuously long way to the dressing station about a mile up the road. Willy became aware of an immense pain in his shoulders, hands, and head as the sensation began to return to his body, and every jostle and bounce of the stretcher was like being kicked again and again.

Willy staggered back to billets later that evening. The sentry outside the gate, a pine marten, stepped aside when he saw Willy's rumpled form shambling up the lane.

Inside the old hotel and up the creaking stairway, Willy shuffled back to room 212 where five cots were set up. Towser, Chumsy, Alby, and David were sitting round a small table with...goodness, were those fresh biscuits!?

"Willy! Where've you been?" Alby called, his tail wagging.

"I've had a dreadful time of it, Alby. The Sergeant damned near crucified me," the older wolf grumbled, grabbing a chair and sitting with a soft groan.

"Old Cordite again?" David asked.

"He's the one," Willy growled, laying back his ears.

"He's been much too harsh on you," David murmured. "Here, have at these biscuits. We've all had plenty."

"How'd you manage fresh biscuits?" Willy asked.

"I found some butter. Towser and I got flour, sugar, and baking powder from some of the other lads. Cooked them best we could."

Willy took a handful of thin, irregular biscuits that were slightly burnt at the edges and devoured them. "Thank you," he rumbled.

"We're going back in the line tomorrow," Chumsy said.

"So soon?" Willy asked, tilting his head.

"Division command sent the order just a little while

ago," Alby explained. "They reckon there's going to be a big offensive, after the balloon and all."

Willy raised an eyebrow. "What balloon?"

"An observation balloon from an artillery post south of here broke free a few days ago. Damned near made landowners of the crew. They reckon it was sabotage."

"Well...I hope it wasn't," Willy said, helping himself to a few more biscuits. "Anyhow, I don't know if I can stand another patrol right now. I'm getting too old for this."

"We all are, except for Towser," David said. "Ypres put years on us."

Willy drew a sharp breath. "Let's not talk about that."

There had been seven of them when they shipped off for Le Havre in February 1915, all of them lads from Hereford, Old Contemptibles who'd been in Secunderabad before the war. They'd lost three in Ypres a few months before, and they'd nearly lost a fourth when David caught a bullet in the shoulder. Towser, the youngest of them, had only joined their little crew after they'd limped back to Dickebusch, well behind the line.

"Do you think the butter will keep?" Chumsy asked, breaking the awkward silence.

"The pests will get it if we don't. May as well give the other lads a fair whack," David said.

Alby nodded. "May as well."

The next day, Willy and the rest of 'A' Company were lined up outside the old hotel, awaiting the order to march.

Down the street marched Sgt. Enstone, a scowl on his flat brow. He was flanked by two brawny, young corporals, a wolf and a badger.

The company snapped to attention. "At ease!" the otter shouted, not breaking his stride as he marched down the line right to Willy.

"I need you to come with me," he seethed, his voice low and dangerous like a hangman. Before Willy could answer, the two corporals seized him and dragged him 'round the corner to a waiting touring car.

"In, you go," said the badger, shoving Willy into the back seat between himself and the wolf.

Sgt. Enstone climbed into the front passenger seat next to the driver, a stag with the Service Corps.

They drove off, Willy sitting in silence between the two corporals, nobody making eye contact. His heart sank. Hadn't he been punished enough? What if they were charging him with desertion? No one from the KSLI had been against the wall at Poperinghe yet. But with saboteurs about...well, maybe they'd make an example?

Willy's mouth went dry when they arrived at a former police station now being used as the brigade headquarters. The corporals dragged him from the car, up a set of creaky, wooden stairs to an office. The office door had a frosted window with 'DIRECTEUR' painted on it in tall, severe gold letters. Inside, a badger lieutenant sat behind a large oak desk.

Sgt. Enstone closed the door behind him and stood beside the desk. Willy stood to attention as the two corporals let go of his arms.

"State your name," the badger commanded.

"Carrick, sir. William Arthur."

"Your rank?"

"Private, sir."

"Private Carrick, do you know why you've been brought here?"

Willy's brow went damp. "Is it because of the stomach tonic, sir? I'm dreadfully sorry. It won't happen again!"

"You know perfectly well why you're here!" Sgt. Enstone snapped.

"That's quite enough out of you," the badger grumbled at the otter. "Private Carrick, what time did you arrive back at billets yesterday?"

"Don't know, sir. Must've been about...nine o'clock Pip-Emma, was it?"

"And where were you between four o'clock and nine o'clock?" the badger pursued, shifting forward, locking eyes with the wolf.

"At the dressing station, sir."

"The dressing station? For four hours?"

"I was in a sorry state, sir. Sergeant Enstone bloody well crucified me."

"You imbecile! I'll see you shot at dawn!" the otter screamed.

"You'll do no such thing!" the badger roared. "Were you there on the medic's advice, Private Carrick?"

"Yes, sir," the wolf murmured.

"I see," the badger replied, casting a bloodshot glare at Sgt. Enstone. "Can you tell us about the bear in the hat?"

Willy tilted his head. "Pardon?"

"You mentioned a bear in a hat yesterday, during your punishment," Sgt. Enstone said. "Would you care to explain?"

Willy shook his head. "Don't know, sir. I wasn't in any state to remember what I was saying."

"You know we have saboteurs about in this sector," the lieutenant chimed in.

Willy swallowed. "Yes, sir. Alby told me."

"Alby?"

"Private Albert James Carrick. My brother. The whole company knows about the balloon, sir."

"Yes, well..." the badger cleared his throat. "As you know, we must take certain precautions. I've seen your service record, Private Carrick, and, frankly, it's disgraceful. Rest assured, if you're lying, we will find out, and if we find out you are a saboteur or you've been consorting with one, you'd better say your prayers."

"I'm not worried," Willy said, trying not to seethe or cast a murderous glare at Sgt. Enstone. "I have nothing to hide. I'm no gentlewolf, but I'm no traitor, either!"

"Put him back in the line," the badger ordered. "That will be all."

"But sir..." Sgt. Enstone protested.

"That will be all!" the badger roared. "See him out."

Willy gave the lieutenant a smart salute and was escorted out, more politely this time, by the two corporals who had dragged him in.

The narrow strait of shell-plowed earth between the German and British lines was about twelve hundred feet across at L'Epinette, the tiny hamlet east of Armentieres where the Shropshires held the line. The summer had been warm and mild, and the trenches were relatively dry in this sector, though it was only a matter of time before a good summer rain would bring all that to a mucky end.

In a dugout, David and Towser were playing cards. Alby slept propped up against the wall. Outside the dugout, Chumsy had a Woodbine dangling on his lips and a concertina in his hands, playing an old Georgian tune and singing:

As I was a-walking all along Ratcliffe Highway,
The recruiting party came a-beating the drum.
I was listed and attested, and, before I did know,
It's to the King's duty they forced me to go.

Well, I quickly escaped, and I thought myself free
Till my cruel companions informed against me.
I was quickly followed after and brought back with speed,
In chains, I was hung, heavy irons on me.

Court martial, court martial, I very soon got
And the sentence they read was that I would be shot.
May the Lord have mercy on them for their sad cruelty,
For now the King's duty lies heavy on me.

So, if ever you're a-walking along Ratcliff Highway,
And a recruiting party comes a-beating the drum:
Don't be listed and attested into the King's army
Or else the King's duty will lie heavy on thee.

"Don't let Old Cordite hear you singing that!" said a familiar, sonorous voice from just round the bend of the fire bay.

"Is that our Willy?" Towser called.

"None other," the tall wolf said, crouching low to keep his head down. He crawled into the dugout and slouched down beside Alby. "Is Fritz behaving himself?"

The younger wolf didn't shift his position. "No more than usual," he mumbled.

"Who's on patrol tonight?" Willy asked.

"Not us," Chumsy said. "Thank God."

"So, it's more of this?"

"Afraid so, Willy," David chimed in.

Willy yawned and pulled the brim of his cap down, just like Albert. "I've no complaints," he murmured, falling asleep in the cool, smoky dugout as the afternoon grew long.

In a slightly nicer dugout, back in a reserve trench, Sgt. Enstone sat on a chair commandeered from a local farmhouse. He had his Victrola and a record of the aria "Where E'er You Walk" from Händel's *Semele* playing, a pipe on his lips, a tin of sardines and a bottle of Claret close at hand.

Simple pleasures like these made the war bearable, almost.

He heard heavy breathing and the sound of footsteps approaching. Nothing at all unusual in these trenches. But when a younger otter with a corporal's stripes stepped into the dugout with a piece of paper in hand, his heart skipped a beat.

"What is it?" Sgt. Enstone asked, running to meet the messenger.

"It's from the Lieutenant, sir!" the younger otter said, raising his hand in salute and presenting a note.

Sgt. Enstone grabbed the note and read:

<u>We are satisfied Pte. Carrick is telling the truth. Our investigation is concluded. We have found no evidence that yesterday's incident was caused by anything except a defect in the cable.</u>

Sgt. Enstone cracked a polite smile. "Thank you, Corporal. Carry on," he said, exchanging the younger otter's salute. The corporal left as quickly as he'd arrived. The Sergeant returned to his chair, lit a match, and took a nice, long draw from his pipe.

So, nothing to be afraid of? Good. But the boys in the line didn't have to know, did they? It might do them some good, after all. Keep them from getting too comfortable.

Especially Private Carrick. He wouldn't soon forget this lesson.

'A' Company were called back to a reserve trench for inspection at six o'clock that evening. Sgt. Enstone addressed them, grasping his swagger stick firmly in both hands as he paced up and down the line of nervous soldiers.

"Now, as you know, we've had some acts of sabotage in our sector. And there is no sabotage without saboteurs. I want you to all rest assured…"

The otter paused right in front of Willy, clicking his heels together.

"...that we have already interviewed all of our suspects, and we are very close to getting to the heart of this matter!"

The otter marched on down the line. "But until we have the suspect safely in irons, I want each and every one of you to do your duty. Remain vigilant! Remember that the saboteur could be anyone in this sector! You are to report anything out of the ordinary to me immediately. Is that understood?"

"Yes, sir!" the company roared in unison.

"All except privates Belmont, Townsend, and Blythe are dismissed!" the otter called.

The three creatures whose names had been called gathered round Sgt. Enstone, who led them to his dugout.

"This way," the otter said, gesturing for the stoat, dog, and genet to follow him into the dugout. He gestured to several crates near his chair.

"Sit down," he ordered.

Chumsy, David, and Towser sat, eyes fixed on the otter.

"Now I want you to listen very closely," Sgt. Enstone said. "The elder Private Carrick, he's a friend of yours, yes?"

"I'd gladly take another bullet for him," David said.

"He saved my life at Polygon Wood, sir! You saw him!" Chumsy declared.

"He's a good 'un," Towser piped up. "Fearless, he is."

"I want you all to keep an eye on him," the otter said. "He's trouble."

Chumsy's jaw dropped. The Woodbine he'd been resting on his lip, unlit and undisturbed, fell to the ground. "Not our Willy!" he breathed.

"Could be," the otter said. "We're gathering evidence now. If he's got anything to hide, he's bound to know his time is running out, and he's bound to do something suspicious. But none of you are to breathe a word of this to another soul!"

"Yes, sir," Chumsy said, his eyes downcast.

"Yes, sir," David murmured, an indescribable pain in his eyes.

"Yes, sir," Towser said with the pitiful sniff of a small boy who'd been let down by his father.

"Right, back to your posts, all of you!" Sgt. Enstone commanded.

The stoat, dog, and genet marched out of the dugout.

The otter cracked a sly grin and packed his pipe with a fresh load of fine Virginia tobacco. *If you want to keep a secret, tell one creature,* he mused. *If you want to start a rumor, tell three.*

Night fell on L'Epinette, dark and moonless, broken only by the odd star shell lighting no creature's land. The deathly lights cast eerie shadows on the trenches.

Ten thousand thoughts raced through David's mind. The genet's tail twitched, ceaseless and restless.

It was Willy's turn on watch. The wolf sat with his rifle pointed over the parapet. It was dangerous work; even making himself as small a target as possible didn't help much. Most of the casualties in this sector came from unlucky soldiers who dared put their heads up, and, for a guard, it was part of the job.

The others seemed to avoid Willy. It twisted David's heart. After all they'd been through, could he really believe it? His Willy? The creature he'd taken a bullet for at St. Julien?

The hours crept by. The star shells became fewer. Not a single shot could be heard. To their left some miles north, a steady rumble emanated from Ypres as the nightly bombardment commenced, but this corner of France was quiet as they came. Too quiet.

Then came Chumsy's turn to go on watch. Willy breathed a sigh of relief and stood down, setting his rifle with the rest of his kit against the edge of the firing step.

"How have you been?" David asked.

They walked into the dugout together. David produced a box of matches and lit the lantern hung from the wooden ceiling.

"Well enough," Willy said. "Just a moment..."

The wolf stepped away to his kit, fishing out a familiar red and yellow tin that once held baking powder.

The wolf came back to the dugout and sat down at the cable spool table, setting the tin between them. "Cigar?" he asked, opening the tin and handing it to the genet.

"Yes, thank you!" David said, taking a cigar and biting off the end. The wolf's family knew what he liked and always sent the very best cigars they could afford, a rare luxury in these trenches. He struck another match and lit the cigar, taking a long pull.

"Nice evening, isn't it?" Willy said, rubbing his neck and gazing down at the floor.

"Isn't it, though?" David said, pulling a pack of cards from his tunic pocket. "Would you mind if I deal?"

"Not at all, carry on," Willy said.

David opened the pack and slipped the Joker toward Willy. On the card was a simple message written very lightly in pencil:

OLD CORDITE THINKS YOU'RE A SABOTEUR.

Willy read the message. His ears folded back. "Still?"

"Still," David confirmed, dealing out the hands.

Willy shrugged. "Well, I'm not."

That was all he said about it. The wolf was entirely unconcerned. Hand after hand, late into the night, the banter never changed, his demeanor seemed the same as always.

Where did this fear that welled up in David come from, then? There was a distance there, a gulf that had never been there before, and it made the genet sick. Willy was a gentle hedonist, a harmless oaf, and candid to a fault. How could he even think for a moment this wolf would betray anyone?

"Is something the matter?" Willy whimpered, snapping him out of it for a moment.

"No, nothing's the matter," David replied, studying his hand. Two deuces, two fours, a five, and a seven.

Willy frowned. "Let's not think about it. Nothing's changed, David."

David sighed and played his hand. "Twenty-four."

Willy's eyes went wide. He played his hand. A deuce, a trey, a seven, and two sevens. "Twenty-four."

David cracked a smile and drew a long drag from his cigar. "Seems we've been dealt a similar hand."

Willy's tail wagged. "Quite. No use in worrying."

The next day came with a bright red sunrise that should have heralded a storm, but, as noon crept upon the land, the day grew blazing hot, the humidity intense but the ground dry. The dust kicked up in thick clouds wherever it was stirred.

Nobody troubled Willy. In fact, most of his usual mates hadn't spoken to him much at all. Chumsy and Towser kept conversation between themselves, and even David was aloof and quieter than usual.

At least, there was Alby. The younger wolf was warm and friendly as they took a rough breakfast of eggs and hardtack soaked in coffee together.

"Do you think they'll make their move today?" Alby asked.

"I don't know," Willy murmured.

"You ought to know. Bloody spy."

It was Reggie Grove, a marten from his company. Not one of his little gang of Hereford lads; Reggie was from deepest Shropshire and kept to his own little band most of the time.

Alby's eyes went wide. "What did you say?"

"Wasn't that what Sarge was on you about then?" Reggie said. "Where're you from anyway? What kind of name is 'Carrick?'"

"I'm from Hereford!" Willy growled.

"I mean originally, wolf!" Reggie persisted.

"We were born and raised in Somerset!" Alby snarled.

"That's no Somerset accent!"

"My father's from Northumberland. Not that it's any of your business," Willy snapped.

"Temper! Temper, lad! What's got you all in a growl?" Reggie said with a sneer so insolent it would make a saint want to polish his teeth with the butt of an Enfield.

"I'm no spy, treeweasel! And I'm English born and raised," Willy huffed.

"Keep these vicious latrine rumors about my brother to yourself, or there's going to be trouble!" Alby chimed in.

"He's always skulking about with that genet, though!" rasped Lawry, a red fox from Reggie's town. "Don't much like genets. Shifty folk! Wanderin' from town to town..."

"David's lived in Hereford his whole life!" Willy protested.

"You would say that! You're English as they come, are you? You don't act English," Reggie said. "We know about your vices, too. Your silly little 'stomach tonic' you like to swill. Had a fine old time in India, did you?"

"Now see here!" Alby screamed, standing up to his full six-and-a-half feet. "One more word out of you, and-"

POP

Alby's eyes went wide. He spun round about a quarter turn, tottering a moment as his

legs gave out. He fell with a sickening, muffled thud like a sack of flour.

Willy's heart twisted. He rushed to his brother's side. Alby was too bloody to tell where

he'd been hit.

Alby coughed and gasped. Blood trickled down his chin.

Willy held his hand. "Alby! Please, stay with me," he sobbed. "Someone get a medic! Get a medic!"

In no time, two medics, a wildcat and a roe deer, were tending to Alby.

"He's poorly," said the wildcat. "Can you tell where he's hit?"

"Bless me!" the stag said. "Right through the shoulder, out the neck. If it'd been an inch to the right, he'd be gone."

Alby gave another wheezing cough, unable to speak. His eyes were wide with mortal terror.

"There, there," said the wildcat, bandaging him as well as he could. "We'll get you out of here soon enough."

Four stretcher bearers carried him away a few moments later. Alby, still unable to speak, locked a pair of pleading eyes on Willy as they rounded the fire bay toward the communication trench.

That look in his eyes fixed in Willy's mind. He slouched in the dust, head in hands, too numb to cry. Gutted. He was absolutely gutted. Was this his fault? Was there something he could do or should have done?

Now he had no one to stand up for him. Even David seemed unwilling to be seen fraternizing with him. The next night would be a long one.

Sgt. Enstone had his head in his hands as well. The younger Pte. Carrick had been nothing if not a model soldier. Better than his brother, for certain. Now he was probably on his way to the dressing station in the vaults of an old brewery on the banks of the Lys. There'd been no word on his condition yet.

There was a cemetery midway between the brewery and L'Epinette where they buried the ones who died on the way to safety or who didn't survive long enough to get to a proper hospital further behind the lines. The thought of old Alby being buried there—all because of some silly argument over his brother that didn't have to happen —that was too much for the otter.

And yet...wouldn't it do for the elder Pte. Carrick to sleep on this for one more night? Just to be sure he wouldn't make trouble again?

The otter took a long, slow pull from his pipe. The thought of punishing poor, old Willy any more came a little more reluctantly this time. But the wolf had shown himself to be too much of a libertine from early on. An indolent libertine with exotic vices, at that. There was no place for creatures like him in His Majesty's service! With no end to the war in sight, it was better to use this chance to break him now than put the others in any more jeopardy.

Another night. The pale sliver of the moon hid behind gathering clouds. Here and there, as patrols crossed no creature's land, the star flares shot up again from the German line, then the British, then the German again. A small volley of coalboxes hit further down the line, knocking the road from Chapelle D'Armentieres to Lille into a bigger heap of dust than it already was.

There were moments of awkward silence, too, when the wind would sweep across the flat plains and rustle the few scraggly patches of grass in the tortured fields.

Willy could have slept if he'd chosen to. He could have huddled in the dugout with his mates. But the poisonous glare from Chumsy and the wounded eyes that David made at him made it clear the wolf was no longer welcome.

Alby...how was he? Willy desperately wanted some news of him, but, every time he would try to get the attention of some passing creature in the trench, they'd speed up and walk away or give him some curt "Don't know." Not a single one of them gave him the courtesy of a moment of conversation.

The wolf felt tears straining at the corners of his eyes but unable to break through. Alone. Totally alone. He could walk into no creature's land, and it would be over. He'd be cut down in an instant. No more worry, no more fear, no more war to be fought. Peace at last.

He peered over the parapet. At the German line, someone was a little too careless with their lantern, and he could dimly make out the outline of a soldier of uncertain species pantomiming the way Alby had spun round as he fell. He heard coarse laughter in the silent gloom.

Rage seethed in his blood. He pinned back his ears, his teeth baring, barely suppressing a snarl. The wolf raised his rifle, drew aim, and took the shot.

The laughter stopped.

"I got him for you, Alby," the wolf whispered as he ducked below the parapet. A single tear finally squeezed through his petrified eyes.

Morning. A long-awaited rain fell hard upon the parched earth, breaking the drought.

In a sodden reserve trench, the lads of 'A' company stood to attention as Sgt. Enstone addressed them.

"Well, lads, thank your lucky stars they didn't come over this time!" he said. "I've some more good news. You needn't worry any more. We've found the saboteur!"

The otter strode toward Willy, his boots squishing in the mud.

Willy felt his entire body go numb, his vision going tunneled. *No. Please. I didn't do anything!* he pleaded in pained silence to whatever god would listen.

Sgt. Enstone stopped right in front of Willy, narrowing his eyes. "I didn't want to believe it when they told me it might be one of my boys..." he paused, drawing out the moment.

"...and I'm proud to say it wasn't!" The otter cracked a smile. "The culprit was a local troublemaker. He has been dealt with."

The collective sigh of relief was held; no one dared let him hear it.

"We return to billets at two o'clock Pip-Emma precisely. There will follow a brief inspection, after which you may do as you please provided you are back in billets by no later than nine. Well done, lads. Carry on."

The rain carried on unabated, and it did the lads a lot of good to go indoors for once, to dry their kit, to change to some dry socks and shirts that didn't have quite as many lice.

Chumsy was the first to apologize. "Sorry I doubted you, mate," he said.

"Quite alright," Willy replied, not wanting to draw the matter out by telling him exactly how disgusted he was by the evil eye the stoat had given him the night before.

"I didn't want to believe it!" Towser whimpered, clutching his cap.

"I knew you were innocent," David chimed in, a note of guilt on his voice.

"Well, it's all over and done now, isn't it?" Willy said. "Any news of Alby?"

"Last I heard, he was at the dressing station, waiting for a transfer to a clearing station," Chumsy said.

"He's not still at the brewery, I hope!" Willy gasped.

"No, the main one," Chumsy said. "We'll have to see him today, though. There's a convoy come to take another round of 'em soon enough."

The sun was low when Chumsy, David, Towser, and Willy arrived at the main clearing station behind the Jesuit school in Armentieres. It was in a red brick building accented with white with ornate gables, a style that spilled over the border from Flanders.

Inside, the nurses tended to row upon row of soldiers in various states. Some were barely scratched; they'd be back in the line within a day or two. Others were on the ragged edge of life.

Midway down, next to a stoat with his head bandaged and his arm in a sling, was Alby. The wolf looked worse than Willy had ever seen him, but he was alert.

He gave a weak smile. "Hullo lads," he rasped, as if the very act of speaking were agonizing.

"Hullo Alby," Willy said, kneeling beside the bed. "In good spirits, I trust?"

"It's a Blighty," Alby mumbled. "But I'll live."

"Say no more," Willy said, taking his brother's hand. "Bless you, Alby. You deserve to go home."

"They caught the saboteur," David said. "You were right to stand up for Willy."

At that, the stoat next to Alby shifted. "There was no saboteur," he murmured. "At least, that's the Colonel's opinion. He says the cable was defective."

"Was it?" David asked.

"Not my place to question," the bandaged stoat mumbled.

"How do you know?" Willy asked.

"I was in that balloon," the stoat replied. "We thought it might be sabotage, but there's no reason to believe it. The investigation was called off the very next day."

"You're fair banged up," Willy said. "Was that from the balloon?"

The stoat on the bed sighed. "No...no. It's...it was a stupid accident. Some bloody fool with the Service Corps...a stag, he was...driving too fast. Knocked me down. And then I had to listen to some otter sergeant yelling at me for getting in the way."

Willy raised an eyebrow. "You don't say. Was he KSLI?"

"I think he might have been? I was in no condition to notice."

"So...Sarge lied?" Chumsy asked.

Alby shook his head. "He did. He lied, and it damned near got me killed" he said. A pitiful snarl of pain was printed on his features, drawn tense and matted with sweat. He caught his breath a moment. "Sorry, lads, I need my rest," he whispered between teeth clenched in agony.

Chumsy, David, and Towser shuffled out. Willy could just make out Chumsy reaching for his coat pocket, no doubt for another Woodbine.

"Do write when you get home," Willy whimpered. "And give my best to father."

"I will," Alby said. "Goodbye, Willy. You've been good to me out here."

Goodbye? That wouldn't do. Willy felt a pit in his stomach. Goodbye was such a foreboding thing to say. He couldn't bear to think of goodbye; not while he and his brother still had plenty of life left in them.

"I'll be seeing you soon enough," Willy said through a forced smile. "The war can't last forever, can it?"

He turned to leave but stopped.

"Oh, one last thing," Willy said. "I got the bastard who shot you, Alby."

Alby's ears splayed. His features sagged. "I'd rather you'd have let him live. Not fair, is it? I get to go home while he doesn't?"

Willy took to wandering for a while. It didn't feel right to go back to billets so soon, and the rain had let up for a little while.

The streets were cast in gloomy shadows. Few lights were lit; the city was beyond range of most of the German guns, but there was no one to light the lamps here.

Inside one of the windows, he could see children playing in a nursery. Two young wolves, one a few years older than the other. Not so different from the way he and Alby had been. On the bookshelf were books. Willy couldn't read them, but they were almost certainly the same thing one would find in any nursery: fairy tales, nursery rhymes, Bible stories, and books about manners.

Those moralizing tales he and Alby had grown up on, that lofty sense of piety and order, what had that prepared them for? A world where there were no morals, no fairness, no justice? A world where his betters could torment him for no other reason than making one stupid mistake?

It was no preparation at all. His generation had been set up, sent to live in a world robbed of the certainty that ruled the world his father had known. Things that seemed solid and steady were gone now, blasted to their foundations. All that was left was a world where cruelty begat cruelty until cruelty compounded upon itself and became the law and religion of all the world.

Willy shuffled along the darkening street, eyes cast down. If he ever made it home, if he ever joined his brother again, what would be left of the world after this war? What would be left of his mind?

Already, Willy could feel his mind starting to give. He'd done a fine job at Ypres, seldom thinking much about the world or the future, staying forever in the moment. But now the cruelty he'd seen was starting to eat away at him.

And when cruelty could only be repaid by cruelty, what was there left for poor, old Willy? To meet the same fate as the soldier he'd killed the night before?

At last, he found the final spark within him that still believed in justice, order, and fairness.

It condemned him

"Goodbye, Alby," he whispered to the wind. "Take care of father for me."

WHEN BALANCE IS LOST, WHO TRULY WINS THE GAME OF LIFE
Ann Crystal

WOLVES AND A KOHKUM SPIRIT
Ann Crystal

The house at the end of a cul-de-sac named Pocket Avenue was a cabin that was older than the ranch style, cookie cutter houses that lined down the same street and made up the rest of the neighborhood. The cabin had a large front yard and was nestled up against a forest that bordered three sides of the property. It was a cluster of trees, the remains of a forest that once dominated the area but now only stretched on for a few miles.

It was not large; the craftsman-style cabin had only two bedrooms and one bathroom. The kitchen was decent, the living room fairly roomy.

"My dear husband, what were you thinking?" Venessa Addams mumbled to herself as she drove up to the cabin her husband had chosen to relocate their family to. Then she stood beside her gray SUV and gazed up at the wood and stone that built up the cabin. "So, this is why you insisted that we come before you, my dear husband."

"Don't worry," Rebecca said, Venessa's nine-year-old daughter, "Mr. Whispers will never find us here."

Venessa stared down at her little girl as she ran the fingers of her left hand through the straight, dark brown strands of Rebecca's hair. Venessa and her husband had tried to keep the truth from their child until gossiping schoolmates had informed and stirred the girl's curiosity about the real-life boogeyman who had prowled the city they were relocating from. A boogeyman who had tried and failed to capture their little Rebecca.

"That's right," Venessa replied, "the only fear we have to worry about here are the wolves."

"Wolves?" Rebecca's eyes widened, and she scanned the forest that began at the back of the cabin.

Those wolves made themselves known that night, their howls joined with the music of the forest, the chaotic yet somehow harmonized music that would be suitable for nearly any ghostly movie.

Mother and daughter bunked together on the living room floor, the embers of a fire still glowing in a little cast iron stove that was to one corner of the room. Venessa watched her daughter sleep. Rebecca had taken her father's fair complexion and her mother's hair, along with Venessa's round face and dark eyes.

"Sleep, baby," Venessa told sleeping Rebecca. "Sleep, now that Mr. Whispers has no idea what town we have moved to." Then Venessa fell asleep in hopes of sweet dreams.

"You thought your little one was safe, that I could be kept locked away," Mr. Whispers' hushed words reached Venessa's ears. "Rebecca escaped my grasp once, but find her again, I will. On my way to you now." His promise was quickly followed by a muffled scream.

"Oh God!" the scream was echoed as Venessa jerked herself awake to a dark cabin. "It was just a dream," she told herself, nearly laughing until she turned her head to check on her daughter. "Rebecca?" A panic rose up within, a sheer terror that no dream could conjure. "Rebecca, where are you?"

"Right here, mommy," Rebecca answered before Venessa had the chance to scream out again. "Did you have another dream of him?"

"Baby," Venessa rolled onto her knees, then half crawled, half slid across the floor to where her daughter kneeled at the head of the hallway that led to the bedrooms and bathroom. "Baby, what are you doing up and about?"

"I was talking with Kohkum," Rebecca said as she turned to look down the hall.

"Who?" Venessa asked, but, when her daughter did not reply, she followed Rebecca's stare in time to see a shift in the shadows at the end of the hallway. "Oh, no, no, no..."

Within a heartbeat, she grabbed at Rebecca, and the two were out the front door into the fresh night air. Their silver SUV was there, barely lit in the light of the quarter room, but the keys to the sports utility vehicle were in the cabin.

"We can't leave," Rebecca told her mother when Venessa slammed her right palm against the driver's window. "We're safe here. Kohkum said we come from her, and this is our ancestral land. She said that, a long, long time ago, she and her people were forced from this area, but she came back like you and me."

"Baby," Venessa shook her head, "you must have been dream-"

"No, mommy," Rebecca interrupted. "Kohkum said her people understood wolves differently than you and I were taught. She said the wolves will protect us the way they protected her."

"Listen to me," Venessa gripped at Rebecca's shoulders, "you are going to stand right in this spot while mommy goes and fetches the keys. Count to sixty. If I'm not back by sixty-one, then you must run to one of the neighbors for help."

"But mommy," Rebecca stomped her right foot, "we're safe here."

"Tell me you'll do as I say," Venessa said, "Rebecca! There is nothing in those woods that can help us." Venessa had to accept a reluctant nod for an answer. "Start counting," she told her daughter as she moved toward the cabin.

The door had been left wide open, and Venessa glanced back to her daughter one last time before she stepped back into the cabin. Slowly, she scanned the room before she darted to the makeshift bed at the center of the living room.

"Where are they?" Venessa tore through the few things that had been brought in from the SUV; no cell phone or keys were to be found.

"Mommy!"

Venessa rushed back to the door and paused just as she exited into the forest-fragranced night air. Rebecca stood where she had been instructed to remain, with her attention held to the rear of the vehicle.

"Rebecca?" Venessa called with an uncertain tone, "What— what is it?"

"Rebecca," someone else called out in a rasp, whispered voice. "Rebecca, I have found you," Mr. Whispers' shadow emerged before he crept out from behind the SUV. His hands, then his arms, reached around the bumper until he stepped out to showcase his signature all black outfit that included a hooded sweater. The hood was to hide away the scar that slashed across his ghostly paled, fish-skinned face.

"Rebecca run," Venessa scream, and the girl did. She ran straight for the forest.

Venessa followed her daughter into the darkness of the forest, nearly slipping twice on damp leaves and moss-slick rocks before she reached Rebecca who had stopped suddenly.

The quarter moon offered no light, yet there was a misty glow that Venessa's mind was too busy to stop and question about. What she did notice was that the music of the forest had paused. There were no howls, not even the hoot of an owl. There was only silence.

"We're safe here," Rebecca said as her mother tried to pull and tug her further into the forest.

"No, we have to keep going," Venessa insisted with another tug of her daughter's arm. "We have to find somewhere-"

"Rebecca, come to me," Mr. Whispers called out with his hushed volume words. "There is no reason to fear me."

"Go, baby," Venessa tried to push her daughter behind her. "Go while mommy takes care of him."

Mr. Whispers seemed to glide across the uneven forest floor, where he was less than four feet away. His black clothing blended with the heavy shadows, all except the stark, pale flesh of his face and hands. A long, stretched out face, and small, stubby hands.

"Come to me," he whispered while he slowly crept closer. "Come, and I will not hurt your precious mommy."

Rebecca giggled, a sweet sound that seemed odd in such a morbid situation. It caused Mr. Whispers to pause, and even Venessa turned to gawk down at her daughter.

"Kohkum called you something funny," Rebecca said. "Kohkum is not laughing though," Rebecca pointed the little index finger of her right hand at Mr. Whispers.

Mr. Whispers twisted his neck as he slowly turned to look behind him, as if he was certain that there would be no one there but was humoring the girl.

Venessa gasped and hugged her daughter to her left side.

There was no grandmother in sight, no woman to take the boogeyman on by surprise. What did stand in wait was a snarling, growling wolf.

With a stumble to one side, Mr. Whispers backed away from the wolf, as well as from Venessa and her daughter. His startled scream was not whispered as other wolves emerged. A pact of wolves crept out from behind trees and from under bushes. They surrounded Rebecca and Venessa while three of the wolves set their attention on Mr. Whispers.

The boogeyman slowly stepped backward as the wolves slowly closed in on the beast named Mr. Whispers.

Rebecca shrieked until Venessa turned her little head into her mother's stomach. The wolves scattered then, their job finished. Or, perhaps, they were frightened off by the high pitched shrill of Mr. Whispers when he stepped into the rusty, old teeth of a long forgotten steel-jaw leg trap, which pierced into his left ankle.

And this is how this story ends; well, not completely. Venessa and her husband decided to remain in that little cabin at the end of the cul-de-sac named Pocket Avenue, where Rebecca would eventually become a big sister to twin brothers.

"The wolves and the spirit of our Kohkum continue to keep a watchful eye from the shelter of the trees," Rebecca would one day tell her little siblings.

A LIFE BEST LIVED
Fenrir Black

Nahuel spotted the deer only a few hare lengths away from his hiding place. If the pack were with him, then it would be a simple task of chasing the small doe down and snapping her neck. He stilled his body and slowed his breathing. No movement. That was the key for a successful hunt. Never let your prey know that they are being pursued. The deer was so close Nahuel pondered if he could attack it from his hiding place. The thought of injury during the chase or even the slim possibility of a misstep vanished the idea. He had not eaten a decent meal in two days, but the risk was not worth dying for. The doe was busy grazing on a patch of grass growing on the forest floor to realize that her life was about to end. Her ears twitched back and forth, listening for any sound of danger.

Slowly, he drew an arrow out of the quiver strapped to his waist. The bow was already firmly gripped in his paw. With the expert skill of a trained archer, Nahuel notched the arrow and focused his vision. One shot would be all it took. As soon as the doe was down, he would go in and finish it with his teeth and claws. He could already smell the fresh meat coursing through his nose. Without a sound, he drew the bowstring back. The doe picked her head up as if sensing Nahuel's presence. This caused the young wolf to pause. There was no way she could know he was there. He was too well hidden, his dark brown and gray fur blended in with the shadows of the forest underneath the setting sun of dusk. Even the black stripes that decorated his body only added to his camouflage. It was now or never.

An earsplitting cry echoed throughout the forest. The arrow leaped out of his paw and sailed toward the deer like a silent missile. However, it was too late. The deer jerked up and bounded into the trees just as the arrow cruised past her light brown coat. It embedded itself in the trunk of a large pine tree. Nahuel froze in stunned silence as his brain slowly processed what happened. He blinked in disbelief at his horrific luck. With a growl, he jumped from his hiding placed and walked toward the tree to retrieve his arrow. He plucked the shaft out of the bark and checked to see if it was still useable. Satisfied that it was, he placed it back in the quiver with the others.

The doe was long gone as were his chances at a decent meal. Tilting his head back, Nahuel howled at the sky in frustration and anger. As if answering his howl, the same cry erupted again. This time, it was louder and sharper than before. Whatever was making that sound was not far from where he was. Nahuel scraped his claws on the tree bark, contemplating what he was going to do to whatever caused him to lose his meat.

He sniffed the air. It was filled with the usual scents of the forests, trees, flowers, grass, the smell of prey, and of course dirt. However, there was something else. A subtle scent that lingered beneath the others. If his senses were not still elevated from the hunt, he might have missed it. The smell of blood hung in the air like a cloud of death. Nahuel sniffed again, trying to determine the animal that was bleeding. Years of hunting different species had trained him to be able to differentiate scents. Everything from fur, blood, and even dung. Yet, this scent was unfamiliar to him. Never had he smelled something like this.

Inhaling the scent, he took off running through the trees. If he bothered to strap his bow on his back, he could have gotten there faster on all fours, but, instead, he chose to run on two legs. He did not trust this scent. Unfamiliarly bred death. The smell of water hit his nose, followed soon after by the sound of a flowing stream or small river. Nahuel slowed down as he neared a slight slope that led to the water. His tail swayed as he peeked through the branches. The smell of blood was so intense his mouth began to water. Fresh kill. Easy prey.

Unfortunately, what Nahuel saw was not prey but something much worse. Laying on its side, clutching an injured arm, was a tall, pale creature wearing a strange pelt that covered only part of its body. The blood dripped down its flesh and into the river where it was carried downstream. Nahuel was not the only predator that would be attracted, he thought. Cougars, bears, or even another wolf would come in search for an easy meal. His paw gripped the bow as he watched the struggling creature. Part of him wanted just to put it out its misery, but he knew he could not. What he was seeing was something more dangerous than any predator in the forest. It was a human.

Nahuel's father, Ujarak, told him of man. Back when Nahuel was still a cub and living with the pack, the elders spoke of humans with great disdain and fear. Although they were weak creatures, they would tell the cubs man had great strength and cunning. They had skills that allowed them to create and adapt to even the harshest and unforgiving environments. Worse was their unequaled cruelty and apathetic nature. They killed without reason or remorse, taking the lives of not only animals of all species, but even their own kind. While those stories instilled fear or anger in the other cubs, they had the opposite effect on Nahuel. He became curious about the species despite the warnings. After all, the wolves had copied and learned from them to increase their own strength.

The human tried to stand up while clutching its injured arm. Breathing heavily, it pushed itself up, only to fall back down with a heavy splash. The impact must have hurt because it unleashed another agonizing cry followed by a pouring of sobs and words that Nahuel were unfamiliar with. Again, the human tried to stand, but, this time, it slipped on the smooth pebbles beneath its feet.

Ears flat against his head, Nahuel turned around to leave the human to its fate. However, he did not make it more than two steps before the human cried again. "Help!" it cried. "Someone help me."

There were no other humans for several treks as far as Nahuel knew. He knew of a human settlement not far from his own pack's territory, but that, too, was several days from here. The human would die if he did not receive some type of treatment. Looking back at the human, Nahuel realized that the human was young. It could not be more than a cub. In the wild, survival meant strength, and those who were not strong did not survive. However, did that mean that he should leave a cub to die alone?

Cursing himself, Nahuel strapped the bow to his back and stepped out of the trees. He slid down the slope and jumped into the water once he reached the bottom. The human turned to him as he moved closer. The smell of fear intensified as the human's small, green eyes widened. For a moment, they both stared at each other. Nahuel stepped forward, closing the distance between them.

"What are you?" the human asked. His voice was deeper when he spoke this time. Nahuel could see that, despite the human's small stature, he was well built. Most likely a male of the species.

He stepped closer, but the human tried to move away. "Stay away from me. You hear me? Leave me alone!" He stuck his hand in the water and threw it up at Nahuel, soaking his fur.

The human was scared, Nahuel knew that, but still, his patience was only so vast. Leaning forward, he bared his fangs at the human in an attempt to keep the cub docile. "If you do not sit still and let me help you, then I will leave you here to bleed out. There are plenty of other animals who will love to tear you apart."

Whether it was fear or shock, the human became perfectly still. He stared unblinkingly as Nahuel kneeled down beside him and tore part of the pelt from the cub's chest. It was surprisingly soft and durable, not unlike fur. *How strange humans were*, Nahuel thought. *They do not have fur themselves, so they have to create their own.* His coat was his greatest pride. The stripes that covered his body made him unique among the wolves of the pack. Carefully, Nahuel used the water of the river to wash the wound. It was severe but nothing that would not heal on its own with time and a few herbs. When the blood was cleared, he tightly wrapped the human pelt around the cub's arm. Satisfied with his handy work, Nahuel stood up and offered the human his paw. Reluctantly, the human took it, shuddering at the touch of it. With one pull, he pulled the human to his feet.

The air was still thick with the smell of blood and fear. More predators would be approaching. Nahuel turned to the cub and spoke again, "Follow me. I know of a place where we can be safe for the night." Without waiting for a reply, the wolf leaped from the river and landed on the banks. The human cub slowly followed up the slope and into the woods, staying close behind him.

They both settled in a clearing among the trees of the forest. Nahuel gathered firewood and started a small fire to help dry their damp bodies. The sun had set entirely, shrouding them in darkness as the flames cast shadows around them. The effect was quite eerie in Nahuel's mind. He thought back to the tales of spirits that were said to wander the forest at night, stalking the lone wolf who believed he was stronger than he was. Nature has a way of making us weaker than we think, his father liked to tell him.

He glanced up at the human who was huddled near the fire. His face was stony and expressionless, but the smell of fear still permeated in the air. Nahuel tossed another stick on the fire and spoke, "What is your name?"

The human looked up at him for the first time since they set down. "Matthew. Matthew White."

"My name is Nahuel." He leaned back, supporting himself on his paws as he stared up at the starry sky above them.

After several minutes of silence, Matthew spoke again. "Why did you save me? You don't even know me. I don't even know what you are."

"Have you never seen a wolf before?" Nahuel asked with a sly smile creeping on his face. The chill of the night blew around them. He pushed himself up and inched closer to the fire.

"I've seen wolves before on the trail, but nothing like you. I mean you can talk and walk like a man. I thought things like that only happened in fairy tales and Indian myths."

"Fairy's tails?" Nahuel asked. "What are fairies, and what do their tails have to do with wolves?"

"Fairy tales are stories people make up about magic and such. My teacher would read them to us at school." He laughed slightly. "There was one called Red Riding Hood. It's about a little girl who goes to her grandmother's house, but, when she gets there, she finds a wolf pretending to be her grandmother."

"What happened?" Nahuel asked. Never had he heard such a story. No wolf would be foolish to dress as a human while in a human dwelling. Such a thing would only get themselves killed.

"The wolf ate the girl, but then a huntsman comes in and..." Matthew's voice trailed off as he looked at Nahuel uncertainly.

He understood where this story was going. Nahuel nodded. "I see. The wolf was killed."

"The girl and grandmother escape the wolf's stomach, but the wolf dies," Matthew said. "Maybe that is not the best story to tell an actual wolf."

"I understand it," Nahuel said, glaring at the fire. "Humans have their stories like we do. It is not surprising to find that wolves are the villains in your tales."

"You still haven't told me why you can talk. You are not like the other wolves who walk on four legs." He pointed at the bow lying by Nahuel's side. "You have a bow. That is very strange."

Nahuel picked up his bow and examined it in the firelight. It was a simple bow made of the wood of a fallen tree that came down one night during a massive storm. When Ujarak gave Nahuel the bow, he told him the bow was special because it carried the power of the storm and nature's wrath within it.

"Why do you need a weapon when you have claws and fangs?" Matthew asked.

"There is a rule of nature that all cubs learn, so you should know it, too." He pointed the bow at Matthew and continued, "Survival is not about only strength, but the ability to adapt and learn. We use our claws and teeth to kill, but that is not the only way to live. Weapons such as these help us to survive and thrive. We grow stronger because we learn from humans and use what they know to our advantage. Wolves never lose sight of past and our nature, but that does not mean we cannot continue to grow."

"Is that how you know how to talk? You learned from humans?"

"Partly. We learned your language simply by observing from afar. We found that, despite your crude words and strange tongues, it is easier to communicate. Communication means survival and increases the well-being of the pack." He studied Matthew for a heartbeat. "That is enough questions. What about you? How did you end up in the river? There are no human territories around here, and yet here you are."

"I was traveling with my father as part of a caravan. We were heading west on the Oregon Trail."

"What is an Oregon Trail?" Nahuel asked. He never heard of such a thing in all his traveling. "Is that like a passage?" Seeing the confused look on Matthew's face, he explained. "When a wolf comes of a certain age, they are sent on a passage or journey in the wilds. They are supposed to learn skills and grow strong so, when they return, they can aid the pack in greater ways."

Matthew shook his head. "It's nothing like that. Is that why you're out here all alone?" Nahuel nodded. He pulled out his sharp rock from the quiver. Picking up a stick, he began using the rock to scrap the wood to form another arrow while Mathew continued speaking. "The Oregon Trail is a route that people take to the western regions. My father lost his job and decided we could not stay in Illinois any longer. We joined a caravan led by the minister, Mr. Jacob Blackwell. He told us there was a place of prosperity for all Christian men and woman out west. We packed up and left two months ago. Last night, it was dark, and masked men attacked us. There was so much fighting and gunshots everywhere. Bodies were all over the ground. People were screaming, and the kids were crying." He wrapped his arms around his body. "I tried to find my father, but I couldn't. I ran off into the woods but got lost. When the sun rose, I spent the day trying to find my way back when I slip and fell into the river."

The sadness in Matthew's voice was unmistakable. Nahuel listened but said nothing. *The cruelty of humans was real*, he thought. How could they kill each other so quickly and leave the innocent to suffer? There seemed to be no reason for it. Wolves only killed for food or if something threatened one of their own. From what he could tell, Matthew's pack was only traveling when they were attacked.

"Wouldn't that be easier with a knife?" Matthew asked, examining Nahuel's work.

"It would be, but I have learned to work with what I have—" He looked up to see Matthew holding something out for him to take. It was a small, thin piece of metal that was attached to a bone-like rock. He looked up at the human who was grinning proudly back. Reluctantly, Nahuel took the knife. It was surprisingly heavy for something so small. He scraped the stick and was amazed by how smoother it was compared to his rock.

"My father gave me that when we first set off on the trail. He told me that, if anything happened, I should be able to protect myself."

"Your father sounds like a wise human," Nahuel said, continuing to carve the wood.

"He is. I wish I knew what happened to him. I don't know if he's alive or not."

Nahuel stopped working on his arrow and looked directly at Matthew. As pleasant as talking around the campfire was, he needed to find out what the human planned to do. "Where will you go now?"

Matthew took a deep breath. "My father said that, if anything ever happened to me and I was separated from the caravan, I should find the closest town and wait for help. He said he would wait for me at Fort Laramie. He told me he would wait for as long as possible. I hope he meant it."

"Do you know how far this fort is?"

Matthew shook his head. "I have no idea. I don't even know where the next town is. Even if I did make it there, I would have to wait for another caravan to take me to Fort Laramie."

Nahuel glanced at the knife in his paw then back at Matthew. He knew the human cub would never survive the journey to the human settlement on his own, even with a weapon such as a knife. He could not even get out of a river by himself. Nahuel could not forgive himself if he left someone like Matthew to die in the forest. He was reminded of the young cubs back in the pack. How they used to run around and get into mischief while the adults scolded them. He was like that, too, wasn't he?

"I'll take you there," Nahuel told him.

"What?" Matthew murmured, his voice nearly lost in the darkness around them. The fire illuminated his uncertainty and disbelief.

"I will take you to the human settlement. You will die out here alone."

Matthew opened his mouth to argue but could not deny the wolf's words were true. Nahuel smiled internally. Matthew rubbed the wrapping around his arm and nodded. Nahuel glanced at his hairy arm. There was a band wrapped around it with feathers stuck inside. Each feather represented one moon since he began his passage. There were three so far. He secretly wondered how many more there would be before he got Matthew back to where he belonged.

Nahuel focused; half a heartbeat later, he let loose his arrow.

It sailed through the air until piercing its target. A small white rabbit laid dead only a few hare lengths away. Forcing down the urge to devour the small creature right there, the young wolf picked up his kill and carried it back to where he left Matthew.

The human cub was sitting on a fallen tree log, carving an arrow out of a stick with his knife. After a week of traveling together, Nahuel decided the human should make himself useful. He would do the hunting, and Matthew could help restock his arrows. It was not the best system, but it worked for the moment.

Throwing the rabbit on the dirt, Nahuel could sense Matthew's apprehension toward the kill. A rabbit was not Nahuel's favorite meal, either, but it was better than the nuts and berries they had been eating. Bending down, Nahuel tore off the rabbit's right leg and offered it to Matthew. He gave a coughing gag and turned away from the bloody morsel. The scent of blood was overpowering. Nahuel was about to eat the entire thing if Matthew did not take it from him.

"Are you not even going to cook it first?"

Nahuel shook his head. He never understood the human custom of cooking meat. Raw flesh was so much better, as the fire only weakened the tissue and sucked away the flavor of the wilds. To prove his point, he took a large bite out of the leg and let the sweet juices flow into his mouth.

Matthew doubled over, gagging violently. "I'll stick to eating my berries," he said. He pulled out a small cloth from his pocket and unraveled it. Inside was a small pile of blackberries they found earlier that morning. One by one, he ate them all before folding the cloth once again. His stomach growled, but he ignored it.

"This is foolish," Nahuel said after finishing off the rabbit. "Human cubs need meat just as much as any other animal. Watching you ignore your natural hunger is something I refuse to do."

Matthew gave him an annoyed look, not unlike one the cubs would give the elders when they were forced to do chores. "First of all, I'm not a cub. I'm thirteen years old. Second, I'm perfectly fine." At that moment, his stomach growled again, louder and unmistakable. His face turned a shade of crimson.

A smile crept on Nahuel's face as he watched the human struggle to contain his growling stomach. Picking up his bow, the wolf gestured for Matthew to follow him. They stood up and left their resting place. After walking for several lengths, they stopped. A rustling sound came from nearby. A sound of a cracking stick and the rustle of leaves. Nahuel sniffed the air and could smell the fresh scent of deer. Perfect. There was something else in the air he could not place. Bobcat, maybe.

He leaned over to Matthew and handed him his bow. "I'm going to teach you how to survive in the wilds. Take that arrow you were working on and notch it."

Matthew stared at him dumbfoundedly. He glanced at the bow in his hand like it was a live viper ready to bite his hand at any moment. "I can't do that."

"Yes, you can. I'll teach you." Nahuel stepped up to a large bush and crouched down. He peered through the foliage and saw it. A buck stood nearby. Not a large morsel but more than enough to satisfy both of their hunger for the next few days. For a moment, he was tempted to kill it himself. It had been a while since he had a decent meal, and Nahuel wanted to make up for the doe he lost the other day. Finally, he decided against it. Teaching Matthew was more important than a good meal. The buck was large enough to be an easy target for a first-time attempt. If they were lucky, then Matthew could injure it sufficiently for Nahuel to go for the kill.

Carefully, Matthew knelt beside Nahuel and waited for the wolf's instructions. "Here is what you are going to do," he told him. "Pull the string back slowly but firmly. Focus your breathing and your vision. You are going to aim for the neck. Hit that, and it will be weak enough for me to finish it off."

Matthew nodded and did as he was instructed. Nahuel watched as the human fumbled with the arrow. He struggled to get it lined up, so Nahuel had to assist him. Satisfied, he held up his paw. The buck was still oblivious to the two, which was good. As long as the dumb creature did not get spooked, then they were in good shape. Nahuel listened to Matthew's breathing. The human took several deep, slow breaths, and he did the same.

Now, Nahuel thought and closed his paw into a fist. Matthew let go of the arrow. They both watched as it impaled the buck but not in the neck. It struck the sizeable brown flank of the creature, causing it to moan in terror and pain. With an angry growl, Nahuel burst from the hiding place and charged at the animal. The buck took off with frightening speed.

Whether it was anger or sheer hunger for a decent meal, Nahuel caught up to the buck. He knocked it to the ground and tore at its flesh with his claws. The deer fought back, giving him several swift kicks to the gut with its hooves. Grabbing the antlers, he pushed the buck into the earth before going for the kill. He bit down on the neck with his powerful jaw. Muscles and tissues tore apart beneath his fangs. The taste of blood flowed into his mouth, numbing his senses. Bloodlust began to cloud his mind. This was his kill.

A footstep crept behind him. Nahuel turned around with his bloody teeth exposed. Lips curled back in a snarl and ears pressed against his head. A threatening growl erupted from his throat as he stared down his potential target. Through his blurring vision, he could see Matthew standing there, visibly shaking. The bow was still in his hand, but he looked like he was ready to drop it and run at any moment. Nahuel blinked several times as he forced the cloud from his mind. He was not a feral animal. He had control. He repeated that to himself until he was safely in control of his senses.

"Good work," he said, standing up. Matthew still looked unsure of him. Nahuel tried to give a reassuring smile but only revealed his teeth again. "That was admirable for your first try." He held out his paw for his bow. Reluctantly, Matthew handed it back to him. Nahuel could not blame the cub for being scared. Bloodlust was a dangerous thing among the wolves. He was always warned never to let the kill overpower your senses, or you would become a danger to the pack and yourself.

"How about you go fetch some firewood, and we can cook the meat this time," Nahuel said. He needed to reassure Matthew he was not a threat. The human smiled broadly at the possibility of real food. Nahuel internally growled at the idea of cooking the fresh meat. He would have to eat his share raw.

"All right, I'll be right back," Matthew said and took off running through the trees again. Nahuel listened to him charge through the underbrush, scaring off all the prey from here to the river, he thought. It was fine. They had their meal. He sniffed the air again, taking in the fresh scent of meat. Yet there was something else lingering. A strong odor that made his fur stand up. It was familiar, but he could not place it right away.

A scream rang out followed by a loud cry for help. "Nahuel!"

Without wasting a second, Nahuel took off running. He learned to recognize Matthew's many cries and yelps over the past few days. This one meant real danger, and Matthew was in trouble. Fear clawed at his fur as he moved. The scent he was smelling before grew stronger, and, as he neared its source, he finally recognized what it was.

He stopped as the smell overpowered his nostrils. It was

a foul odor of moldy fur mixed with wet bark. It could only mean one thing. Cat. Sure enough, standing just a hare length from where Matthew was cowering was a large male cougar. The cat had light brown fur with black spots on the side of his muzzle along dark hair on his tail tip. His lips were peeled back as he stared down at Matthew who looked like he was either going to scream again or pass out. Nahuel had seen cougars before on his travels and with the pack. However, this one was no ordinary cougar. He stood on his hind legs and wore a broad leather belt around his waist. In one paw was a crudely carved tomahawk made of wood and a sharped rock. It was not much but could do some damage.

"Galen!" Nahuel shouted. "Step away from the human."

The cougar turned to him, and his eyes narrowed. "Nahuel, what do you think you are doing back in *my* territory? This area is mine, and you had the nerve to kill *my* prey. I should kill you and this human right here."

Nahuel slowly pulled out an arrow from his quiver. He knew Galen from when he first came through this area. They had a skirmish but decided neither one was worth the other getting hurt, so they parted ways on the condition they would never see each other again. The cat was large and powerful but not as fast as his feral cousins. He gripped the bow tightly in his paw. In his mind, he knew he could shoot Galen, but it would not be enough. He would kill Matthew before Nahuel could take him down. Biting down his frustration, he decided their best chance to get out of this would be with words.

"Let the cub go. He's with me."

Galen looked from Nahuel back to Matthew. "I know. I've been tracking you both since you entered my territory. I should have killed you right then, but my curiosity got the better of me."

"You know what they say about curiosity and cats," Matthew said. A growl from both animals immediately silenced him.

"This has nothing to do with you, Galen. Let the cub go." In the blink of an eye, Nahuel notched the arrow and pointed it directly at Galen's heart. The odds of getting a clean kill were not in his favor, but he had to do something. This was his fault. The cougar's scents were all over the area, but he was blinded by his own hunger to recognize it.

"Maybe I will let the cub live," Galen said, stepping away from Matthew. "Instead, I'll take your head instead." He lashed out with his paw, claw unsheathed. Nahuel let the arrow go, but Galen was expecting it. He twisted, and the arrow missed by a hair. The cougar struck Nahuel and sent the wolf tumbling backward.

He rolled to the side as Galen pounced with amazing speed and agility. "Run. Matthew, get out of here!" he screamed. Matthew did not need to be told twice. He flailed around and stood up. In the corner of his eye, Nahuel could see him drop something where he was sitting. Within seconds, he was racing through the trees as fast as his legs could carry him.

With Matthew gone, Nahuel could focus on the fight. Galen swiped again, but he dodged by rolling backward. He was never good at close range combat. The smell of his blood hung in the air. The pain would come later, he thought. Galen pounced again with a horrific screeching sound. He landed on Nahuel, and their furry bodies entangled with each other as they fought.

Clamping his jaw down on Galen's arm, Nahuel got the upper hand. With a single kick, he knocked the cat off his body. Something glistened in the sunlight streaming down around them. It was Matthew's knife. He smiled inwardly. The cub was clever when he wanted to be. His claws were sharp but not as sharp as a human's knife. Galen swiped again when Nahuel was distracted. The wolf flew sideways, striking the tree with a heavy thud. He fell on the gnarled roots, feeling them press into his bruised body. His claw gripped the knife tightly, and he stood up again. Limbs as heavy as stones, Nahuel somehow stayed upright.

Galen growled maliciously, his lips twisted in an amused snarl. He swung his tomahawk this time. *Going for an easy kill*, Nahuel thought. Two can do that. He dodged the swing by ducking under Galen's outstretched arm. The cougar had size, but Nahuel was lithe and faster. He swung the knife and struck it into Galen's chest. The cougar screamed as the blade tore his chest. Nahuel removed the knife once he was satisfied with his handy work. A sizeable, bloody gash was now visible on Galen's chest. Not enough to kill him most likely, but it would never heal properly. He would forever have a scar that showed how a wolf defeated him.

Nahuel took off after Matthew. He could hear Galen's angry roars behind him, but he ignored it. Killing the cat would be pointless and only cost him more injuries. The only thing worse than an angry cougar was an injured one. They fought twice as hard. The pain was slowly making its way to his brain. Everything hurt, and he was sure he was bleeding in more than one place. His fur stuck together in a sticky mess. The urge to lick the wounds was overpowering. He sniffed the air, trying to find Matthew scent. It was easy to pick up, and the human was easier to find. He was kneeling on a tree stump in the middle of a field.

As Nahuel approached, Matthew stood up and ran over to him. "Nahuel, are you all right? My god, look at your injuries. We have to take care of them right away."

The human's worry warmed Nahaul's heart. It was nice to see how much he cared. Whether that concern was from their friendship or because he was Matthew's guide was left to be seen.

"I'm fine. This is not the first time I've been injured, and it will not be the last. Part of living in the wilds is learning to overcome injuries like this," Nahuel said. He handed Matthew his knife back. "Thanks for that. It came in use." He felt dizzy all of a sudden. He sat down on the cool grass and laid back. The cool breeze blew around him, but it did little to relax him. The pain was intense. Dark clouds appeared, blocking the sun. Shadows danced around him, and he wondered if he was dying. He closed his eyes and listened to Matthew's increased heartbeat.

"Stay with me," Matthew cried. "You can't die on me."

"I am not going to die," Nahuel murmured, but, at the moment, he was not sure. He did not even have the energy to lick his wounds. "I need you to get some water. Wash the wounds and wrap them in leaves. Can you do that?"

Without seeing it, he knew Matthew was nodding. "Water and leaves. I got it. What else do you need? We need medicine, but I don't know what kind."

"I can help you with that," a voice said sweetly. Nahuel cracked open an eye and turned his head. Padding out of the woods was a fox. She walked with the grace and power of someone who had control and intelligence. Nahuel tried to growl or show his fangs but couldn't.

"What are you?" Matthew asked.

"A vixen," Nahuel replied before the fox could. "A trickster fox, am I right? You take advantage of the injured and the weak to get what you want."

The fox sat down and wrapped her tail around her legs. Her eyes burned darkly, but she stayed calm. "Think of me as you wish, but I can help you."

"For a price," Nahuel spat. He learned of the trickster foxes from the elders. They warned that a talking fox could not be trusted. They were the worst kind of animal. Even worse than the coyote.

"My price is not your concern right now, my dear wolf," she said softly. "You need help, and I am here to offer my service and, more importantly, my knowledge."

"Let's just hear her out," Matthew whispered.

Nahuel was not sure. He did not take his eyes off her. She smelled like fresh pine and berries. A scent most likely used to establish a sense of trust with those she came across. He knew these foxes had some type of magic, but it was never clear what kind.

"Listen to the human, Nahuel. You could use all the help you can get. You both do."

"How do you know my name?" Nahaul demanded.

She licked her paw innocently. "Call it foresight or foreseen knowledge. However, I heard the human call you that before I appeared.

"So, you've been watching us?" Nahuel was growing more distrusting of her by the passing second. "For how long?"

"Just since you entered the cougar's territory. I wanted to see you two fight. I have to say it was quite amusing."

"What do you want?" Matthew said, cutting off Nahuel's angry retort. "How can I help him?"

"Water and leaves will do the trick. However, you need the right kind of leaves. You need yarrow and comfrey. Crush them and apply them to the affected areas. Bind the wounds, and they will do the job."

"Got it," Matthew said before turning back to Nahuel. "I'll be right back."

"Do you know what they look like?" he asked. "What about Galen? He's going to be out for blood."

"The cougar is licking his wounds. He will not bother you as long as you do not go too far. What you need is within your reach. All you have to do is find it," the fox said.

It was not much of a plan, but it was the best they had. Matthew crept through the trees until he was out of sight. Nahuel was alone with the fox and entirely at her mercy until he could get the energy to move.

"What do you want for your help?"

"I already got my prize. That fight before was more than enough payment." She stretched her long legs and flicked her tail. "My life is so mundane. The animals around here are simple creatures. The cougar scares off any of the interesting ones. You are the first creature to stand up to the brute in quite a while."

"I don't believe you would be that sincere. To help us for such a reason goes against everything I was taught about your kind."

The fox padded closer to him. "Believe what you want, wolf. However, I have helped you, and I'm asking for nothing in return. If I wanted something, then I would not have given that knowledge so willingly." She leaned down and whispered in his ear. "As a show of good faith, I will tell you this. The human will come to your aid one of these days at a time when you are at your most desperate. In return, he will need your help. The darkness in his past will come to light, and death will follow. Whose death is up to you."

She licked his ear, which only caused a chill to run up his spine. It was cold like frost. "Farewell." She ran off into the field and disappeared into the tall grass. Not even her scent remained. As Nahuel waited for Matthew's return, he wondered if she was ever real or not.

By the time, Matthew returned, the sky had become shrouded in dark clouds. The rain drizzled on them. Matthew ran over to Nahuel and knelt beside him. He unfolded his arms and dumped several plants. More than the fox requested.

"I was not entirely sure which one was which. I grabbed whatever I could. I couldn't find water, but, at least, it's raining." With that final word, the sky thundered, and a bright light flashed overhead. The rain went from a drizzle to a downpour.

The weather did not distract Matthew from his work.

He used the rainwater to clean and scrub the blood from Nahuel's fur. He only paused as the thunder grew louder and more intense. When the wounds were clean enough for his satisfaction, Matthew held up each plant and asked if Nahuel knew which one was which. He learned the smells of different plants from his time being healed, so he was able to differentiate each plant. Matthew began crushing the right plants on the stump. He used Nahuel's sharping rock to do the task. The rainwater helped create a fine paste that Matthew applied to the appropriate wounds. Yarrow for the cuts and scrapes, then the comfrey for the bruises. When that was done, he carefully wrapped long leaves around the wounds and used thread from his clothes to tighten them so they would not come loose.

Matthew helped Nahuel stand up. His body still ached, but the medicines were already alleviating some of it. They gathered their things and sought shelter from the storm. By the time they found shelter, the day had faded into night, but the storm had not ended. A small cave in the hillside served as their temporary shelter. Matthew gathered the driest firewood he could find, which was not much. Nahuel started a small fire, and they tried to warm up. They were both soaked to the core of their beings. Nahuel wanted to shake his fur but could not risk damaging the bandages. Matthew took off his damp clothes, but he apparently was not happy about undressing in the company of another.

Nahuel frowned down at the fire as Matthew set across from him. The sound of the rain striking the ground outside did little to improve his mood. He was the one who was supposed to be taking care of the human, not the other way around. The fox's words still haunted him. Why would Matthew come to his aid again? What did the fox know that he did not? He did not realize he was chewing his claw until he noticed the strange look that Matthew was giving him.

His paw dropped to his side. Chewing his claw was a bad habit he had since he was a cub.

"You seemed stress about something?" Matthew asked. "Do you want to talk about it?"

The last thing Nahuel wanted to do was talk about his feelings. It was not something wolves did. Instead, he tried to change the subject by asking, "How do you know so much about herbs and plants? Given how little experience you have in the wilds, I am surprised."

Matthew's eyes dimmed. "It was my mother who taught me. Back home, she had a garden where she liked to grow different plants and flowers." He folded his hands together, intertwining his fingers. "I remember walking beside her as she pointed out the different flowers and told me their names. She would even tell me stories about them. Some I think she made up, but others I think came from her tribe."

"Tribe?"

Matthew nodded. "Not many people know, but my mother was half Indian from her own mother. My grandmother belonged to the Shawnee tribe." He looked at his pale skin. "You can't tell from looking at me, though. Anyway, I loved those stories. Every Sunday, she would go out and pick a bunch to place on the table where we would eat supper together."

Nahuel could tell this story did not have a happy ending. "What happened to her?"

"There was an epidemic. It swept through the town, and many people got sick. One day, she was there, and, the next, she was gone. Minister Blackwell said it was God's plan." His voice turned bitter and cold at the mention of Minister Blackwell. "He told us that the good are taken too soon. I don't believe in God. Even if he is real, does it matter? We're on our own."

"Is that why you left your home? Because you lost your

mother?"

"Partly. My father wanted a new life out west. It was not hard for Minister Blackwell to convince him to join the caravan. There was nothing left for us there. The day we left, I went to my mother's grave and left her a bouquet of wildflowers." He smiled sadly at the memory. "What about your family? Are both your parents still around?"

"My father is one of the elders of the pack. My mother is one of the best hunters. I miss them. I know they will be waiting for my return once my passage is over. One day, I will show them I am worthy of their heritage and become a proud member of the pack. That is why I am on this journey."

"How do you know when the passage is over?" Matthew asked with renewed interest.

Nahuel sighed. "They only told me I could return when I was ready to take my rightful place in the pack. I would know when it was time."

"I feel like I'm keeping you away from them. I'm holding you back from your quest," Matthew said. There was a tinge of sadness there.

"That's not true," Nahuel said swiftly. "My passage can take me anywhere." He pointed at the feathers strapped to his arm. "Each feather represents one full moon since I left. It does not matter how many more I collect. I will know when I am ready. Protecting you and seeing you get back to your kind is only one step."

Matthew smiled, and Nahuel felt a small bubble of bliss rise up inside him. He never noticed how lonely the journey had been up to that point. Having someone to spend the nights with made him happy. Wolves were meant to be part of a pack. Even if was just for the moment, Matthew was part of his pack.

"Slowly, take one foot at a time. Do not be afraid to use your hands as well," Nahuel instructed. As part of his training, Nahuel was attempting to teach Matthew how to navigate different kinds of terrain. It was a fundamental skill all cubs learned from the time they could walk. Mountains, hills, forests, rivers, and lakes were all open territory for the wolves if it meant finding food or avoiding threats.

After traveling for another ten days after their night in the cave, Nahaul had taught Matthew several skills. Everything from how to properly use the bow, swimming, how to stalk and track prey, and now how to climb rocky terrain. Matthew took to each of the tasks with the excitement and enthusiasm that Nahuel had seen in the cubs of the pack. Despite how often Matthew complained about being referred to as "human cub," he was more like a cub than an adult.

As instructed, Matthew slowly edged across the small ledge he was standing on. Nahuel picked a location where the heights were not lethal in case the human fell. The fall would cause injury but should not be fatal. He had to learn on a cliff much higher and much steeper. One step at a time was what his teacher told him and now what he said to Matthew.

A cry from a hawk caused Nahuel to look up at the sky. He did not see Matthew slip until it was too late. He screamed as he flailed around for something to hold onto. His fingers caught an outcropping rock after falling down the side a few hare lengths. Nahuel did not waste a moment before climbing down after him.

"Hold on and do not let go," Nahuel said as he moved down one paw at a time.

"Was not planning to, but I am slipping," Matthew shouted back.

"There has to be a ledge." Nahuel's gaze scanned the area. Sure enough, there was a large ledge not too far away from where Matthew was hanging. "You are going to have to swing yourself to the left and let go. It is not a far fall, but if you miss, then it will be."

Matthew twisted his head slightly to try to see what the wolf was talking about. He could barely see the ledge below him. He glanced back up at Nahuel who nodded reassuringly. Inside his chest, Nahuel's heart was beating rapidly. He did not want to see the human die in front of him.

Closing his eyes, Matthew started swinging his body. After the third swing, he let go of the rock and fell. He landed on the ledge and rolled on his side. Nahuel quickly climbed down after him, thankful for his claw's ability to grip the surface better than the human's stubby fingers. As he neared Matthew, his ears were pricked up to listen for the human's heartbeat. After a second, he could hear it beating fast as the adrenaline wove through his system. He landed beside Matthew and bent over to check for any injury.

"Are you all right? Can you move your limbs?" Nahuel asked, sniffing for any blood. There was none, which was a good sign.

Groaning, Matthew pushed himself up on his arms. He flipped himself over and tried to catch his breath. "I think I'll live. However, I never want to do that again."

Nahuel nodded. He sniffed the air again. The fur on the back of his neck stood up. There was something wrong. The wind direction changed, and it carried the smell of something rotten. It smelled like fish that had been sitting in the mud under the summer sun. His ear picked up a slight sound, a small clicking.

"Get down!" Nahuel shouted and knocked Matthew flat as an arrow sailed past them and embedded itself in the rock just above their heads. He did not say anything as he looked around. Sure enough, a large, hulking figure stood several hare lengths away on one of the mountain ledges. At first, Nahuel was not sure what he was looking at. The creature was large but blended in with the rocky wall. The smell of mud confirmed his theory. The beast was camouflaged. The mud not only hid his scent but helped him become one with the area. A crossbow in its claws. It drew another arrow and aimed it directly at Nahuel.

Without a second thought, Nahuel leaped from the ledge and started climbing up the side of the mountain. He felt another arrow fly past him, the wind lightly touching his fur. *I have to keep him focused on me*, he thought. It would be bad if the creature decided that Matthew was the target he wanted.

Upon reaching the top, Nahuel grabbed his bow and an arrow in a single, flowing movement. He drew back the string and aimed it at the creature. With astonishing speed and power, his target jumped up so it was on the same ridge Nahuel stood. Seeing it up close allowed him to determine whom they were dealing with finally.

"A bear. What is a bear like you doing out here?" Nahuel asked, not taking his eyes off the massive animal or his claw off the arrow. "Why are you shooting at us?"

The bear stood up on his hind legs, which were not uncommon for bears, but, the way this one did, it seemed more natural and more comfortable than that of a feral. The mud was missing in several places, leaving black fur exposed. The size was that of a male with broad shoulders and a large head. His crossbow was still in his grip, but he did not have an arrow ready. They were still in the quiver on his back. Nahuel glanced at the bear's waist. Around it was a pelt of some kind. It took a second before he realized it was a wolf pelt. Whether it was feral or not, he could not tell.

"Surely, you can tell why I'm here," the bear said with a deep, throaty voice. "A wolf of your breed is a rare treasure. Something that is worth your weight in gold."

Gold? Why would a bear need gold, Nahuel wondered? Gold was something that only humans cared about. Then it struck him like a blow from behind. "You're a rogue animal." His fingers tightened even more on the arrow that was still pointed at the bear's chest.

"That is such a negative way of saying it. I prefer an innovator." He laid the weapon against his shoulder. "You should know this is a changing world. The humans are more widespread now than ever before. It is only a matter of time before the wilds are gone."

"You would sell out your kind to be a part of that. I know rogues only care about being human even though they will never accept our kind. They will kill you the moment they get."

"Only if I don't bring them what they want," he said slowly. "I, Everest, will always deliver." He charged at Nahuel with incredible speed. For a moment, the wolf was caught off guard. When Everest was almost on him, he let go of the arrow. It struck the bear's shoulder, but it did not slow him down. He swung a massive paw, catching Nahuel in the stomach. The wolf was sent through the air and fell hard on the ground.

Within seconds, the bear was on him. Before he could move, Nahuel was pinned under the bear's incredible weight. Everest roared in triumph as he raised his paw for the kill. Nahuel closed his eyes and waited for his death. The sky was torn by another roar from the bear, but, this time, it was one of pain. Nahuel felt Everest move off his body. He glanced up to see the animal struggle to knock something off his back.

For a moment, Nahuel could not believe what he was seeing. Matthew was clinging to the bear's back and, in his hand, was his knife. He stabbed the bear's flesh repeatedly as Everest roared and growled in agony.

"Get off me," he growled and slammed his body into the rock wall. Matthew yelped in pain and was forced to let go. Before he fell, he knocked the quiver off Everest's back. It fell on the ground with its contents spilling out. The bear turned to Matthew who was slumped against the wall. "Now you die!" Everest raised his paw, the black claws like knives sparking in the sun.

Nahuel picked up one of the arrows that fell out of the quiver and did not bother using his bow this time. He jumped up and stuck it into the bear's side. Taking a claw full of fur, Nahuel pulled Everest away from Matthew. Shifting his weight, he threw the bear on the ground where he slid to the side of the ledge. Nahuel went to finish the job, but Everest was not done. He struck out again with his paw, striking Nahuel's face. Three long gashes appeared as the pain made his muzzle feel like it was on fire. He lay there clutching the side of his head as Everest lumbered over. Anger and hatred burned in his eyes as he stood there.

"Hey, you big beast. Over here," Matthew shouted. He stood up and waved his arms. That did the trick. Everest turned to him, and, at that moment, Nahuel took his chance. He kicked out with both his legs, knocking Everest off balance. Matthew rushed over and slammed his shoulder into the bear's stomach. Everest fell backward and slipped over the edge. Matthew moved back as the bear fell out of sight. Nahuel listened as the sound of a massive body hit the ground below. There was a horrible cracking sound which meant that Everest had at least a few broken bones.

Nahuel jolted slightly as he felt Matthew's hand touch his arm. "Are you all right?" the human asked.

He nodded before saying, "We need to get out of here. I don't think that will be enough." Nahuel stood up, ignoring the aching muscles and sore limbs. He was still recovering from his fight with Galen and now this. Matthew's face was full of concern. Nahuel put on a strong front to reassure him. The last thing he wanted to do was show weakness to a human cub. However, he could not help but feel thankful once again Matthew had been there to save him. "Come on.

It's a long way back down."

After another long two days, Nahuel and Matthew had arrived at Fort Laramie. The sun had begun to set, making the sky look like fire and blood. Not wanting to be seen by humans, they decided to wait in the small grove of trees just outside the town. Nahuel examined the area. It was just as the elders described a human settlement. Large, oddly shaped dens made of stone and wood. A few humans roamed around like lost cattle. Horses grazed in the fields like dumb animals who had long since been broken. Why Matthew had journeyed so far to get here was beyond Nahuel's understanding. He stared at the human who was gazing at the fort in the distance. It was the largest structure in the entire place. A colorful piece of cloth hung from the top as it danced in the evening breeze.

"I wonder if my father is here?" Matthew asked in a hushed whisper. Nahuel wondered if he was asking him or simply asking himself. There was something in the way he asked it. Fear, but something else. Regret, maybe. Nahuel felt the same way. After coming so far together, it would be hard to see the human cub leave. He felt like part of the pack to him now. Losing Matthew was like losing a limb or a claw. Nahuel needed him more than he wanted to admit or ever would.

"There is only one way to find out," Nahuel said and pointed towards the fort. "You have to go make yourself known."

Matthew stared at the dirt beneath his feet. "This is goodbye, I suppose," he said. Nahuel nodded as Matthew continued, "I could have never done this without you. You have my thanks and...I don't know. I've never been good at this."

"Then do not say anything," Nahuel said bluntly. When a wolf died, there was no time for mourning the loss. Sadness was not the way of the wolf. Instead, they honored the memory of the fallen by becoming stronger and remembering only the best things about them.

Matthew held out his hand. Nahuel stared at it, confused. "You shake it. Place your paw next to it and grip it tightly," Matthew instructed. The wolf did as he was told. Matthew gripped his paw and swung his arm up and down. It was a strange custom, surely, but he was glad that Matthew shared it with him.

"There was something my father liked to tell me," Matthew said. "A life best lived is one of adventure."

Without another word, Matthew turned away and walked out of the trees. Nahuel stood there in the shadows and watched. The human was different than when he first saw him in what felt like a lifetime ago. His clothes were torn to shreds, scratches decorated his skin, and his body was caked in dirt. He was barely recognizable, but it was not just his appearance that changed. It was the way he moved. He held himself up with confidence and strength that Nahuel had not noticed until that moment. Thinking back, he could not remember the last time he heard the human scream for help. He smiled; the human was no longer a cub.

As Matthew walked toward the town, Nahuel stood behind the trees and watched him. He needed to make sure the human was safe without him. One of the structures opened, and a large human stepped out. He wore a long, white shirt and brown pants. The human's body was large like a bear but fattier like a boar. His face had what Nahuel could only describe as a caterpillar above his lip and another one directly above his eyes. Atop his head was a hat with a feather sticking straight out. Matthew saw this man at the same time the man saw him.

Even from where Nahuel was hiding, he could hear them both. "Matthew?" the man asked. "Is that you?" There was something strange about his voice. Although he seemed to know Matthew, he did not sound happy about seeing him.

Matthew, on the other hand, was overjoyed to see this man. "Mr. Blackwell." Matthew ran to the older human and stopped only when he was about to collide with him. "It's so good to see you."

"Yes, I'm sure it is," Blackwell said. Nahuel remembered what Matthew said about this man. He was some leader of the humans that Matthew and his father were traveling with. From the looks of him, Nahuel would never assume this man was a leader of anything. He seemed weak and prone to injury.

Matthew looked around as if trying to spot something that was being kept hidden from him. "Where is my father? Is he here?"

Blackwell 's face darkened. A shadow was cast over his face, blocking him from Nahuel's view. His whispered something, but it was still loud enough for Nahuel's ears to pick up. "You better come inside and get cleaned up. You can tell me everything that's happened since we parted ways."

Blackwell turned and walked back into the structure. Nahuel assumed it was some type of human den. Matthew followed, but there was uncertainty in his movements. He looked back at where Nahuel was hiding one last time before stepping into the den. The door was shut, blocking them from Nahuel's view.

That was it, then, Nahuel thought. He moved away from the tree and looked out at the open fields. The sun had almost entirely set, and the first stars began to appear in the sky. He wondered where he should go next. Nothing would be the same now that he was back on his own again. He ran his paw through the fur atop his head. His tail twitched slightly. A sense of unease settled over him. Despite how much he willed his legs to move, they would not listen. It was like his body was telling him something. He turned back to the town again. What was this feeling? Wolf instinct was never wrong, and his told him that he needed to stay a little longer.

The full moon rose in the sky as Nahuel crept from the woods. He crouched low as he moved. Humans still roamed around the town, carrying small lights in their hands. They were watching for something. Other humans, most likely. Some carried weapons. Long metal tubes. Guns, he remembered they were called. Weapons that shot fire and steel that could tear apart any living creature no matter how big. It would be dangerous to be hit by one of those.

He moved undetected to the den where Matthew and Blackwell were staying in. His ears perked up to listen to the voices coming from inside. He instantly recognized Matthew talking. Kneeling under one of the open windows, he listened while keeping watch for any humans who may see him even in the darkness.

"After that, I made my way here. It was hard, but I managed to survive," Matthew said. He was purposely leaving out details of his assistance, Nahuel thought. He could not help but grin. Matthew knew better than to reveal the existence of the wolves and other talking animals. "It was the things my father taught me that helped the most." He paused. "Where is he? I mean, what happened to him after we got separated that night."

Nahuel stood up slightly and peered through the window. Blackwell was standing over a small hole in the far wall. Inside was a burning fire. He leaned over it with his head pressed in his arm. In his hand was a long metal stick with a sharp pointed end.

"I have to say I'm impressed that you were able to survive alone in the wild for so long. Moreover, you even made your way here," Blackwell spoke. He turned around to face Matthew who was sitting at the table. "No one helped you or knew you were out there?"

Matthew hesitated at first but shook his head. Blackwell picked up a bucket from the floor and poured the contents on the fire, extinguishing it. The room was cast in darkness with the only light coming from the moon.

Blackwell smiled cruelly. Nahuel felt his fur stand up. It was a look he had seen only on the faces of predators about to kill their prey. Blackwell spoke again in a lower voice, "Lying is a sin. God punishes sinners. However, that does not matter now. No one will hear your lies after tonight."

"What are you talking about?" Matthew asked. His body tensed. Nahuel could see him reach for something in his pocket under the table.

"I don't know who helped you, but it does not matter. No one will know you were ever here. You are just another victim of a bandit raid gone wrong."

Matthew's breathing intensified. Nahuel could hear the boy's heart beat faster like it was it was about to burst from his chest. "That was you're doing." It was not a question but an accusation. "You led us into a trap."

"Smart boy," Blackwell said and moved closer to where Matthew was sitting. "Your father seemed to figure it out before I shot him."

A savage growl rose from Matthew's throat, not unlike a wolf. He kicked the table up as Blackwell charged at him with the metal stick raised above his head. The table hit the man, knocking him sideways. Matthew rolled out of the chair and landed on all fours just like Nahuel taught him. Blackwell recovered quickly and charged again. He held the stick like a spear, ready to run it through Matthew's chest.

Nahuel could not stand back any longer. With a murderous howl, he jumped through the open window and tackled the human. Even with his strength, the human's size proved more formidable than he anticipated. Blackwell fumbled slightly but swung his arm with the stick, missing Nahuels' head by a hair.

Blackwell stared in horror at Nahuel's hairy form as he stepped closer to the human. "What the hell?" Blackwell cried. "What kind of demon have you called, boy?

"Nahuel!" Matthew said excitedly.

Nahuel's eyes glowed dangerously at Blackwell. There was nothing but murder in those yellow orbs. His ears were flat against his head as he bared his fangs. Whatever fear Blackwell had upon seeing him vanished. He charged again at Nahuel, swinging the stick with surprising agility and skill.

"I'm not about to let a monster ruin my plans," Blackwell screamed.

Nahuel growled in frustration. He tried to reach for his bow and arrows, but he could not grab them and dodge at the same time. Blackwell swung again, and Nahuel rolled to the side. Grabbing his bow, he tried to get an arrow out of his quiver, but Blackwell was on him in less than a second. The end of the stick was pointed directly at his eye. There was no time for an arrow, he thought. Nahuel swung his claw upward, but Blackwell was expecting it. He moved out of the way and jabbed the stick at Nahuel. Thankfully, he jerked his body so the stick only struck his shoulder. Nahaul howled in pain.

Blackwell smiled wickedly as he withdrew the stick and readied it for another blow. At that moment, a shape jumped out of the darkness and attached itself around Blackwell's neck. "Leave him alone!" Matthew screamed before jamming his knife into Blackwell's beefy neck. Blood dripped down as Blackwell screamed. He gripped Matthew's arm and threw the boy at the wall of the den where he lay there unmoving.

With a burning rage, Blackwell stalked to where Matthew lay. Nahuel had to act fast. Matthew cracked open one eye just enough to see Blackwell standing over him with the stick raised above his head. "Now you will go to Hell, just like your father."

Nahuel notched his arrow and pointed at Blackwell. He focused his vision. His mind was completely clear except for one thought that kept appearing in his head. "A wolf always protects his pack," he said.

He let the arrow loose, and it flew directly into Blackwell 's back. It pierced through the human's heart before he could even react. He dropped the metal stick, and it clattered on the floor. Blackwell toppled over and hit the floor where he shuddered only for a few seconds before the last light of life faded from his eyes.

Matthew slowly moved towards Blackwell 's body and checked to see if the human was alive. As he stood up, he was visibly shaking. Nahuel tried to catch his breath. His shoulder ached, but it was not nearly as bad as the other injuries he had received since he began his passage. Sounds came from outside the den. Nahuel turned his head as his ears perked up. More humans were coming to see what the commotion was about. Matthew heard them, too, because he stuck his head out the window. Nahuel rushed to the window and jumped out. He looked back at Matthew and offered his paw to the human. Matthew nodded and took it. He jumped out the window and landed beside Nahuel.

"What is that thing?" They both turned to see two humans pointing and gaping at the duo. "It's some kind of monster. Quick, somebody get a gun."

"We got to go," Matthew and Nahuel said simultaneously.

They ran away from the den and into the cover of the trees. Neither stopped or looked back until they were safely away from the town. Matthew stopped and doubled over to catch his breath. Nahaul listened for any sign of the humans, but he was sure they were not going to find them.

"You came back," Matthew said after he could successfully breathe again. "Why would you do that?"

"A wolf always protects his pack and takes care of his own kind," Nahuel said. His teeth shined in the moonlight.

"I'm glad you did." Matthew reached in his pocket and pulled something out. At first, Nahuel thought he was getting out his knife, but instead, Matthew held up a feather. He recognized it as the same feather that was in Blackwell 's hat. Seeing the confused look on Nahuel's face, Matthew explained. "You said that you get another feather every full moon. Well, here you go."

Nahuel had completely forgotten about his ritual. After everything that happened, that was not surprising. He looked up at the moon, then back at the feather. He accepted it graciously and placed it in his armband with the others. That made four.

He looked back at Matthew who was staring at the ground. Tears rolled down his face as the realization that his father was truly gone finally sank in. He had no one left, Nahuel thought. No, that was not true. He placed his paw on Matthew's shoulder. The boy looked up and stared directly into his eyes. Nahuel finally understood what his passage was about. It was time to return to the pack.

"Let's go home. Both of us."

WHERE IS MAMA

I woke one day and looked around;
Mum was nowhere to be found.
The den was dark and colder still,
but Mama always said these words:
"Wait here, don't wander. I'll soon be back."
For despite having taught us the One True Way,
cubs we were and thus may stray.

Hours passed, and our bellies growled,
and soon the will to listen passed to roam!
Tumbling over each other with leaps and bounds,
our paws and tail soon got in the way.
Nips were followed soon by yelps.
The dominant ones went out ahead.

Out into the summer air we loped,
tongues and ears turning all around.
Our freedom gained, we stretched our legs
and looked about in a world so huge.
How colorful all this looked!
Oh, how wonderful all things smelled!
If all was such and all was so,
why did Mama keep us down below?
Nothing did we have to fear;
we're Freedom and Strength, high up the chain.

Though the world was huge with things abound,
we knew well the scent of Mother dear.
We followed the trail that led uphill,
marveling at streams that flow down below.
The forest that never seemed to end,
the sky that's ever all so blue.

But all the beauty we saw can't compare
to our Mama whom we found asleep.
Hackles shining with the morning's glow,
her eyes closed tight as she lay upon her side.
I nosed her twice but got no answer.
Try hard we may, try hard we might,
Rouse not could we from her deep slumber.

The scent of something different hung in the air,
sharp and unfamiliar, not of this world.
It tasted foul and felt more so,
with the tramp of feet and a bark of voices.
They came upon us, sneering a fit,
with muzzles flat and teeth so blunt.
Nip them we did, and struggle we had,

but biped by stature, furless to boot,
our foes were far stronger and much taller.

I knew then why mama always hid us,
keeping us safe from danger, safe from foes.
The world was beautiful in all its wonder,
cast not in stone, but neither in marble.
For dangers abound, and, around the corner,
therein lies our darkness in man's greatest hour.

—HJ Pang

THE WOLF OF GUBBIO
Dana Sonnenschein

The wolf was not as old as *la montagna*, but he was long in the tooth, and his hips were sore, so he rose awkwardly and his back legs turned out when he walked. He'd been driven from his territory high in the Umbrian Appenines when his massive size and jaws were no longer enough to hold his own against a stranger's challenge. Without his pack, he could no longer hunt chamois and deer, much less wild boar. So he wandered, subsisting on small game, his form growing gaunt—until he arrived at the *campi* near Gubbio. Fields of sheep and tender lambs! The people who watched over them ran even faster than their flocks when he loped over a hillside or out of a strand of trees. Even their dogs fled. So he denned in a grotto during the day and came out at dusk and dawn to hunt and to drink at a nearby spring. When shepherds or other men came too near his resting place, he frightened them away by howling suddenly from within a thicket or charging at them, head low, growling. They were not like wolves who would have seen his stiff-legged bluff for what it was. But *homo homini lupus*, for they turned upon one another sometimes with blows and knives and cut away the little, chinking bags they carried. He gnawed a corpse or two, understood why they'd been left, then lifted his leg to show what he thought. When the bodies were discovered, the people laid their hands in his tracks, and then they left him in peace.

Until a man in a brown robe came and, behind him, others muttering and stinking of fear and anger. The man was calm, like a buck too big to be harried, and arrived with a whiff of meadow-sweetness. In one hand, he held some long-dead animal skins and in the other a bundle—what could it be? He spoke quietly and rustled the old hides, and then he knelt down and unwrapped—ah—tasty-smelling things! The wolf was reminded of the way he'd brought his pups a freshly-killed hare when they were just getting big enough to learn where meat came from. He stretched and came out of his lair. Slowly, he padded toward the offering, keeping the brown robe between himself and the man's pack. Then he snapped and jumped back; in a bite, the wedge of cheese was gone. The man remained motionless as a tree, so the wolf came forward again and stood his ground to crunch down a clutch of eggs, shells and all. He looked over at the man's hand, sniffed, then brushed it with his nose. Saltiness. The man stopped making noises. Then he leaned down, the wolf jumped to lick his chin, and the man caught *il lupo's* giant paws in his hands.

Mio fratello, he said. My brother.

And, in time, the wolf was. So when the man led him into town one day and offered his hand, the wolf touched it with a paw, lowered his head, and looked away.

"Hunger has made thee do much evil," the man said, "but no longer shalt thou suffer such pangs. Let there be peace."

And, afterward, the people called out *La pace* and *Il lupo di Francesco* whenever the old wolf paced the town's narrow streets, receiving alms at every door. Two years later, when he died, they brought his body down from the hills and buried him with honor beneath a slab of stone. Now his bones rest in the shadows of his brother's church, and, once again, the howls of his kin haunt the *Appenino umbro*. Let there be peace.

WOLVES
Virginia Romero

SONG FOR A DESERT HOLLOW
Shannon Barnsley

Wolf, you call me. Smaller than some of my kin, maybe, a different coat perhaps, but a wolf all the same. And, over the years, I've been many things to you, done many things for you, had many things done to me. I've been worshipped, wanted, feared, hunted, sterilized, studied, protected, caught, tagged, released, legislated, listed, unlisted, loved, romanticized, watched, tracked, counted, hated, driven off, and hunted again.

Vermin, you call us, saying we don't belong here. But this is our land. We have always been here. It is you who is the newcomer, the foreigner, the invader to the land of our forefathers and packmothers. Our bones filled and fed this land long before you made it our graveyard to clear the way for your farm.

Through acts, whether to exterminate us or to save us, you have shepherded us, corralled us, contained us, relocated us, taken us, used us, imitated us, outlawed us, killed us. You've stolen pups from our dens to sell, made souvenirs of the bones you picked clean, worn us as jewelry and fashion, and even taken our dead. But, though our lives are short and our lines broken, we remember. We sing the old songs in the desert night and remember your old songs that once filled that same desert, a painted haze of color, bleached under an unforgiving sun and cooled under an unfeeling moon. Frozen in time yet always shifting as your territories changed and expanded, ever pushing ours back.

We remember a time before English, when Spanish hung on the night air like the scent of honeysuckle. And we remember before it was Spanish. When older tongues raised with ours to celebrate beneath a desert moon. We remember when we were the only voices.

We mourned with you many times through the years, through famine, through drought, through war, through sorrows beyond words in any of the languages you brought with you. And we mourn still, our pain fresh as the blood on our pelts and the words caught in our throats as silence descends like a desert storm.

Too many songs are lost, and too many voices are gone. Our old game is scarce. Our old seasons are changing. Our old rivers run dry. Those that remain boil over with rage as the desert paints itself for war. Our old roads are blocked by complexes and compounds, concrete, and convoys. Our old hunting grounds riven with metal jaws and planted with poison.

We are hunted, chased, driven away from the only homes some of us have ever known. We grew accustomed to cruelty as cruelty became your custom. But we were not prepared, even so. Not for the day our pack tried to return to another home, to follow the seasons and the sources of water and food, the footsteps of those who walked these paths a thousand times before us. The day we found our way blocked with a dead end.

A scar raised upon the back of the desert, running deep into its marrow, cutting our souls to the quick. We stand stock-still before this monstrosity, this miasma, branding the land, and for what? To protect sheep from an imagined danger even as the men with pitchforks prepare them for slaughter? A wall to shut out everything that isn't you. Until you're alone with only skeletons and ghosts left to sing with you. So, you block out their words and bury your head.

I hear my brothers' and sisters' cries on the other side of the divide. I hear pups howling for their mothers, mates for their lovers. We raise our voices together. In mourning. In song. In resistance. Somos lobos. Cuetlāchcoyōtl. We are wolves. Whatever side of the wall we're on.

No matter what you do, we were here. Your guns may tear through our bodies. Your walls may cut through our territories. Your laws may split our families and crack open our hearts. The growing heat may bake our deserts until nothing can live here, not even you. But that great expanse of wilderness that endless time and patient rivers carved, now cracked as shattered glass and red as torch fire, was our home long before you claimed it. This land was ours first. We were here before you.

We know it. And you know it, too. You know it in your bones and by the bones you made your trophies. May our desert lullaby become an anthem of resistance, echoing over millennia of our bones and a desert that wasn't yours. May it haunt you all your days. A song of broken hearts, a song of hollow hearts.

MEXICAN WOLF MEDITATION

M1133, WCC Webcam 6/26/18

Lobo, you are all long lines, back and shoulders
mantled in streaks of black and gray, pale sides
and legs, your face a bone-white mask of fur

as if you rose from the dust of your ancestors.
Loping across my screen, you're a flickering
pixilation of bark, leaves, and dirt; a blur,

a living ghost, descended from the first wolves
who crossed the land bridge to this continent
and the last five to survive traps and long guns.

In a world out of balance, slow cattle graze
where you hunted fleet deer and mighty elk;
your dens are holes collapsing in the hills.

No wonder, when you sleep, you choose to lie
camouflaged against tree trunks and granite slabs.
Today, as usual, you arc your spine

and tuck your muzzle into the bushy tail
wrapping one haunch. Front legs and paws folded
to chest, rear legs drawn up against belly,

your speed and strength drawn in, centered, a mound.
I glance away and back for a moment, sure
there is no figure huddled against the ground

where you lie. Then I see the edges of your ears
and sigh. There's an emptiness you fill, curled
around yourself, until nothing is farther

apart than the distance between guard hairs.
When you sleep this way on a summer afternoon,
you're the keystone in the arch of the hemisphere.

—Dana Sonnenschein

WE'LL NEVER HAVE PARIS
Hermal Rana

Corporal Williams was exhausted. He was hungry. He was in pain. He was homesick. He was nearly deaf. He was stressed out. He was pissed. And he was dying.

Or, at least, he hoped he wasn't. He was putting as much pressure as he could on the left side of his belly where the bullet grazed him. He didn't think it went through him, but he could still feel the burning sensation, nonetheless. He could definitely feel the blood dripping down his side. He didn't know where he was going; he just needed to find a safe place to rest.

Finally, he found a tree surrounded by bushes. He figured this would be a good place to camouflage himself from the Huns. It took him awhile, but he was able to sit himself down on the base of the tree and rest his back on the trunk. He let out a soft sigh of relief. The ringing in his ears had finally stopped, and his wound didn't hurt as bad now. But he could barely walk, and he needed to get this wound treated before it became infected. He took out the pad that he used to put pressure on the wound from under his coat. It was covered in blood. *Great.*

Jessie focused on catching his breath and regaining his

energy so he could get back to headquarters. But, until then, he needed to hide himself. He had no idea where he was. There could be enemy soldiers patrolling the area at that moment. There could also be wolves. Wolves? Yes, wolves. The French soldiers warned them of wolves eating the carcasses of dead horses. But they didn't eat the bodies of living people. Right?

Jessie muttered a prayer under his breath. He prayed for the Good Lord to get him the hell out of Northeastern France and back to Harlem. Back to Zoey. He promised her that, once the war ends, he'll take her to Paris. The City of Lights. The City of Love. The City You Had to Experience to Believe.

He hoped his veteran status would help him obtain the funds necessary to bring her here. He hoped the war would end before Christmas so they could spend the holidays here. He hoped the white people here would treat them better than those from back home. He hoped to propose to her on the Eiffel Tower.

But the sudden burst of pain on his side brought him back to reality. He's a twenty-year-old soldier far away from home. He just saved himself from being ripped apart by German artillery, only to be deafened by the noise and then shot at by Prussian sharpshooters. He wandered away from the battlefield to get himself together, but now he was lost, the sky was turning to dusk, his wound was festering, and he could hear the sounds of something coming.

Jessie made himself as still as possible and slowly turned his head to where the sounds were coming from. Sure enough, Jessie found himself staring at a muscular wolf coming out of the shrubbery. Man and wolf stared at each other as the wolf inched itself closer to the disabled man. Jessie knew he had no way to escape, so he dared not move so as not to provoke the beast.

The wolf got so close to Jessie they were nearly touching noses. The wolf sniffed the soiled man up and down. Many thoughts went through Jessie's head. *Can wolves smell fear? Dogs can. So why not wolves?* Suddenly, the wolf stopped sniffing Jessie and let out a howl that could be heard all throughout the battle-scarred landscape.

Corporal Moneau continued his so far uneventful patrol with ease. Most soldiers would have shirked at volunteering for a solo patrol with the enemy so close, but it was nothing to it for the sulky NCO. Like the wounded Corporal Williams, Joseph Moreau was a twenty-year-old corporal trying to survive the final weeks of The Great War. But, unlike the American soldier, Joseph has been at this war since he was eighteen. Certainly, his face wasn't that of a twenty-year-old. Three years of mud, loss, and killing made sure of that.

Joseph was tired; he wanted nothing more than to go back home to the countryside where his sweetheart was. *Valentina.* Joseph remembered how, so long ago, he promised his love that, once the Huns were driven back across the border, he would take her to Paris. The centerpiece of their great nation.

He had barely seen her since he made that promise. He didn't get much personal time. The Army always seemed to need him specifically. He joined as a Private, but he figured by now he had enough experience to lead a regiment instead of being second in command of a group of teenage recruits. But that didn't matter. What mattered was getting back to his love and fulfilling his promise to her. So much had been broken in the past few years. Friendships. Trust. Lives. But he couldn't break this one promise. It would break him if he did.

Joseph figured it was time to turn back when he heard the howling. Joseph instantly knew what it was. He was a farm boy. Wolf hunting was a skill he had mastered since a young age. He never imagined he would use his wolf hunting skills to kill humans. Joseph got his weapon ready. At least, this would help his home sickness. With his rifle pointed in front of him, the corporal started walking slowly towards the howling.

Jessie didn't know how he was able to prevent himself from screaming. His body's survival mechanism, he guessed. He continued staring at the wolf as the creature finished its song. The wolf gave the American soldier one last look before walking back to where it came from. Out of sight and gone forever.

"What the hell was that about?" Jessie blurted out once the wolf was gone. Then, Jessie heard the bushes moving again. Tears began pouring down Jessie's face as he cursed his luck. From the brambles came another soldier wearing a different uniform and pointing his gun at Jessie's face. Jessie was about to give his last stand by cursing the blue uniform out when he put his rifle down.

No one was more surprised than Joseph when his wolf hunting venture resulted in him finding a wounded black soldier. When Joseph realized he was pointing his gun at an American soldier, he put it aside and ran towards the man. Joseph knelt down to Jessie and started asking him how badly he was wounded.

Jessie had no idea what this French soldier was saying, but tears continued to go down his face because now he knew he was safe. Jessie tried to give Joseph made-up hand signals that he couldn't understand him. When Joseph got the message, he laughed, and he helped Jessie get to his feet. He then put Jessie's arm around his shoulder and supported him as they began the trek back to headquarters.

As the two corporals continued their journey back to safety, Jessie looked back and mumbled a "Thank You." A "Thank You" to the wolf who first found him and signaled for help. Thanks to the creature, Jessie could now focus on Zoey and bringing her to this great country once the carnage ended for good.

THE HOWLING TEMERAIRE

We sailed for days and days, the sun and moon
Chasing each other's tail among the stars.
After three days, the fleet from France nigh' noon
Comes cresting over waves, void yet of scars.
My pack lets up a howl. I raise the flags.
The fleet responds in kind, flood-gray and keen,
With cannons aimed, our captain's tail now wags.
His orders roar, the flagship to careen.
Gunpowder floods our senses: paw to sword,
We charge the foxes, claw meets flesh then blood—
Our swords may clash—but send them overboard!
One day, we all will meet Poseidon's flood.
   But now, today, we beat the Temeraire.
   Every wolf did his duty, fangs bare.

—Jonathan W. Thurston

NEW YEAR'S ADVENTURE:
A PETER GRAY TALE
Nathan Hopp

New Year's Eve. Earlier that day, part of me was half-tempted to storage myself in one of the number of charity houses still open that night, but I couldn't. I hadn't been in one since I left the orphanage, and I didn't want to try them out today. Stories of burglary and unpleasant Furren often escaped from their walls onto the streets.

Besides, I grumbled while pulling my coat closer to my nimble body, *those places stink more than a clam seller on the South Street Seaport.*

From the lightworks and abundance of Furren waltzing through the snow with expensive winter gear, I could tell I was somewhere south of Park Row, where most of the lights shone through the snow. I had to be near City Hall Park, where the best of it could be found.

An otter couple's conversation beside me grew softer and softer until they went down another street, while a gentletiger in a burly winter coat strolled by puffing on a thick cigar. Walking ahead of me, he puffed out a lungful, and the wind blew it into my muzzle.

"Ack!" I coughed like I'd smoked an entire pack of whatever he had, then groaned, "Watch where you're puffing!"

"Sorry, my boy!" he laughed without even looking back. "Happy New Year!"

"Grrr," I barked, "I'll show ya a 'Happy New—fwa!" Without looking, I slipped muzzle deep into a pile of snow, and the gentletiger's silhouette disappeared into the white haze.

I gathered myself up before limping down the street again, where a bizarre variety of odd sights could only be seen in Manhattan; two feline drunkards fighting over a pack of cigars around an alley corner, one hunched wolf in worker's overalls waddling with an armful of bags, and a few peddlers trying to sell the latest items ransacked from abandoned homes.

Despite the laughable weather, that didn't prevent other New Yorkers from flocking the cold streets. A few too many Furren sang drinking songs, some threw soot-filled snowballs or skated along patches of ice, while the rest of Manhattan—those like me—went on to see the firework show. All around me, windows shone frozen and filthy under new layers of dusty sheets. A thousand voices trumpeted from everywhere, making it harder than usual for me to navigate the streets. Sure, the cold air stung from recent rainfall set in late December, but nothing hurt more than a broken chorus in a wolf cub's ears.

After wandering around for a vendor still out this late, I finally found a street peddler selling ice cream—in winter, no less. The thought almost made me laugh aloud, but the sudden noise of my growling stomach dissuaded any doubts. Food was food, after all, and I'd rather have cold morsels than no morsels at all.

"One cone is ten cents..." the hawker, a cougar in a warm

coat, told me. "Otherwise, get lost."

I tried pulling into my pocket for whatever change I held. Once I did, though, a pawful of pennies dropped onto the cold cobblestones. My fur hitched high through my coat, and I tried grabbing each of them before presenting what I could gather to the cougar.

"Hmmm..." he counted them as my eyes wandered to behind his cart. When the peddler finished, I nervously smiled. "You're short a penny. Now get lost."

"Please gimme something!" I whined, clutching the pennies against my sore stomach. "I haven't eaten since yesterday, and it's one measly little piece of copper...Please—"

"Get lost," the tempered feline repeated to me, "or I'll make you."

With downtrodden ears, I stuffed the pennies into my pocket before wandering off. Oh well, I still could try to find food in the marketplace the next day, even if it were only the bits and scraps leftover. Either way, I didn't want to be missing the fireworks tonight.

Passing through an intersection lit by dimmed streetlamps, though, movement caught one of my eyes. As well as voices which made my ears twitch. Further down the joining road by one of the street posts, a group of older cubs surrounded two younger Furren—a female leopard and a male jackal— wearing strange, patterned robes.

"What're ya wearing?" one of the bullies, a wolf who looked to be a few years older than I, sneered down at them. Around him were two huskies who looked to be taller despite their species being known to be smaller and cheerful. "Hey, Hank, are they wearing dresses?"

The jackal guarded the leopardess and shouted something in a foreign tongue toward the wolf. He and his friends laughed, though, pointing at the dog.

"Speak English, friend!" one of the huskies growled.

"Ya got that right, Hank!" the other cackled.

At first, I didn't know what the other cubs meant, but then I recognized the female leopard and jackal. Their clothing looked like that from Arabic immigrants from the harbor's ships. On the few occasions I decided to watch them sail from Ellis Island to the city, I was partly surprised by how differently they dressed. Some wore styled quilts, other migrants having wrappings on their heads like the Egyptian mummies I heard about in the newspapers, and how long some of the elder men's beards went.

With the cubs cornered against a streetlamp, I couldn't help but feel my inner strings begin to pluck left and right. Their parents must've allowed them to see the New Year's celebrations, and now my city saw them as easy prey.

Part of me wanted to turn tail, because I didn't want to miss seeing the fireworks starting off. Still, my noggin' won the battle along with my heart. Though I'd told few of my fellow Furren, I wasn't born in Manhattan but in an orphanage in New Jersey. My parents didn't want me when I was born, and even the nuns nor the other orphans wanted to have me around.

Seeing the leopardess on the verge of tears, hiding behind her companion, pulled at my stretched heartstrings. And if there was one thing I knew after escaping the orphanage a few years ago, it was that no Furren out there—no matter where you were from or what you looked like—deserved to be bullied for being themselves.

No one.

"Hey, church bells!" I growled at them loud and clear. "Pick on someone your own size!"

All four of the bullies swerved around at me, with even the jackal and leopardess eyeing me in surprised revere. I glanced to the jackal, who gave me a questioning stare that made me certain about what I was going to do.

"What do ya think you're doing, pup?" the wolf asked with a growl, turning away to focus again on the two younger Furren. "Get outta here before ya join these two camel herders."

"You're giving us wolves a bad name!"

He laughed. "I'd say the same to you, squirt!"

Without a single beat, I scooped a pawful of snow off the icy ground and threw it directly at the black wolf as he grabbed the jackal. Bulls-eye.

"Ow!" he yipped, rubbing the back of his sore noggin'. "Ow, ow, ow!"

I threw another snowball, this time hitting square on his rear. Before I could tie up my tongue, I let loose every curse I knew by heart as an honest street urchin of New York City.

"Leave 'em alone and pick on someone your own size, ya pigeon-livered, mumbling-coved, hornswoggling, wag-tailing, gibfaced, pinheaded flapdoodle!"

At first, I couldn't help but smirk at how good my aim had gotten and wrote a mental note to use it the next time the local cubs and I got into a snowball fight in Lance Turner's neighborhood. Then I'd show his twin brothers not to pour melted ice down the back of my shirt!

Even if the Arabic jackal didn't understand me, the leopardess must have. Because she was giggling, but neither the huskies nor the black wolf laughed.

They were royally pissed—at me?

Like an angry bull, the wolf's nostrils breath visibly flared.

"Get the runt!" he barked. "I'm gonna give you a blinker!"

With fallen ears and blood rushing from my cheeks, I bolted in the opposite direction.

Luckily for me, I knew the best ways to avoid being caught in a chase, and years of practice in the winter had given me the smarts to give my two pursuers a run for their money. I dodged each pedestrian, ducked between every footpaw in my path, and all while the wolf and huskies struggled reaching me.

Up ahead came a flat street of frozen ponds and puddles. An idea popped in my noggin', and I reached for the nearest moving cart before gripping its back. Like magic, my paw pads slid over the ground as the horse-driven wagon barrowed down the lightly-darkened road.

Unfortunately for me, it suddenly stopped at an intersection, causing my momentum to make me run into the wagon.

"Ow," I winced, rubbing my sore muzzle. "Ow. Ow."

"Hey!" the cart owner sneered at me from up front. "What do ya think you're doing?"

"There's the little snot!" boomed another voice from behind me. "Get him!"

I nervously grinned. "Gotta go! Thanks!"

Stumbling up, one of my eyes caught sight of a ferret newsie near another intersection. As always, even in the cold, he began chanting the news with shivering teeth.

"H-Happy New Year to New York City! Read all about it! C-Come tomorrow, the Bronx, Brooklyn, Queens, and Staten Island'll be one of us! R-Read all about it!"

And behind him could be seen a crowd of other Furren on the street leading to a large, open area aglow with lights and music. City Hall Park. And not too far near another street connected to this one could be seen four or five coppers on patrol for the evening. Some of them looked eager for anything to happen from how bored they visibly seemed under a streetlamp

Grinning ear to twitching ear, I yanked a quarter out of my pocket before sprinting past the newsie. Before the unsuspecting ferret could react or thank me for the extra fifteen cents, I pointed him to the three canines and whispered, "Shout that they stole a paper to the four coppers, and it's yours!"

I grabbed one of the papers and tossed the quarter into his paws. Right behind my tail, the sounds of footpaws followed, but I remained focused on the rooftops above me. With a firm nod, I darted away and glanced back as the three passed the ferret.

Three, two, one...

"Police! Police!" the ferret recited at the top of his lungs, "Stop them!"

On cue, the police sprinted for them behind me. As I swiftly zipped through the uncrowded streets, I glanced back to see both huskies were grabbed by a larger policecat, but not the wolf. He didn't stop running for me as the other two coppers followed, and I feared being within the elder cub's claws.

My legs didn't quit running like their owner's skin depended on it, but the chunks of icy cobblestone continued providing difficult foothold. As I spotted a fire escape nestled against a building on my left, I leapt atop a misshapen woodpile and jumped.

I felt weightless and desperately climbed onto the first level of the fire escape while gripping the newspaper in my paw. And below me, the fellow canine managed to catch up with the policewolf on his trail.

The older wolf growled from below. "Come down and fight like a real wolf!"

I laughed. "Nah, I like it up here. You should join me to watch the new year!" Snarling like a nasty wound, the other wolf tried jumping up. "I was kidding! I was kidding!"

Right as I spotted a policewolf heading down this dark alley, I dropped the newspaper into his confused paws. "What the...?"

"Stay still, sons!" the copper shouted like an echo. "Give back the paper!"

Without waiting, I began climbing up the fire escape as the two wolves argued he never stole anything. As the debacle continued, I ran up a set of icy metal stairs and past windows peering into office rooms until, minutes later, I made it to the top.

At last, I jumped up onto the roof and grunted while pulling myself onto the stone ridge. Like a howling banshee at this height, the higher winds wailed across my muzzle and furry cheeks. My tail curled against my leg under my coat, and I struggled standing up as the exhaustion and cold crept back into me from during the chase.

However, they soon disappeared once I saw the view.

On the rooftops, little could be seen save for the Brooklyn Bridge's shadow looming through the fog. Standing atop an office building overlooking the entire celebrations, though, City Hall Park lay bathing in light. The New Year's Eve festivities could be seen and heard in every single direction, while the scents of food and beer blurred under cold rain that began turning to fresh snowfall. Behind the wakes of an earlier parade, crowds of Furren New Yorkers circled lit fireworks on the street. Brass bands and choirs sung carols of the new year vast approaching, and all as the fireworks and streetlamps illuminated every building in City Hall Park.

Most of Manhattan had tucked themselves inside their homes since Christmas, save for tonight. Everyone celebrated tonight despite the cold, from the northern parts of Manhattan all the way from the harbor. Tucked openly from the masses of Furren, there were a few gentlewolves I could guess as city officials scurrying near the City Hall's grand stair case giving speeches about the city's unity.

I even noticed a few street sweepers beginning to clean from the previous parade and half-expected to find two certain ones—a tall red fox and a small mouse by his side.

I hope Eddie and Hansel are keeping warm tonight, I prayed, hugging my arms to my chest as I sat down to watch it all. *Lancie's probably doing well with his family, I bet. Hopefully, David and Mrs. Kinnick are fine, too...*

A quick glance to my pocket watch told me 1898 was only a minute away.

As we all watched the fireworks in awe, I wondered about the two immigrants who led me to getting chased by the bullies. Unknown to my knowledge until tomorrow, I'd see the same young leopardess as I bought editable scraps in the open marketplace. She was escorted by an older male leopard in larger robes, but I recognized her from a stone's throw away. One moment, our eyes would meet, and the next she'd smile at me before disappearing with her guardian.

In the present, though, I couldn't help but laugh as more snow began to fall.

Well, I thought in pleased bemusement, *this is one way to begin the new year right.*

PETIT MAL,
Adolph Murie's Villanelle

Denali, 1939-41

My senses sparkle like snow in sunshine—
it's how I know a seizure's coming on.
The she-wolf lifts her head, looks back, and whines

from a far slope. Then wind blows through my mind,
filling her tracks with white. She's gone. I'm gone.
My senses spark. Ill, like snow in sunshine.

For days, I follow her, hiking from ridgeline
to riverbank, until I spot the den.
The she-wolf lifts her head, looks back, and whines

as she trots away. I crawl up the incline
and in. Her kind! How could I not take one?
My senses sparkle like snow. In sunshine,

I glance at eyes that will be as blue as mine
when they open. On me. Then I climb down.
The she-wolf lifts her head, looks back, and whines

for the pup that I'll call Wags and love like my kind
but leave, locked in a pen, when she is grown,
my senses sparkling like snow in sunshine
as the she-wolf lifts her head, looks back, and whines.

—Dana Sonnenschein

WOLF'S SONG FOR A FALLEN SNOW CAT

A precipice where an odd couple may have stood,
wolf and ice cat where only wolf stands now,
alone; as the storied past may have shown, he takes a bow,
remembering only the things that could...

could have happened, had he known you better,

Every day, the thought, bitter
now that only one can remain,
cat versus dog, the old refrain,
the chase, the skitter,

of claws, you, the intermitter,

imagining, eyes a-glitter
as dramatic pause takes place,
only to never hear your reply...
Left constantly asking why...

Had they only spoken,
who? Maybe both,
what would the wolf have found...
but his own tears on the ground...

By bloodied, accident bound,
the wolf, rituals due,
due north,
uncrowned,

and declares your legacy forever renowned,
Snow cat, severed too soon,
the wolf's eyes, misted, cries to that moon,
"Had I known...your life would be so profound"

—Ivic Wolfe

INSTINCT
HJ Pang

She made her way up on stage with the grace distinctive of her species, her headfur swaying luxuriantly with every step up the podium. A dip of her head and a glimmer of a smile with just a hint of a twitch upon her black lips greeted the audience, firm and yet diplomatic. Her immaculately groomed tail swished as she stood behind the lectern, her voice filling the hall as she addressed the audience, notes of a song flowing freely about the acoustics of the hall.

She spoke of the irreparable state of the planet, incurable as we had made it so. How people had selfishly plundered the streams, the forests and the deserts to further their own stretch in the world. Indifferent to the feral brethren that lives within their depths, only to be flushed away from their homes, their very destruction our progress. Perhaps one should pause for a moment and reconsider what it would be like in their place. Take the ongoing war in the Eastern Deserts for one. Feel how you would in the eyes of a refugee in a war long fought, seeing your entire family scattered before you, displaced like leaves before autumn. Only to realize that your very existence is pitted on the whim of those who are blind to the pain they cause, ignorance begetting indifference.

Just as all men used to say they are brothers, so must we that all living creatures are in this together. Be it wildlife, Morph or human, all life is special. Never forget that.

Kheng watched as Enq stepped down from the podium, a mere scattering of applause following her descent. He watched intently as she accepted a glass of water from a nervous usher no older than 16. Kheng barely noticed as the next speaker was called up, watching Enq lap up the water in her glass. Those near her shot her looks of annoyance at her seeming uncouthness.

It came as a relief when a break for lunch was announced. Kheng followed the line of people in his row out of the convention Hall, stopping briefly to consult a placard locating the lunch reception. He made his way past an Alsatian Morph, whom he recognized as a speaker in a panel addressing Non-human Equality, and headed to a crowd gathered around several buffet tables. Dispersed throughout the foyer were countless tableclothed stand tables, with a banner declaring this the buffet reception of the 2050 NWCC, or Natural and Wildlife Conservation Conference.

Kheng wasn't hungry, so he grabbed a single sausage roll off a waitress. He looked around to see if there was anyone he recognized from his workplace and past conferences. Noticing where a small crowd had gathered, he tried to catch a glimpse of what they were gawking at.

Reporters and cameramen from both local and international news agencies surrounded a pair of Morphs who stood together, closer than colleagues ought to be. It was the wolf speaker Kheng had listened to earlier, along with a male wolf, a snowy, black-clawed paw across her shoulders. Unlike the occasional wolf Morph Kheng had seen in the street, the two of them had shorter, tawny fur across the back and tops of their heads, unlike the more common thick, mottled manes found in the North American or European color strain. The female, however, had a considerably darker fur tone than her male counterpart.

"Miss Enq, how was your time in Singapore so far?" asked a reporter, thrusting a microphone towards her. Her large, sinewy ears twitched as the click and flash of cameras erupted.

"It has been splendid, thank you," the wolf replied. As with most canid morphs, her lips parted as she spoke, showing a brief glimpse of her fangs, her nose twitching as it did. "Though I must say it is rather humid, keeping up with the evidence of Accelerated Global Warming."

The onlookers laughed politely. "Another question, Miss Enq," spoke up a different reporter, a female one this time. "Before you came here, we understand you were doing conservation work in your native homeland of Mongolia. So what brings you here? Any other plans aside from the NWCC?"

Enq peered intently at the reporter with deep amber eyes, and Kheng swore that the reporter flinched, despite the fact it wasn't necessarily a hostile gesture as far as wolves went.

"Although the conservation of my feral brethren is far from done, I will now be stationed here," replied Enq as the reporter finally looked away. "Due to its international reach, I believe that Singapore will be the ideal location from which to spread awareness of not just Mongolian wildlife, but also that of other endangered groups. That said, I had also considered getting back together with my family who had moved here two years ago—"

"Would you say you're an endangered species as well?"

A hush fell over the gathered crowd. Even the click and hum of the remote hovercams stopped. Kheng could see that it was a youngster with his chin thrust out in defiance. His hair was still immaculately black, so he had to have only recently graduated from university. The lack of finesse was always a sure sign.

"Endangered is a relative term, Mr Reporter," said Miss Enq, tilting her muzzle upwards as she fixed her gaze on the offender. "Just as a species of Ibex may become endangered due to one's ignorance, so can an individual when they detract from courtesy. Does that answer your question?" Enqs lips drew back just enough to show the whites of her fangs. Her companion licked his lips contemplatively.

"But of course!" flustered the offending reporter. Everyone laughed.

"Well then, if there's no other questions, we'll be heading for lunch!" said the male wolf with a wave, his tongue out in a grin. "Thank you, and see you around the conference!"

As the reporters and camera crew dispersed in confusion, Kheng inched his way forward to get a closer look at the two canids who were now in hushed conversation. Without warning, the male wolf turned towards him. Kheng stopped, not quite sure whether to proceed. He had no intention of getting in between a couple. Everyone knew that wolves were protective of their spouses, being monogamous and all.

"Hey, come over! We don't bite." exclaimed the male wolf. Miss Enq turned to look at Kheng with her eyes slitted in challenge, ears laid back against her head.

Kheng averted his eyes and tilted his head down in submissiveness. He stepped forward slowly, vaguely aware that the two wolves were now watching him curiously.

"Hi, my name is Kheng," said Kheng confidently without changing his stance, lifting his right hand up for the wolves to scent. "Chan Boon Kheng. Pleased to meet your acquaintance."

The male wolf gingerly took Kheng's hand and sniffed it cursorily. "Umm, sure, Kheng. You know, you are the first hu—I mean—person to accord us our cultural greeting. You really don't have to do that. Enq, please sniff the poor guy's hand already."

A wet nose tickled Kheng's hand with snuffles, and he finally looked up. "Pleased to meet you," said Miss Enq, her voice overlaid in a multitude of tones. "It's good to see that there are at least a few of your kind who understand us. I take it you're a linguist?"

Kheng laughed nervously. "No, I'm a zoologist actually. I, err..."

Something about Enq's scent intrigued him. In the underlying currents of her musk, there were also rich tones of cinnamon and something intangible that made him feel warm inside. Up close, Kheng could see that Enq's thick mane around her neck and top of her chest leading into her safari shirt was cream white, almost the same hue as a Samoyed's. Although the slant of her ears suggested that she was still suspicious, her lips were no longer drawn back, which meant she no longer considered him as big a threat as the reporter was. Her slow and deliberate movement and upright body posture emanated a certain confidence he respected. Although her eyes were deep amber, as were those in most every wolf, her pupils were similar enough to that of a human. She was dressed in a khaki safari shirt and pants, brown paw wraps wrapped tightly around her digitigrade hindpaws. Despite the coverage provided by her pants, Kheng could see the muscular contours of her thighs and shins, threatening to burst through the fabric.

"Well, Kheng, it's nice to meet you, too," said Miss Enq, and Khengs eyes snapped back up. "As you probably heard from the paparazzi, I'm Enq Chinua, and this is my brother, Oyu. He studies Sociology at the National University of Singapore."

"You're siblings?" said Kheng in surprise. "Oh, sorry...I just thought..."

"Now Kheng, there's no need to be all flustered up here.

You're among friends now," said Oyu soothingly, holding his hand—no—paw out reassuringly. His paw pads were rough when Kheng took it, almost like untanned leather. "So you're a zoologist? That must mean you work at the Singapore Zoo! Which department?"

"Frozen Tundra," said Kheng. He tried to ignore the stares passersby were according him; few humans actually spoke to Morphs for extended periods of time as the perceived cultural differences usually unnerved anyone who tried. "It's the section with the polar bear and wolverines. We've recently built another section for a Grey Wolf pack and are studying how to best assimilate them within their enclosures..." Kheng paused at Enq and Oyu's intent looks, and only then realized he was broaching a sensitive topic. "I like how you answered the reporter," he replied as an afterthought.

Enq tilted her head. "The one who took conservation status lightly, believing that juicy news means much more than respect?"

"Yes, that was rather uncalled for," said Kheng. "I mean, I wouldn't like it if someone asked me if my right to live is determined by whatever I had accomplished! Life may be different, but it is all precious, isn't it? Me, I never truly got over it when Nanook died. He felt just like part of my family."

Kheng couldn't help it, but his tears just came as he thought back to the years he had spent observing Nanook, only to have him lie still one morning, never to move again. He quickly brushed his eyes and, with a brief "Excuse me," made his way quickly to the exit of the Marina Bay Sands Convention Centre. A guard asked him what was the matter, but he merely uttered an apology. Somehow during his haste, he ended up exiting through the door leading to the palms beside the Singapore River rather than the one leading to the main road. Stumbling towards a bench right beside the river, Kheng put his face into his hands and sobbed, tears mingling with the wood by his feet.

He had just made a fool of himself before not one, but two Morphs. Ever since Morphs existed, Kheng admired them for their tenacity in the face of a society reluctant to accept them. They came not just in different ethnicities and species, but found solace in each other, building communities wherever they found themselves in. Humans couldn't stand their being around, but that wasn't anything new, wasn't it? Ever since humankind existed, they had found countless ways to discriminate against one another, each new reason as justified as the other. It was so ingrained, so deeply-seated that it's too much to expect not to carry over across species. The way Enq held herself before a mistrustful audience was exemplary to say the least. Kheng had met Morphs up close before; many of them in Japan where they were first conceived, with the US being a close second. Many Morphs had no other choice but to brave the snub of society, living their lives at the mercy of those who'd created them, the unwanted children of a large family. There had been the occasional protest and fightback, but this had always given humans the ammunition they needed for their hatred.

The Republic of Singapore had been a relatively new country to participate in the Morph Assimilation Initiative, a UN mandate seeking to better integrate Morphs into society. Although many people in Singapore exhibited racial tolerance, it has yet to extend beyond species. Only last year, a human Morph rights activist named Hassenhoff was murdered shortly after a bill to form a Morph community was passed, with his Morph assistant shot shortly after. The assistant had survived, with the attacker identified as a Police Staff Sergeant. There was no guarantee that the law could protect anyone, and the fact that they were decreed and enforced by Humans meant that Morphs could only depend on one another, along with the scattering of human sympathizers that existed from Hassenhoff's movement.

Kheng had been fascinated in Morphs ever since he had heard of their existence; after all, weren't they a people in their own right? They formed communities. They had families and friends. They protected their own. The instincts that had been brought over from their feral ancestry strengthened them more than any cultural identity had. It was known that a cheetah Morph would gladly protect a fox cub like her own, if only because of group identification as a whole. Their interspecies unity transcended what was unheard of in the wild, a sample of what the world would be in complete cohesion. Perhaps this solidarity is what the world needs to be truly at peace...

Someone plunked onto the bench beside Kheng with the tickle of hair, the subtle scent of baked bread washing over him.

"Hey, Kheng," said the newcomer. Kheng turned and stared at the wolf seated next to him, her well-groomed arm fur having brushed against him. Kheng turned away, his face flushing. He wanted to leave with his dignity intact, but he couldn't do even just that.

"Listen, Kheng, I'm sorry if I upset you." said the wolf firmly but, inquisitive all the same. "Nanook must mean a lot to you, and I understand if you are not comfortable discussing him. But I followed to see if you're okay. You were in no state to run, stumbling around like a cub."

"It's not you," breathed Kheng. He looked ahead at the One Fullerton building across the water, a light breeze brushing his cheeks. He didn't feel like heading back into the convention center, not with him in this state. He won't hear the end of it from his co-workers once they saw him. These days, everyone had ten forms of social media to make it all the more painful, including live-streaming to one's chatgroup.

Enq turned curiously at him, obsidian nose twitching. "It's

about Nanook then? Who was he?" she asked. Her gaze was intense, but Kheng felt compelled to look back into it, if only for a moment.

"Nanook was the last polar bear in the world that we had at our zoo," started Kheng. He knew Morphs avoided discussing their feral counterparts in captivity, but it had to be done. "He was the very first polar bear to be successfully born from the stem cells of a species no longer in existence. I personally took care of him in his last few months."

Kheng blew his nose on a tissue Enq passed him. *Why do girls always have them?* he wondered.

"Nanook was fine until late last year. Then he started having these cramps and wouldn't even eat what he was given. He hardly ever moved from his cold room, such that my guys and I had to place his meals right before him. One day, he just stopped.

"All of us loved Nanook—many keepers see their wards as their own kids, and Nanook was no exception. It's hard to describe the connection we keepers and exhibit staff have to those under our care. It just isn't possible to ensure the well-being and care for a living thing and not feel like they are your kids in a way. Kids that you bring up and get worried about when they run a fever. Nanook was more than that to me."

Enq sniffed. Or was that a snuffle? "Whatever do you mean?" she asked. Her ears were now peaked towards Kheng.

Kheng shook his head, breathing in the salty tang of the river as his nose cleared. "As the first polar to be born of a little-understood scientific procedure, Nanook represented hope. The hope that even in the face of adversity, all living things can still thrive. When Nanook died, that hope died with it. There are no other polar bears in the wild left to hope for. He was the last."

Enq bent over and whined, much to Kheng's surprise. For

a moment, he thought she was hurt, then realized she was crying. Not for a feral of her descendance, but for a complete stranger she couldn't have known. Her whine drew out, and Kheng found himself placing an arm around her, his shorter arm barely reaching around Enq's larger shoulders. He swayed along with her sobs, awkwardly aware that others nearby could hear them. Enq's whimpers reverberated across his frame, each syllable with the resonance of a storm. He leaned his head into her mane, and soon he found himself crying along with her, two mourners of a friend long gone.

"So how old was the cub when you left?" asked Kheng as he stirred his *Kopi-Si*, which was coffee sweetened with evaporated milk. Realizing that they were starving, the pair had adjourned for lunch at a nearby roadside café. They weren't in any state to return to the convention hall.

"A month and a half," answered Enq. They were talking about a feral cub Enq was in charge of at the conservatory. She didn't order Kopi but had *kaya* toast which Kheng and her shared. "He had only just begun to recognize me! I didn't want to leave, but my pack needs me here with them, as well as my job."

"Don't worry, I'm sure he's in good hands," assured Kheng. "How many are there in your pack? How did you meet?"

"They're my family, actually," Kheng froze, but Enq didn't seem offended at his words. "So there's four of us, including Oyu and I. My father wanted him to stay and study at the National University of Mongolia, but Oyu convinced him that the Sociology program here was more comprehensive. My parents weren't happy about that, but they came along anyway, leaving me to work at the research center back home. Sometime later, I realized that there wasn't much I could do from Mongolia itself. With Oyu's persuasion and contacts with the faculty, I came down when I heard there was an opening for the local charter of my organization. You know the rest." The wolf leaned back into her chair.

Kheng nodded, looking closely at Enq's face. He could see the black specks that ran down from the side of her cheek ruffs, ending across her sleek muzzle. Up close, he could see the more subtle nuances of her visual gestures. The oh-so-delible slick and twist of her ears, the quivering of her whiskers as her lips rippled over the crunch of toast—

"So what do you do at work, Kheng?" Enq broke in. "You already said you studied Zoology and Life Sciences at NUS and work at the Zoo. But what do you actually do there?"

Kheng coughed as the crumbs of toast caught in his throat. Direct and to the point. "Well, I mostly write journal papers and propose policies for better care procedures for the wildlife in my section. It isn't strictly protocol, but I make an effort to assist the keepers in their tasks as well. It's only through getting your hands dirty that you truly understand the conditions faced by the animals, you know."

Enq leaned to the side, her paw scratching at the side of her mouth. "Any policies regarding Morphs?"

"Morphs? No, we don't really handle that," said Kheng, surprised at the change in topic. "I've published a peer-reviewed paper on my observations on Morph society within an urban setting, but I'm not getting much results on that. The only reviewers I get on my work are mostly other Morphs, including that Alsatian who got shot last year...what's his name, Gottlieb?"

"I'd love to take a look at it," said Enq, and once again, a warmth Kheng couldn't explain spread through him. "I want to know, Kheng, what makes you so interested in Morph society? How long has it been?"

Kheng thought for a moment. "Since my last year of Secondary School, actually," he confessed.

"Oh? Why so?"

"Well, there was this guest speaker my school invited during Tuesday assembly," said Kheng, trying to recall. "A Professor told us of the breakthrough in bioengineering and how Morphs could live among us as a valued member of society. At that time, I was thinking, 'Why not?' If those who are different could live alongside one another, wouldn't there be true unity throughout the world? From then on, I read whatever I could find on the topic: Science magazines, editorial reviews. I must be the geekiest guy alive."

Enq looked back at him, her face inscrutable. "Would you call advocating human rights the ramblings of a geek?"

Kheng stared back. "What? No, of course not!"

"So you would define interspecies unity as such?" Her question was now interlaced with the hint of a growl.

Kheng was at a loss for words. "No...I mean, yes, it's certainly important. Wait, you're leaving already?"

Enq had crammed the last of her toast into her snout and stood up. "It was nice meeting you, Kheng. I'll see you at the conference." With barely a dip of her muzzle, the she-wolf ambled off, her black-speckled tail swishing behind her with each step.

Kheng stood up to give chase, then thought better of it. He cursed himself inwardly at his lack of tact and hastily gathered up the bill. As he did so, a recycled plastic card placed below it fell into his plate.

Kheng wiped the stains off on the sleeve of his shirt. It was a United World Trust business card, complete with Enq's full name and accolades (*MSc, Ecology, Environmental Sciences*). No phone number, however; with only a CloudMail address. He knew that he had to find Enq again, if only to apologize for his insensitivity. He brushed the crumbs off himself and left the lone remnants of a shared lunch behind him.

"You come here often?" asked Enq as they walked step in

step beside the river. Boat Quay was a collection of lights after dusk, multiplied by two upon the surface of the river. Several River Cruise cell-powered bumboats hummed past, boatloads of tourists gawking around them. Few of the colonial-era buildings still stood, contrasting sharply with the 4th Generation skyscrapers. Near to them was the Parliament house, as well as the digitized statue of Sir Stamford Raffles, founder of Singapore.

"Only when there's an exhibition on," said Kheng, gesturing towards the direction of where the Museums were. "But I always make a point to walk beside the river, you know? There's a kind of peace to be found in it, knowing this is where everything started."

"All because of this guy?" teased Enq, pointing at Sir Raffles. A group of kids giggled as the statue quoted the year of his landing at their approach.

"Along with everyone else who came before," affirmed Kheng. "Most of us here can trace their history to the river. All the immigrants and traders landed on the very banks of this river, followed by many others. My great-great grandfather worked as a coolie in the warehouse that used to be there." He pointed towards the far end of the open-air restaurants that made up the west side of the river. "That's a kind of physical laborer, by the way."

"So you have returned, just like the salmon to his birthplace..." commented Enq, tail flicking in amusement. Her tongue lolled out in a smile, and Kheng couldn't help but feel good about that.

Kheng smiled. "I quoted that exact phrase in my final year thesis, but my lecturer wouldn't agree with it. You ready for dinner?"

"If I wasn't, would I be here?" She gave a wolf-pout, mouth closed with her eyes lidded, and Kheng had to marvel at the way the Chinuas took things in their stride. They were direct and to the point, although Oyu himself was more assimilated into human culture. It wasn't easy to find out which panels Enq attended, but Kheng had managed it with the help of his contacts at the conference. She had been impressed by his resourcefulness and perseverance, and after discovering they had plenty to talk about, they had met for every meal during the conference, but due to their own hectic schedules, could only manage a date on the night the conference ended. No longer decked in her safari clothes, Enq now wore a loose-fitting dress that was effective in breaking up every suggestive contour of her body. Kheng had ditched his working clothes for a polo-tee and jeans.

"There are other necessities aside from sustenance." pointed out Kheng.

Enq laughed. "Come on, let's not be lascivious, shall we?"

"I'm not!" protested Kheng as they made their way toward the nearest bridge. "There's water and companionship, for one thing."

"You really are a geek, you know that?" teased Enq. She turned to the river and leaned forward on the railing. Closing her eyes, she lifted her nose and inhaled, her breath a series of sniffs. Kheng stood beside her with hands in his pockets, peering into the flickering depths.

"Tell me, Kheng," spoke up Enq, her eyes still closed. "What do you smell?"

Kheng lifted his nose and breathed. "I smell salt. And cinnamon."

"Cinnamon?" asked Enq, turning to him in surprise. Her nose caught against the side of his lips, knocking him sideways. In his surprise, Kheng lost his balance and fell, landing butt first. As he threw out his arms to break his fall, his elbow scraped hard against the rough granite. Kheng groaned, propping himself up on his hand and jerked back, realizing he had cut his palm as well. Blood ran down the entirety of his hand, the river of blood from elbow meeting his palm.

Enq's paws went to her mouth as she slouched forward, ears and tail down. "You all right, Kheng?" She bent over to pull him up, only to have him jerk back as she grabbed his smarting arm.

"I'm fine," winced Kheng as he tried getting up. "I just need to wash it and—what are you doing?"

Enq had bent over, lapping hard at his sandy cuts with thick, deft strokes of her tongue. "Just got to clean these up before they got infected," she mumbled. "Hmm, it tastes good—"

"Enq, you gotta stop it, it isn't clean. Come on—" There were people around staring, so Kheng pushed hard at her shoulder.

Without warning, Enq snarled, her jaws clamping twice over his arm. Kheng yelled, stumbling back from the wolf. He could hear screams from people around him, but fear for his life kept him looking forward as he crawled backwards.

For a moment, Enq snarled back at him, her black lips drawn back with all teeth bared, fur across her neck bristling. Then a look of confusion crossed her muzzle, and she fell back against the railing, tail drooping. Her ears dropped flat against her crown, and a low, soft whine could be heard as she slumped to the ground, her eyes averted from Kheng.

"Enq, what just happened? Are you okay?" asked Kheng uncertainly, placing both hands forward as he stumbled upright. Part of him wished to run from this and pretend it never happened, but his zoologist side needed to know. "Enq, we got to get you back home. Just follow me, and everything will be fine—"

The flash of torches blinded him, and he threw up an arm to shield himself from the glare. "Police! Get on your knees!" yelled someone behind him. "You, too, wolf!"

Kheng tried and failed to look past the beams. "Officer, I'm afraid there's been a misunderstanding..."

"On your knees! Do it now!" yelled another officer. Knowing that he wouldn't be asked a third time, Kheng dropped quickly to the ground, locking his smarting hands behind his head.

"Don't worry, Enq, it's not your fault." Kheng whispered even as the police surrounded them. "We'll soon be out of this mess." As he said it, Kheng wondered just how true it was.

After detaining them in two separate guardhouses at the nearby parliament building, the Morph Crimes Unit came to take Enq away to the Police headquarters, Kheng close behind in another van. Kheng's mind raced as a paramedic treated him.

Running through earlier events, he knew that there was no way that Enq had any intent to murder him. If she had, she wouldn't have tried it right next to many other people, what with Parliament House close by with its permanent police garrison. He recalled how she had reacted when the stimulus for her anger had been applied by his push and quickly removed soon after his backing off. Kheng had worked with enough canids to understand their mannerisms. If he didn't know any better, Enq was reacting to her natural instinct to be aggressive towards physical contact, like how one's own dog would still bite should you disturb it during a meal. To make matters stranger, this seemed to have been retained despite a Morph's modified gene strain. Kheng had never heard of Morphs reacting this aggressively to an unprovoked push, and they'd been around for a while now.

They pulled up at the police headquarters at Irrawady Road, and Kheng was brought to an interview room for questioning. Numerous witnesses along with SmartCam footage made it clear that Kheng had been the victim, but the Investigation Officer on duty wanted answers. What was his intent of being with her? What were they fighting about? Furthermore, will it be safe for the public when the wolf walks among them, assuming that bail was approved? Despite Kheng's protests, he was sent for a breathalyzer and urine tests, as he no doubt knew Enq was, too. How would Enq feel with four walls around her? Will she fly back into the rage which the police so wanted proof of for her incarceration? He didn't even know if this joint had staff trained for such an incident. One underlying problem with the handling of Morph suspects was that they saw and thought things differently than humans, and what could be acceptable for them may be uncalled for to their human counterparts.

Eventually, the IO and the other detectives got tired of questioning Kheng and allowed him to wait in the lock-up waiting area, no queue numbers for him. Kheng leaned back against the creaky, worn Plastmetal seats, wondering how this would all end. The cops had nothing else for him, but he couldn't leave Enq all alone to face these guys who barely understood her. Even today, Morph behavioral training was given only to a small percentage of police officers, and these were almost never Morphs themselves, meaning that the training was of limited use. It wasn't uncommon for Morph-related crimes to be prosecuted with the same intensity as human-related crimes, despite the fact that they had their own behavioral and cultural norms.

The door to the front desk creaked, and waves of musky scents washed over Kheng's nostrils, including one he recognized. Turning round, Kheng saw three wolves and recognized the youngest as Oyu. He stood quickly as the oldest wolf approached.

"Mr. and Mrs. Chinua?" said Kheng meekly, lowering his head and ears the best he could in submissiveness. "I was with your daughter when she—we got arrested."

The old wolf was much larger than Enq was, and she beat him by at least 6 inches. His expression was the most inscrutable of all canids Kheng had ever encountered, feral or otherwise. Unlike Enq or Oyu, his chest fur was yellow, with the tips of each and every strand of fur tinged with the white that came with age. His wife, or mate—depending on how one saw it—was smaller, but no less unapproachable in demeanor. Oyu stood slightly behind them, his muzzle averted, and Kheng remembered that this was Enq's entire pack.

Mr. Chinua sniffed the top of Kheng's head. "If you're human, don't greet us with our ways," he snorted, sneezing as he did.

Kheng raised his gaze. "Sorry, I just—"

"Listen, human," Mr. Chinua stepped forward, and Kheng was forced to move back as his muzzle came close. "I don't know what intentions you're harboring, going out with my daughter as you did. You had both met at a conference which may have brought together like minds, but not like attitudes. By attempting to date another not of your species, you are an affront not just to us as a people, but an instigator of warped perceptions your kind have against us. As the Patriarch and Alpha of the pack, I order, no—command you to cease all dealings with my daughter. Is that clear?" Mr. Chinua lifted his lips, just enough to show his still-intact row of fangs.

"But Mr. Chinua—" stated Kheng and fought back his panic as Mr. Chinua bared his sharp fangs with a snarl. The Sergeant could no longer be seen in his booth, and Kheng knew the police didn't want to get involved as long as the Morphs were around. It wouldn't make for good PR.

"Oyu will show you out," snarled Mr. Chinua with a click of his teeth above Kheng's ear. His ears flicked, and he looked twice his size with his fur bristled. "I believe we understand one other." Mr. Chinua drew back, and Kheng only just realized he had been pressed against the wall all this time.

"Come on, Kheng," Oyu caught hold of Kheng's hand and dragged him through the main reception area. He pushed their way past two officers, and, for a brief moment, Kheng wondered if Oyu was going to take him into a nearby alley for a vendetta killing. But the wolf let go of him just outside the doorway of the station. Several officers sat a distance away on break, but otherwise paid them no heed.

Oyu checked that there was no one near them and turned to Kheng. "Listen, Kheng," he said in a voice much gentler than he would have expected. "Forgive my father. He's highly protective of his pack, you may say. Despite what you may think, he would never dream of harming you. But it really wouldn't do well for you to get in his way; he fought more than his fair share of people at the laboratory."

"Laboratory?" asked Kheng, but Oyu shook his head vigorously. Now wasn't the time.

"I take it that these bites were caused by my sister?" Oyu lifted Kheng's right hand, the one he had pushed Enq with.

"Who else could it have been?" snapped Kheng. "Didn't the police tell you about it?"

Oyu shook his head, his cheek ruffs fluffing. "No. Our family simply got a call that Enq assaulted someone. We've come down to post bail and answer to any charges, if there's any."

"I didn't know you needed the whole family to bail someone."

"We're her pack. We support each other not just alone, but as a family." said Oyu, holding both paws out. "That's how we do things, for the strength of the wolf is the strength of the pack, if you quote Kipling. But that's not what I wanted to talk to you about."

Kheng folded his arms tenderly, supporting his right arm with his other. Oyu paced around agitatedly, his tail smacking hard against his brown work pants. The glare of the spotlights around the station threw harsh, unyielding shadows around him as he moved. When he finally stopped and turned back to Kheng, half his face was shrouded in shadow.

"I've been in human society far longer than any of my family have, Kheng. That's how I understand why your people do things that we have no reason to do. But you have to understand one thing about my family." Oyu fixed his amber eyes in Kheng's. "We weren't always Morphs."

This was a surprise. "But Morphs are born as Morphs, aren't they?" He had researched extensively on the subject, largely in part of his own interest. "There aren't any cases of ferals becoming Morphs, or humans for that matter. Not yet."

"That's where you're wrong, Kheng," said Oyu, gesturing with a finger for emphasis. "Ever since Morphs were bioengineered from scratch, certain researchers around the world took this principle further. Have you ever wondered why, despite certain species going extinct, there are still Morph equivalents of them?"

"I did, but I thought they were engineered straight from the extinct gene stock."

"Well, let me break it to you." Oyu placed his paws on his hips. "My family were ferals."

"What?" Kheng jerked back in surprise. "How's that possible?"

Oyu's ears flattened from his outburst. "Everything's possible with modern science. Surely you of all people know that. Not that my family had a choice."

"But surely I would have heard something about it!" Kheng's mind whirred as he took stock of this revelation. "My organization keeps up to date with the latest bio-technological developments, from stem cell research to Spec-cloning! How can we not have heard of it?"

"Keep your voice down, Kheng," growled Oyu, his eyes flicking to the group of cops. "Of all the research done in the world, just how many of the findings ever come to light? How much of it do you think is even legal? You can never imagine. Who knows how many breakthroughs could have been halted if the government or WHO doesn't approve, or if the area's head of religion comes down hard? Whatever you see or hear through news or journals is just the tip of the iceberg. Not to say there're many left." Oyu flicked his tail despairingly. Global warming had reached new heights in the last half-century.

"So what's that got to do with your family having been ferals?" asked Kheng. "Unless you're saying..."

Oyu sighed and leaned against a lamppost. "We were transmorphed from ferals to Morphs."

Kheng merely stared as Oyu continued, his eyes avoiding Kheng's. "My family was living around the northern steppe region of Khetti Aimag in Mongolia. My littermates and I were only five months old, and there were originally four of us, not counting Pa and Ma.

"You must understand that by then, we were old enough to learn to hunt, so Ma made sure to bring us out of the den. Times had always been lean, and the fact that we could never escape the ever-reaching grip of humans meant that we lived near them. I remember cowering in our dens whenever the humans came around with their tree-eaters and ground-pullers, never more than fifty meters away. I still remember Pa wanting to move, but Ma telling him they had cubs to feed, and that it would be the same everywhere. We were all in our den when they found us."

Kheng held his breath. He knew the trauma wildlife experienced whenever they were ripped from their homes, their collective experiences no more different from refugees in the Warring Zones. Except that refugees had much more hope of getting away from all that, even if it be through death.

"We didn't know for sure, but the scientists that grabbed us were probably tipped off by the redevelopment crew that worked in the area. There weren't many of us left in the wild or captivity, so it was quite a find for them.

"Know that research institutes are by far and wide varied. Some, like the Singapore Zoo, spans resources beyond that of one's country, while others are more like private practitioners, scientist wannabees if you will. Unlike national or multi-national corporations, these guys usually perform controversial research unsanctioned by the government. That was where we landed up in."

"And you could still remember all that even though you were all in your feral forms?" asked Kheng uncertainly.

"Being feral doesn't make us dumb to what's going on around," huffed Oyu with a glare, nostrils flaring. "Seriously, man."

"No, of course not!" assured Kheng hastily. "It's just that I don't understand how..."

"Fair enough," said Oyu, and Kheng was relieved he wasn't anything like his father was. "As I was saying, the theorem the scientists wished to test through us was that of Pre-cognizant Evolution, which is to say, evolution to before the point of that species' full potential. You ever heard of the Mongolian belief that all men were descended from wolves? Well, Ahsai, the Professor in charge, was a strong believer in the legends and only needed to confirm it.

"We were placed together in a chamber and subjected to control testing, including some sort of energy bombardment. You won't believe how much pain we felt. Our limbs and joints ached, our ears and backs hurt; even our noses weren't spared. All this happened for a total of two days, if I guess correctly, and, by time they were done, Palik and Cheka were dead."

Kheng then understood why he only saw Enq and Oyu. "Oh my, I'm sorry, Oyu," he whispered softly.

"My only consolation is that they suffered less than we have," replied Oyu as his ears drooped. "But we were no longer the same. We found that our paws could hold, and that our weight and spine shifted towards the back, such that we could stand on our hindpaws, albeit clumsily. We were also more clear-headed in our thinking, though I and Enq were still little more than cubs.

"Ahsai's theory was that, by subjecting us to Accelerated Evolution, or AccVolv for short, we would eventually evolve to humans," recalled Oyu, the fur on his back standing as he spoke. An ambulance siren peeled in the distance. "However, he saw the potential of utilizing incomplete evolution as a means of creating Morphs, which during then would fetch quite a sum as skilled labor. We were thus kept in containment cells, still together as we still needed our parents with us. From what we could see from our cells, Ahsai also experimented on other animal types such as Ibexes and also succeeded in creating Morphs out of them.

"Now, I knew not how the authorities got wind of us, but the Police stormed the facility two days later. Perhaps a lab associate tipped them off after he was beset by his conscience. Maybe he was bribed. Whatever the case, Professor Ahsai and his research were rounded up, along with all the AccVolved Morphs.

"The Police didn't know what to do with us. Although we were technically still partly feral in mind, we were still classified as Morphs, all other things considered. They knew what Ahsai wanted to prove with his research but were aware of the political implications. To inform the public that humans evolved from a host of other animals could lead to conflict with existing religious and international doctrines, as well as others who may seek to replicate Ahsai's research.

"The Government thus sent us to Morph education facilities to train to be what Morphs were originally bioengineered for: useful workers. My family was originally trained to be military personnel, but after the International Morph reinstatement act in 2031, Morphs became citizens. We had the choice to do what we wanted with our lives. I went on to study sociology, so I could better understand why you guys act as you do, while Enq studied Ecology and Environmental Sciences to help protect our feral brethren. As for Pa and Ma...they didn't see things the way we did."

"What happened?" asked Kheng.

"They didn't adapt well to the change," said Oyu, his tail drooping. "They were AccVolved when they were four and three years of age, you see, equivalent to an adult in human years. They were already set in their ways and didn't see the point in conforming to a culture they believed wasn't theirs. They turned to hunting in what little was left of the forests, as was what my ancestors had been doing since we existed. But they couldn't survive on that, so they tried livestock farming for a while. Enq and I bettered ourselves through the education system, and, the moment I got my degree from NUM, I applied for my doctorate. This meant that my parents could come along with me so that I could keep an eye on them. As you know by now, Enq continued her conservation work before following us here. Eventually, the pull of the pack was too strong for even her."

Oyu looked hard at Kheng. "Do you now know why Enq bit you?"

Kheng thought for a moment. "Instinct? From the time when you were all..."

"That's right," affirmed Oyu, pointing at him. "So you have to understand that you are not simply dating another Morph, but someone who follows what comes to mind. Not that she was trying to harm you, mind; she was most likely trying to protect herself as anyone would. No one can fight their instinct and reflex, as I'm sure you well know, but one can choose who they want to be with. Enq's going to suffer as long as you expect her to behave according to human norms. My family does their best to conform to society, but each and every one of us has our moods and impulses we cannot hope for any of you to understand."

"Why don't you report what happened back in Mongolia?" demanded Kheng. "Someone has to know about it and do something!"

"For what, exactly?" asked Oyu, throwing his paws up. "So that we can be segregated and treated as a curiosity? So that we can be kidnapped and locked away in another lab no different from that of Ahsai's? That's not what we want, Kheng, and the freedom to live our own life means more than anything else. I'm only asking you to understand us as we are, and not what we are supposed to be in society. Enq likes you, Kheng, that much I know about her. But I completely understand if you don't wish to continue going with her. Heck, I'll even let her know on your behalf, no questions asked. So what do you say?"

Kheng looked back at Oyu. The wolf had his whiskers and ears down, though he made an effort to peek them up when he saw that Kheng was looking. His tail slumped so low that it nearly brushed the floor, and Kheng realized that, as much as the wolf feared for his own safety, Oyu didn't want him to break up with his sister.

"Oyu, why are you doing this?" asked Kheng. "I would have thought that you would want your sister to date another Morph. Why a human? Why me?"

Oyu slid his hands into his pockets and paced, such that Kheng had to keep turning to track him. When he finally stopped, he looked uncertain, looking at Kheng out the corner of his eye. Kheng knew that look; it was exactly the same one his last dog Milo gave when he did a number on his socks.

"Enq told me that you smelt right," confessed Oyu. "If there's one thing we pride ourselves on, it's our sense of smell. How else do you think we avoid a confrontation in the wild? I smell it, too, but Pa's too narrow minded to go beyond appearances. Furthermore, if you and Enq ever got together, it proves to the world that true love spans even across species. Where are you going?"

Kheng stalked off without turning back. "I'm not someone to be experimented, you know that?" Oyu could only stare as Kheng disappeared around the corner of a building, lost in the darkness of the night.

Kheng threw his cellphone onto the table, bouncing it across the polished surface. His door hummed shut even as he slammed himself down onto his sofa. Before him lay the fresh remnants of a meal, probably Toman or Threadfin fish steak.

"Kheng?" called a voice from the main hall. Kheng jerked, turning to the source. A lady dressed in a shower cap and dressing gown appeared, looking much too alert to have been asleep.

"Hi, Ma," said Kheng. "You're up late."

"Late night at the hospital," said Ma. Her eyes widened. "Hey, what happened to your arm? Let me see!"

"I'm fine. The paramedics took care of it," said Kheng as Ma bustled around him, lifting and feeling it in places. "I really don't want to talk about it. But I'm kind of confused."

"What about, son?" asked Ma softly, sitting on the sofa beside him. The feel of the weight on the cushion reassured Kheng, even as he fought against the urge to tell her what happened. Will she really understand how he felt as he spoke with Enq, two minds in symphony as they discussed their life dreams and hopes? Ever since Father died five years back,

Mother was more pushy than ever, always encouraging him to find someone to share his life with. But what if that someone was someone she didn't expect? What if that someone wasn't a human, someone he might not possibly have kids with?

Kheng sighed, leaning back against the backrest. "I dated someone today," he started.

"That's wonderful!" cut in Ma, grapping hold of his hand, stopping when he winced. "Why didn't you tell me before? What's she like?"

"Different from us," said Kheng. That part was true.

"Okay," Ma didn't look at all upset. "Where's she from?"

"Well..." Kheng wished Ma would go already. "She's Mongolian. Her name's Enq."

"Oh. Respectable job and education?" asked Ma, bending forward with a smile.

"What's that got to do with anything? She got her master's degree in NUM and works in conservation," said Kheng, wishing Ma would stop probing already. "I first met her at the conference since it began two weeks ago, and she seems to be interested in the same world issues as me. I met her today for dinner, but her parents didn't like me."

Ma seemed confused. "You met them for dinner?"

"No, we met them somewhere else," Kheng's stomach rumbled, a grim reminder of what he'd missed. "I'm not sure if I should go out with her anymore, Ma, it's so damn complicated! I dunno, maybe I should just stay single. Let someone else complete her life."

Ma crossed her arms. "But is your life complete?"

"What?" Kheng looked back at his mother. Never before had she asked him that, even before breaking up with his past girlfriends. There had been Saskia, and Tai Sun, but Ma never asked after them when Kheng broke up with them. They had always been against his views, believing that humans are vastly superior to animals, such that respect need not be accorded even to Morphs. The last date with Tai Sun had ended in a shouting match of sorts when she made an anti-morph slur. No turning back from that.

"Kheng, I'm your mother. I've known you all my life, and you can bet I'll guide you as long as I live," said Ma, crossing her right leg over the other. "You were never happy with Saskia and Tai Sun, good riddance to them. Ah, you think I don't know?" She nodded knowingly as Kheng stared. "I've never seen this girl of yours, but when you speak of her, there's definitely something there. This is someone that will complement you!"

"She has mood swings," said Kheng, showing Ma his right arm. "I mean, from what I understand, she has little control over it. Her family's like that as well, except her brother, and I've known him longer. Is it really worth all that trouble and hurt to be with someone?"

Ma looked hard at Kheng. "Is it some mental illness of hers?"

"No, it's more of...cultural differences." Kheng looked away as he said it. Damn, any further probing and he would have to say how fluffy Enq's pelt was.

"So there's nothing wrong with it! Accept her as she is!" encouraged Ma. "Will you love Nanook less if he were to be hyperactive and damage the walls of his enclosure? Will you love your home less if the paint is peeling and the automated cooling is out? Why should Enq be any different?"

Ma gripped Kheng by the shoulders, and he jerked in surprise. She stared deep in his eyes, and, for the first time, Kheng felt that she understood, neither judging nor deciding.

"My mother had a saying; It is only through having another to live with that you have truly lived life. For without having done so, you have nothing to look back to." Ma glared at Kheng. "Do you want to look back at this point in your life and wish you had never let Enq go? Do you want to wrinkle your nose in disgust when you find someone crass and demanding, wishing you had a better choice?"

"No, Ma!" Kheng sat upright now.

"Then ask her out again, son, and apologize for any misunderstanding caused," said Ma, hugging Kheng tight. "Her family may not accept you, but you will be able to make the changes you need for it to be so. It is solely your choice and hers, Kheng, remember that. Know that I love you, regardless of who you choose to spend your life with." Her hug deepened, and, for a moment, Kheng felt like he was five once more, safe from all the troubles of the world.

Kheng paced in the common corridor of his apartment floor, pondering the crossroads he had arrived at. He stared at the traffic flowing across the nearby expressway, his thoughts lost in the blur of movement. He wasn't completely lost and alone in this dilemma but was ultimately the one who had to live with the consequences of a decision. Was it his own safety he was concerned about, or was it something else entirely? He had no doubt Enq was fine with him the way he was, but could he truly understand her, regardless of whatever he had learned in his studies and time with her? Despite what he had studied and observed in the field of zoology for the last few years, nothing could come close to that of actual Morph psychology. Notwithstanding the fact that psychology tainted one's perception of those you dealt with. He would no longer be looking at Enq as a potential lover, but as a subject under scrutiny. His view of her world would be sharper, but how much of it does she actually want him to see? Everyone has their secrets, even if it was yawning with their jaws wide open, and, as far as Kheng was concerned, they had the right to keep them.

As for her parents. They had been brought up as ferals. Enq had not. Can their perception of what's right for their daughter actually be trusted? Her parents would sooner pair her up with a feral as soon as a candidate presented himself. That wouldn't be fair to Enq, or anyone else that got caught between them for that matter.

Morph discrimination had occurred time and again, but was getting steadily less as public awareness increased. In all the times he was with Enq, there had been humans and even Morphs who didn't like the fact that they were together, forget anything else they might be doing. But discrimination wasn't exclusive to the human world. Kheng knew of many occurrences in nature of which members of a pack or pride bullied another merely because it looked different rather than it behaving differently from the rest. He had plenty of research and Animal Planet documentaries to back it up, assuming anyone so wished to hear his case. Heck, Enq's parents were already a real-life example to speak of, hating him merely on the basis of being human.

Discrimination existed, but whenever it happens, it strengthened the individual's responsible, be they human, feral, or Morph. It made them fight hard to be accepted and gave them a challenge to petition for equal rights where there otherwise would be sloth. Is he going to let discrimination strengthen the bond he and Enq had, or is he going to let it pull them apart as easily as leaves by a passing wind?

Kheng pulled out his cellphone and dialed, hoping Enq would give him just one chance.

She looked about her surroundings, uncertain but firm. Her fur threw the reflection of the colored streetlights as she moved, graceful even in her uncertainty. Ears and nose twitched as she sorted out the scents that assailed her, her tail lifting somewhat as she found it. She stepped forward, slowly, hesitantly quickening to a brisk stride.

Kheng stepped forward slowly and deliberately. Dressed

in a polo T-shirt, with his most worn jeans to match, he had done away with deodorant and aftershave, letting his scent reflect his true self. He noticed that Enq wore her safari clothes once more and realized that she had the same idea. He stopped several meters away, giving her the space she needed.

"Come walk with me, Kheng," said Enq, her low growl betraying none of the agitation her tail showed. It wasn't an angry growl, but that low "rrrrr" that seemed to follow through with her words, like the wind passing through a forest. Kheng dipped his head and kept in step with her, tracing the edge of the river as they moved.

"You chose to meet by the river," said Enq, and Kheng realized it was as much a question as a statement.

"Just as it represented the start of my ancestor, so had I wished it was so with us." replied Kheng.

Enq peered at him through the corner of her eye. "Do you think up of all these analogies by yourself?"

"Yes. Why not?" Kheng smiled back at her. They walked along a stretch of the river where it was far away from the tourist spots, a spot where only lovers reigned. Far across the black, rippling water stood the luminescent profile of the Marina Bay Sands hotel, the towering guardian of the city. The twinkle of the Singapore Flyer dwarfed it, a mere retainer in the wake of a great lord.

Enq hopped in step, her lips pursed. "My brother told you what my family were," she said, eyes flicking to Kheng. Her eyes practically glowed in the dim light, seeming to peer within his soul.

"That, he did," said Kheng, looking back into them. "But I see no reason to judge someone on what they cannot control. Would you deny me my dignity if I can neither smell the scents you enjoy, nor hear the sounds beyond my ears' purview? There's more to life than that, Enq, and I came here to tell you that."

This time, Enq stopped and turned bodily towards him, arms crossed. Once again, Kheng was reminded of how much taller she was.

"There are many things we can tell about someone, be it through intuition and scent," spoke Enq, her voice challenging, yet curious. "I know you are sincere in your intentions and reasons, Kheng, but I have to know this. What do you see in me that you don't in others of your kind? Besides the obvious, I mean."

Kheng turned to meet her gaze, gazing back at her eyes in equal footing. He looked back into those amber pools, feeling himself drawn in as steadily as the seconds passed, the windows of both souls open to one another, binding and intertwining together like minds and like spirits. "I see another who shares my fears and concerns of the issues of the world. When you understood what it felt to lose one you have cared for, I knew you were the one. When your family came down as a collective caring unit, all in the aid of a pack member, I knew I wanted such a life. I've always envisioned a world where each and every one cared for one another, and I would like to live my life knowing that we are all connected this way. I would like to spend my life with you, Enq. I mean it."

"Even if it meant withstanding my outbursts, as well as that of my family's?" asked Enq, her nose peaked in questioning. Her muzzle was now curious. "I'll do my best not to let the instinct override my judgement, Kheng, but you know as well as I do there's little to fight it. The next time round, you may get a lot worse than a bite. Are you really sure about this?"

"I'm sure." replied Kheng.

Enq pounced on him, her heavier bulk pinning him down to the ground. Her arms and muzzle closed around his neck, her tongue and whiskers scratching across it. For a moment, the world was perfect, with nothing able to ruin the moment for them. The couple drew their arms around each other in a passionate embrace, none of them wanting to let go lest it all ended.

Enq lifted her snout from Kheng, drawing her tongue hard across the nose. "You weren't even startled. You really trusted me," she giggled.

"I always have, Enq," replied Kheng, stroking his palms across his lover's cheek, relishing in the warm feel of her fuzz against his skin. "How about you give me another chance to make it up to you?"

Enq paused, her whiskers twitching in contemplation. "Fine. But this time, I get to choose the place!"

Kheng sat on a grass patch next to the river beside his Wife-Mate Enq. Little Milan and Yugen chased after Sena, their yips filling the windy silence. Nearby, Thesha growled, keeping his eyes on his tail before pursuing it. His black fur was a whir of black smoke as he spun, much to the laughter of his parents.

Kheng leaned his head against the curve of Enq's neck, nuzzling gently as he did. "A good litter we have here, my love. They're as beautiful as you are."

"It was as much your doing as mine, Kheng," huffed Enq, nosing his ear as he laughed. "Look at Thesha there. He takes after you, you know that? Not just about being a loner, but..."

"Having a thinner pelt?" said Kheng, watching his son tumble to the grass. "Yes, I know. I was surprised they all have near-complete wolf traits. But I've consulted my curator, and she thinks she knows why."

"And?" Enq turned briefly as Sena squealed, but kept her ears trained towards Kheng.

"Any evolutionary form which precedes that of a later one has gene dominance, insomuch as what she knew," said

Kheng. "That means your genetic strength is greater than mine and is a bigger contributor to the turnout of our cubs."

"But without you, we wouldn't have any," purred Enq, giving Kheng a lick on his cheek.

The cubs, including Thesha, suddenly stopped their play and turned, dashing off to someone in the distance. With barks and yaps, they rushed towards him, oblivious to the human families who stared at them uncertainly. As the figure neared, Kheng saw it was Oyu, who now had the cubs trailing close behind him, nipping and tugging at his knees. He wore a polo tee, which was a big change from the usual working clothes he wore in addition to a wolfish grin.

"Nice pack you have here," said Oyu, settling down near them. He brushed muzzles with Kheng and his sister before passing the cubs a pack of steaks, and they took off quickly, snapping and growling at each other. "Not that I ever doubted you," Oyu said to Kheng, tilting his muzzle apologetically.

"I never thought that," said Kheng. Oyu merely waved a paw in acknowledgement, and once again, Kheng was reminded how easily he transited in between the social realm of Morphs and Humans, adapting his mannerisms to the situation. A true adapter, as all wolves were. Regardless of climate or habitat, from the tundra to the cities of humans.

"How's Ma and Pa? They doing okay without me?" asked Enq.

"Sure," answered Oyu with a shake of his fur. "They weren't crazy about your leaving, but it had to be done. As long as you aren't with the pack, they don't care who you spend your life with. And I think it's great! You two make a great couple."

"You teasing us?" snarled Enq, and the two wolves stood up and faced off, growling and snapping in sibling rivalry. Kheng fought back his laughter as they danced around each other, the cubs watching them.

"Hey I'm Uncle Oyu!" yelped Yugen. "I'm going to be a

fighter some day!"

"Oh yeah? Then I'm Mama Enq!" snorted Sena. "I'm gonna bite your tail off! Rarrgh!" Sena leapt on Yugen, and Milan joined in, lost in a tumble of fur. Enq yelled and broke away from her brother, hastening to separate the cubs from each other. Oyu laughed as he helped Enq, the pink of his tongue bright against the grass and sky.

Kheng looked up as Thesha came and sat next to him, fixing his eyes up at his father. The feel of warm fur always pleasant, and Kheng reached out to brush the grass off his son's head, the sounds of Oyu and Enq in the distance.

"Pa, why do we look so different from you?" asked Thesha, and Kheng jerked, looking back into the bright, brown eyes of his son. Although the other cubs always looked away whenever he made eye contact and had yellow eyes just like their mother, Thesha was different, at ease with looking back at him. It had caused problems with Enq in the first few months of their upbringing, and the parents eventually had to pass it off as something they had no control over.

"That's because your mother's beautiful, Thesha, and we wanted the best for you all," answered Kheng. "Why don't you play with your brothers and sister? You're always doing things on your own." He nudged his son lightly.

"They keep saying I'm different from them, Pa, and I think they're right," said Thesha, his ears and tail drooping against his father. "How can I play with them if I'm different?" His question died into a whine, and Kheng immediately held his son close.

"Thesha, listen to me," said Kheng, nuzzling Thesha's ears such that he sighed. "In this world, there are many types of people, be they humans, Wolf Morphs, and other Morphs. It is through coexisting despite our differences that we are accepted for who we are. How else did you think your mother and I got together? Never ever forget that, son."

Thesha wagged his tail slightly. "But how you do know that you wanted to have a family with Ma?" he asked, and Kheng realized that, after all this while, there was only one answer for everything he had gone through with Enq, the reason why he had deviated from the course of action most people, Morphs or otherwise, would follow. Some called it love, while others called it an impulse. But there was no denying the real reason for what made all living things choose to do.

"Instinct, my son. There's no stopping instinct. Trust in it, and you can never go wrong." And Thesha knew just what his father meant.

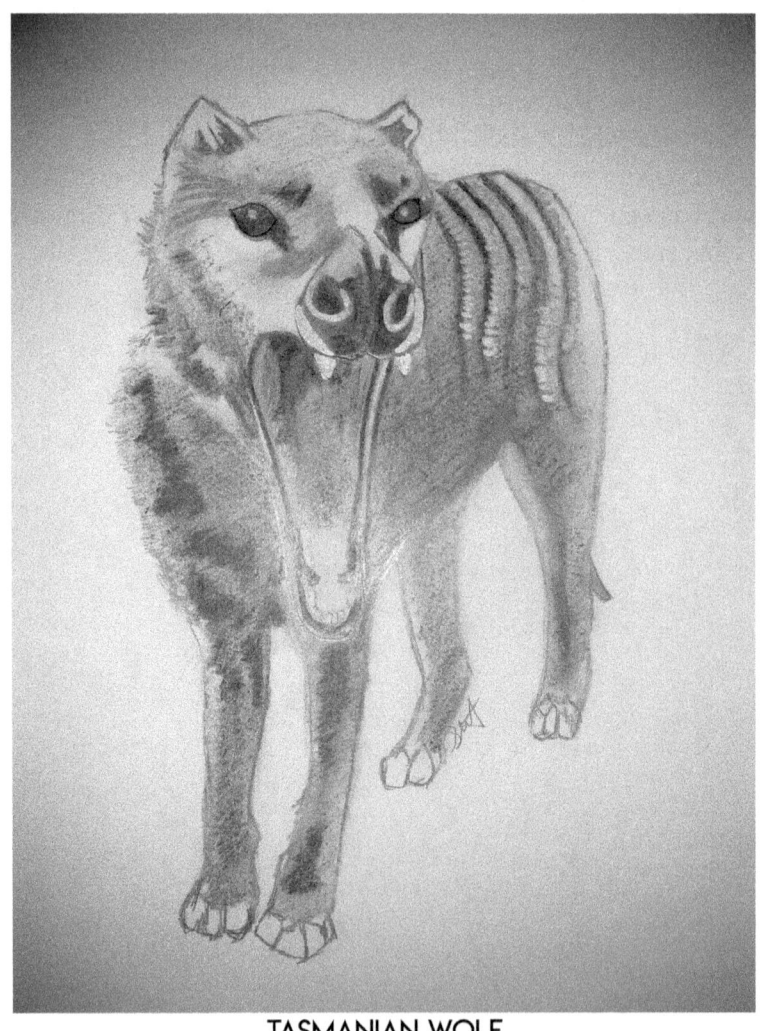

TASMANIAN WOLF
SL Westerfield

ROCKY MOUNTAIN ROSE
J. Daniel Phillips

And there, they waited. The ridiculous story had been told and the clerk sent home to brood, for Sherlock Holmes and his faithful servant were on the case. A weekend, they promised, a weekend and nothing more. Come Monday, Holmes instructed his companion to call for the police, for he had solved this conundrum once again. They were back at the street, at the building where their client was copying from some encyclopedia I'm unfamiliar with. No, no, not that building, but the bank next door to where the poor fellow owned a store...

I've always enjoyed the stories they write out in jolly old England. It's like a world far removed from the one I've inhabited for countless years. Brilliance and sophistication are celebrated, while here... Well, at the Cat & Kettle Saloon, a hog has just thrown up in the spittoon. I glare at him over my yellowing copy of the 'Adventures of Sherlock Holmes' with unsurprised familiarity. Wiping the muck from his face, he stumbles out the front door into the cool autumn weather. It's mostly known for that.

In the corner, a piano is being tuned, and yet music wafts

through the expansive establishment. A new windy box, the name of which escapes me, serenades us from the corner, expertly attended by a bartender who otherwise couldn't fry an egg in a pan. But here, at the foot of the Rocky Mountains, about as much can be expected from the dregs who call this place home.

Keeling isn't known for paved streets and brand new gas lighting. Then again, I didn't choose to move here because it boasted such amenities. I moved here for the peace and quiet, to get away from a life so different than the one I lead now. One that lets me live in solitude, where I can walks the streets without so many swiftly averted stares and the quiet insult of someone rushing across the street to avoid passing by my shoulder. That, at least, Keeling does provide. The weather is mild, the people keep their noses to themselves, and I'm left to buy books from passing stagecoaches bound for San Francisco without so much as a second glance.

For a looming wolf with fur like freshly-dug coal and eyes of smoldering ochre, that's about as much as I can ask for. It's a town that consists of perhaps two dozen scattered buildings—not including sheds and privies—and four times as many beasts. It's main street has six stores, a bank, an inn, a Western Union office with telephone and telegraph, a rather sizeable train station for the wagon trains of ore and timber that come out of the foothills, and, of course, the Cat & Kettle. The best and only watering hole in fifty miles.

From out the window beside me, I can gaze straight across the wide street to where iron horses and stagecoaches alike are attended by overworked hands. Beasts of all shapes and sizes mingle on the platform or wander across the dirt road to grab a quick drink or a bite to eat at the last stop before Great Salt Lake. And despite their gaudy, expensive Chicago attire, very few stick their nose up at it.

It's a building two stories high, sitting at the end of the

street, the head of which is the train station. Across in the other direction are a dry goods store, a general store, and the burgeoning skeleton of a Methodist church. A porch wraps around much of the building, below a catwalk on the second floor that grants access to the crisp, refreshing evening air, or a balcony from which adversaries may be thrown.

Inside, it's about as traditional as they come. Warped, wooden floors pocked with liquor and spit, sturdy frontier furniture which will remain long after the building returns to the earth, and a bar which runs from one end to the other just inside the door constitute its guts. At least here, they have a player piano—and a player when he isn't drunk—some tasteful paintings, mounted fish and fowl, and gas lamps. At the center back, below the stairs which wrap up to the second floor, the hearth crouches, dark and dormant. Two Kentucky rifles form a makeshift crest above the mantel from which mortar shakes as the trains rumble by, whistles blaring.

Today, thankfully, it is quiet, and I'm left to read my book, unmolested. It only cost me a nickel and a few minutes of haggling, but I'm always glad for any book I can get my mitts on, even if the pages are already beginning to yellow. Despite my desire for personal peace, I still love the melodramatic adventure novels. It makes the things I've done appear more romantic than they were. It paints them brighter. Sometimes, it even makes me long for them.

The bartender, an otter with ruddy brown fur, places a beer before me with a silent nod and wanders away. I flip to the next page just as a coach rattles by out front, swinging across the intersection and coming to a stop beside the train station. The bitter liquid passes my lips, and I sigh with relief at a good drink and of someone who feels stupid once he's been provided the answer to a puzzle.

They were tunneling into the adjacent bank through the fellow's pawn shop. His apprentice and his thieving friends just fabricated this nonsense about red fur in order to leave his property vacant as a staging ground. Quite clever. I would've never come to such a conclusion, even with the information I was provided. How does he come up with such tales? I sigh and turn to the next page. The story is called 'A Case of Identity.'

The illustration is pretty, featuring Holmes, the dashing badger, speaking to this aging heiress, a mare, in her finest clothes and pearls. A bit of laughter yanks me from my fantasy. Yes, I suppose I'm not alone here. A group of travelers off the Union Pacific idling at the platform outside occupy the bar. The barkeep entertains them, regaling them with nonsense stories. Suddenly, their eyes dart in my direction, and I conceal my face behind my book. A stone travels down my throat. No laughter this time. In fact, the silence is a thunderclap.

It's the cost of owning a home here, I suppose, and buying it off the landlord here dirt cheap. I stand out in a place like this, where I'm one of only a handful of carnivores. Even among the carnivores, I'm a sore thumb. It naturally raises questions, about where I came from, who I am, what are in the boxes I took into my house. In order to stem any outlandish tales, I informed the bartender on my first night here that I was a soldier, a Vanguard with a long rifle, and I've come here to retire. And I made it clear I wanted to be left *alone*.

Doesn't stop them staring, though, making up dime novel stories about me. Whisper, whisper; snicker, snicker. I shift in my seat so I'm angled toward while reading the same sentence ten times. Lowering the book, frustrated, I wipe my hands down my vest and adjust my belt and coat. Across the way, the coach is being serviced, baggage yanked from the roof by the four-horse crew that guided it into town. They're fighting over who can do it fastest. Fools.

Meanwhile, a female drops from inside the stage, donning

clothes intended for males. A wolfess, young and strong. From under a cream hat, she turns and barks commands to the crew and then grabs the arm of the stationmaster as he attempts to skirt her attention. After exchanging harsh words, a hand is hiked towards the bar. With a nod, she pushes him away. Then her march across the half-busy street commences.

My interest wanes, and I take in another mouthful of the beer given me. Then I lift the book and try to focus. I'm perhaps a handful of paragraphs in when the door bursts inward with great force. My nose pressed intently to the pages, I listen as pawsteps harshly cross the room. The crowd of gawking travelers has fallen silent.

"Can I help—?"

"Which one'a you's the soldier?"

She has a voice like nails down a chalkboard, a schoolmarm in the body of a girl just out of puppyhood. I risk a glance over my book. The bartender, Carl, I think, timidly raises a paw and points towards me. I put the book between us just as her head swings around. Even though I don't meet her eyes, it doesn't mean she didn't see me. And it's not like there's anyone else on this side of his saloon. The deliberate, fervent steps approach.

"You the Barghest?" the wolfess screeches.

For only a moment, I pretend as if she isn't speaking to me. But then I lower it ever-so-slowly. The Barghest? A thin, pretty face stares down at me from but a few steps away, her hands akimbo and her hip jutted to one side. It accentuates the wide bandolier that loosely hugs her waist of intricately, flowery machined leather studded with fresh bullets begging to be shot. That, and a tarnished Colt Peacemaker, blued, with a rosewood grip.

My eyes wander up, taking her in inch by inch. Her fur is like dirty snow, grays and blacks mottled in with clearer white. Her eyes are fresh clover, sort of like my ma had. And like my mother, this wolfess looks like she should be wearing a sheriff's badge, the way she carries herself. Despite it all, she's beautiful.

"No," I tell her, "go away."

And the book is raised again. That doesn't stop her, however, from yanking a chair back opposite me and plopping into it. After a moment, accepting that neither her leaving nor I resuming my stories will occur, I lower the book so it's held just above the table and look across to her. She's wearing a tight, white shirt with blue flowers stitched on, a brown jacket over that. Worn gloves protect her hands, and that hat isn't nearly as clean as I thought it was out the window, bent and cut up.

"What do you want?" I finally demand, flatly.

"My name is Rosaline McGinty," she answers without being asked, "and I came here to hire you."

I scoff and peer out the window at the stage she arrived in. It's nice, but I'm beginning to notice it's not as pristine, the luggage not as new. Who is she, so brash and bold? Why'd she search me out?

"I didn't see a work wanted sign in the window, did you?" I sardonically ask. "Besides, there's lotsa other folk here looking for work. Why don't you go bother them?"

"Don't want them," Rosaline immediately responds. "They wouldn't do no how no way. This is too dangerous for no fools to be sent out to their deaths. I need a professional."

"You need a professional for what, exactly, little lady?"

She purses her lips, offended, and jabs a gloved finger up at me.

"Don't you go patronizing me there, fella; I know who you are, I know the work you do," she hisses through her teeth. "And I need someone in your line of work."

I retreat from her as she retracts her arm and reclines in

the seat across from me. The chair creaks, and conversation resumes across the bar when I cast a withering stare at them. In the meanwhile, the box has stopped playing music, prompting the bartender to wander over to it and slip a new tube on. He winds the box, holding the table firm, and, with some grunting effort, music resumes, something new. It's like magic.

Now focused on my uninvited guest, I ask, "And what exactly is that?"

"I need a couple'a fellas kilt." When I don't immediately respond, she adds, "I got money."

I scoff. "You need some beasts killed? Then wait until the evening. There'll be a whole gaggle of desperados in here to select. They'll eagerly line up to take your gold."

"And they'll go on up there and get themselves killed," Rosaline retorts, leaning forward again. "Get other beasts killed, too. No. I need someone of your skill. Someone who can shoot the flame off a cigarette at a hundred paces; someone who can draw on a beast and kill him before the bell stops ringing; someone who's taken bullets through the heart and lived."

A cold chill races up my spine, and I drop the book onto the table, its pages open for the world to see.

"You mean of my *legend*," I snap before I can catch my tongue. I pound my fist onto the table and close the book as her face lights up like a firework.

"Ha, I knew it!" she cries. "I knew I was right! They told me in Cheyenne, they told me you go on up to Keeling, and you look for the Barghest, and he'll help you. They say you're the best and, fella, I need the best."

"God—look!" I reply, leaning forward. "I dunno who you think I am, but I ain't that. I'm too old and too retired to be traipsing around creation with murderous intent. Now why don't you go back to Cheyenne and tell those idiots who sent you here the *Barghest* is closed for business. Now, if you'll excuse me, I've got a book to read." Before I can open the book again, though, Rosaline has snatched it from my hand. "Hey!"

She twists around so my hands can't get to it no matter how far across the table I lean, and she hums to herself. Her face twists as she reads, unimpressed.

"You sit here reading dumb police stories?" she mockingly asks. "The great, bad Barghest is sitting in some rundown inn in some nameless town reading *books*? You're right, I *don't* know who you are." She returns the book, which I tear back and hug to my chest, grimacing at her even as she grins, quite proud of herself. "Why don't you tell me? I don't even know yer name."

We sit in relative silence for a moment before I ask, "You aren't going away, are you?"

"Nope."

"And I can't say or do nothing to scare you away, can I?"

"Not unless you wanna catch lead." She grins wickedly, trying to make me unsure of how familiar she is with the gun she so proudly displays at her hips. She wants me to second guess myself on whether or not she'd be willing to draw it on me. She does that, her story ends here, of course. And yet still...

I frown and shut the book after laying the little string down into the pages. I grasp the beer and swallow what's left of it before casting my eyes outside, catching sight of birds as they take flight from the post holding up the telegraph wire above the train station. I guess it has been getting boring. Sighing, with fingers wiping down my chin, I turn towards her.

"Fine," I say. "My name is Edward Harrow, Captain, United States Army, retired."

"Good to finally meetcha, Captain," she says and snatches

my hand up from the table. "Took me all of a day to get up here, you know."

"So you're from Cheyenne," I ask, stretching my fingers to regain the feeling in them, "Miss Rosaline?"

"Naw," she replies. "Just came via it, what with the railroad and all. Thought I'd find me someone good and talented down in Cheyenne, but Wild Bill's dead twenty years, and the Earp brothers might as well be."

"So you came looking for me?" I ask, a tad amused. "You know how to make a wolf feel special." And not bad, for once.

"Well, you used to do work for Marshal Collins, and you done ran Indian and bandit alike into the dirt, so you came highly recommended. Collins and this fella I met, Colonel Bert Hayworth, both said if you can't do it, it can't be done, that you's the best shot that lived since William Tell held a bow."

Yeah, I'm definitely not running her off. She believes the myth too much. Exhausted, I resign myself to this fact, and into my chair, too. With my arms crossed tightly, I cock my head to one side and look sidelong at this little lady. Tough as nails, this one. Got a look in her eye like she'd crush whomever it is she wants dead if she had but the knowhow to do it. Hope it's not over money.

"Tell you what," I surrender, "you buy me a drink, and I'll listen to your proposal."

A very large part of me hopes that, in the respite provided by her departing the table, I would discover I'd developed the ability to become invisible and slip away while everyone's back is turned. The truth is, I haven't had a gun in my hands for years, though skills like that never go away. I prayed it would stay that way. The other part of me expects exactly what happens.

Rosaline turns around and whistles at the top of her lungs. "You! Boy! You get on over here with a bottle and two shots, or you'll be eating one of them!" she hollers. "And you make it snappy, or I'll get snappy!"

The otter looks up with immense disbelief but ultimately complies, despite the muffled giggles of his other patrons. A handle of whiskey is retrieved from the middle shelf, and the proprietor shuffles across the empty room to serve us. The liquid bobbles in the half-full bottle as he places it between us. Then he presents us each with a glass.

"Will that be all, Miss?" he asks, sourly.

"For now," she replies without glancing up. "I don't think I'll be here long. I think we'll be heading out soon."

Scoffing, Carl rolls his eyes and wanders away, wiping his hands on his apron, muttering something about him owning this place and he can have her thrown out. He could call Sheriff Nelson, too. Nelson wouldn't touch her with a ten foot pole and probably has enough sense to just lower his hat again and return to the nap he's taking behind his desk when Carl got done talking.

Either way, I shake my head and flip my shot glass over.

"You're confident." A little too confident, if you ask me.

"I get what I want," she says, the cork swiftly loosed and the whiskey distributed. "By hook or by crook. That's what my daddy taught me." She replaces the bottle and slams the shot without a chaser. "I ain't got time to deal with no hogwash running one of the biggest mines this side of creation, so I take no guff and I give none, neither."

"You're a mine owner?" I ask, surprised.

"Ayup," she says and pours another shot. "Copper Creek, couple days' west'a here. Mostly silver, but we've brought up some iron, too. It's actually why I'm here." Ah, I think I see the point, and we're coming up on it at full tilt. She downs another shot, shivering and shaking. "Hoo, that's some nasty stuff. I'll have'ta order me some." I only drink the shot once she's settled down. It's like drinking acid. "Couple'a days ago, we were attacked. Whole bunch'a shooters come out the woods just after dark, or at least I assume, 'cause by the time we knew what was happening, they were shooting folk in their sleep. By the time me or my daddy figured out what was goin' on, five miners were shot dead, and another three were killed hitchin' up their pants. We thought they were just after the fresh ore. We had lined up an order for Denver, and a train from the Union Pacific had arrived to be loaded. But after we fell back from the base camp and shafts, leavin' all the silver, they just ignored it.

"We couldn't even mount a defense. It was like an old Indian raid. A-hooping and a-hollerin', firing madly, at least a dozen of 'em. Wasn't long until Daddy and me and what remained of the miners were down in the dell where the comp'ny buildings, rail station, and loading docks were. And they nipped our heels the whole way. We tried to hold out around the locomotive, but we lost that, too. Then it was just me, Daddy, and a couple'a miners holed up in the office, prayin' we'd see daylight again. But God weren't with us then. They started shooting up the buildin', and Daddy got us out the back window while we shot them through the window. I think we killed four of 'em, but it was like they were endless. I was just outside when they kicked in the front door. That's when I saw him.

"It was our old forebeast, Gerald Davison. He was a cruel creature who took pleasure hurtin' others. We had fired him the month prior for throwin' a worker down an incomplete shaft. I guess he wanted some payback. And it wasn't enough to just rob us or ruin us. He wanted our lives, our livelihoods. And that was all in the company safe, in the office with Daddy. But he and his beasts couldn't get in. It's a new one, heavy, and they didn't wanna blow it for destroyin' what's within. They forced Daddy to open it, but he couldn't. It takes two keys, and Daddy only had one. Davison wouldn't listen, beat Daddy bloody while I crouched under the windowsill. Then he dragged him outside and screamed, screamed that, if he didn't have that key afore the full moon, he'd hang my daddy, blow the safe to smithereens, and burn everything to the ground."

In the ensuing silence, I pour Rosaline another shot, which she greedily takes.

"That's in two days," I tell her.

"Thank you for the reminder," she sardonically swipes, the shot glass returned to the table.

"And you want me to kill them all?"

"I want you to help me save Daddy, save my company," Rosaline hisses, shooting daggers. "There were twenty-six beasts of all ages who worked there. I escaped with five. Davison needs to die for what he's done, the cruelty he's inflicted. And if that means burying a dozen beasts, so be it."

She retreats into silence and I to deliberation. When Rosaline's mouth isn't moving, she becomes someone else. Her eyes soften, her grip loosens, her shoulders no longer squared for a fight. She becomes a scared, little puppy who misses her papa and only knows one way how to handle adversity. Hitting it. Except this is something that hits back. Now she needs a bigger hammer.

And I can't find it in myself to tell her "no." My eyes wistfully gaze at the closed book upon the table, and I mentally admit she's right. I should help her. But I'm not wrong when I said I'm too old, too retired to be doing this. If it has to be done, it has to be done right. This is one of those situations where, if you screw it up, you die. Painfully. But the mist she hides in her eyes says that's already come and passed for her. I catch myself nibbling my lip.

"What are you offering?" I finally ask.

I brace myself for a barbed retort, accusations laced with acid, but none of them ever come. Instead, Rosaline leans forward and draws a silver chain from around her neck. Glimmering in the afternoon light, a large, golden key appears from within her tight shirt. Her hat swiftly removed, she guides the safe key around her neck and places it softly upon the table. Then Rosaline's Irish green eyes meet mine. My jaw sets.

"Alright," I tell her. "I accept your contract. But it comes with conditions."

"Name 'em, mister," Rosaline states without hesitation.

"You don't get in my way," I explain, to a reluctant nod. "And you do exactly what I tell you, when I tell you."

Rosaline's jaw sets hard, her lips becoming black lines hidden in creamy fur, but then her brow loosens and she stands up forcefully. Her hands snatch up her key and hat, which are roughly replaced. A handful of loose coins are dumped gracelessly onto the table to pay for that bitter swill we've consumed.

"We leave in a couple hours," she loudly declares, running her claws along the brim of her hat. "Just try not to get in my way, either. I know what you see when you look at me, and I ent weak, and I ent helpless. I killed two of them as they were barreling down on us, and, if it weren't for the gaggle of miners I had under my wing, I'da killed them all!"

Then, just like that, she's already marching out the door. I'll try not to, lady. I shake my head, my mind still playing catch up with my ears, and retrieve my book, trying to salvage at least a portion of my day. I crack it open to where I was and get perhaps a few paragraphs further before the door opens up again. Rosaline thrusts her head back in.

"Oh, and incidentally," she announces, "the lady's suitor's just her stepfather in disguise, and he's thieving her inheritance."

It's like being backhanded, and I wind my hand up to throw the book with as much force as I can muster. "Oh, you little—!" But she's already gone.

There's not much for me to collect before leaving, really. Some clothes, some provisions, and a big steamer trunk I lifted into the cramped attic years ago. It's heavy enough that, as soon as I have it down the stairs, the coachbeasts pulling Rosaline's modest purveyance help me get the thing out and onto the roof. I swear, it didn't use to be so heavy.

After that, I'm left alone to wait for her to return. The four horses that work for her roughhouse with each other in the street, and I look anywhere but at them. I've always felt strange about hiring coaches. I don't like being moved about by other folk. It gives me the distinct feeling of standing on someone's neck, despite evidence to the contrary. Doesn't matter. If it can be helped, I'll travel by rail or walk before I consider hiring a stage from Wells-Fargo or J.D Kinnear.

I'm sitting shotgun when the little wolfess finally returns. A box is under her arms, wrapped in paper and twine. Without so much as a word or an insult, she mantles up over the dash and thrusts her package atop the mountain of luggage behind us. With a whistle, her crew take their position, and we're off in a cloud of dust and debris.

Wyoming can be a downright beautiful place the right time of the year. It's a land that's as wide open as the plains but not nearly as featureless. It's a land of rolling rock, dense forests, and roaring rivers, with the imposing, snow-capped spine of the Rocky Mountains visible virtually anywhere. In the summer, it can be temperate and comfortable. In the winter, deadly. It's a land that takes much more than it gives without preference, where only alphas survive and prosper.

It's why I'm so unsurprised that this little lady has a personality like an agitated porcupine. Anyone weaker dies in the snow or at the mercy of bandits that call the craggy valleys and impenetrable forests of this untamed land home. And its settlers their prey.

"So what'cher story anyways, Captain?"

Angling my head back, I glance over to her. It seems the magazine she'd been perusing no longer holds her attention. Sherlock Holmes has taken a rest, stuffed into my steamer for later, and I've resigned myself to a little nap. Or what substitutes for one on this godforsaken road, seeing as every few minutes we clear a rut wide enough to rouse me. It doesn't help the crew keep pestering each other like a gaggle of unruly pups.

"What do you mean?"

She shrugs. "Well, like, there's a reason I came to you. Both Collins and the Colonel said you was the best there was but wouldn't really elaborate, such. And all I got out the drunkard soldiers what hung 'round the bar just told tall tales about you running down whole war bands of Comanche, killing the whole Culver-Warp gang in one evening. They said you killed Geronimo as his tribe was charging down the plateau in Arizona, one shot, right between the eyes."

She gets so animated with each additional load of lies that, by the end, her fingers are splayed wide and her eyes are wild. A sputtering laugh slips between my lips, and I lay myself back again, returning my hat to my eyes and my world to darkness. My hands slide under my neck. I've heard the first two before. But killing Geronimo? That's a new one. I'm not sure what she'd say when she learns he's in prison somewhere out east.

"You shouldn't listen to rumors," I chastise her, still grinning. "You shouldn't believe anything you hear and only about half of what you see anyways."

"So you're saying they lied and I hired me a moron, *Captain*?" she quips, trying to get my goat.

I scoff. "No," I parry, "I'm just saying stuff like that is hardly rooted in truth. One guy tells his neighbor, his neighbor tells his friends, his congregation, and soon a story about a drunken argument that ended with one broken bottle turns into the O.K Corral, with fireworks, a dozen deaths, and a fire to boot."

She's silent, but her silence is oppressive, accusatory. I can actually hear her put her hands to her hips and furrow her brow in disdain. It's enough to make me roll my head back in order to glimpse her face from under the brim. Yup, I'm right. When I finally meet her eyes, she hikes an eyebrow and sighs.

"Well, alright, Captain, why don't you tell me the truth," she requests, more politely than I had anticipated. "I wanna know who it is I was told to hire. And, well, it ain't like we ain't got time. Still about a half a day until we make base camp, and I can't think of a better way to pass it."

With lips pursed, I return to a half-doze and weigh the options presented to me. It's been a long time since anyone's asked about my past in earnest. Usually, it's some boozehound looking for a myth to latch onto or a gambler trying to knock me off my game so he can win back the shirt I took off his hide. She has nothing to gain from me by asking, and yet thinking about a lot of it still makes me prickly.

Far out to my right, we exit a copse of trees into an expanse of plain. Off in the distance, hill and tree climb against the horizon. Clouds skip along the mountaintops, caressing them, pocked with birds of all shapes and sizes that turn cartwheels, fighting over territory or cruising for food. The peace of this place is why I chose to move here. I suppose it's softened me.

"I, uh," I begin, my lips tripping over themselves. I cough and readjust my hat. "I served in the United States Army as a scout for a detachment of cavalry outta—well, I spent most of my time between Fort Laramie and the Arizona Territory. We were a bulwark against the Lakota, the Sioux, the Cheyenne, and I served from about '75 through 'bout the end of 1890.

After that, I left and started using my scouting and rifle skills to hunt bounties out of Cheyenne and Denver. What with the gold rush and the railroad, I was never wanting for work. That satisfy you, Rosaline?"

"Not really," she sourly replies. "Hardly any interesting or fun stories in there."

"'Fun!?'" I demand, jerking upright. "You think that military service is supposed to be fun or amusing?"

"Well, no," Rosaline defensively insists. "Every soldier and bounty hunter and gunfighter I've run across between home and Cheyenne has a dozen stories about their exploits, their adventures. Just thought you'd have one to share, too, since we're not exactly going anywhere!"

Half of a growl slips through my teeth as I turn towards her, throwing open my riding coat.

"My service wasn't *fun*, Rosaline!" I chastise her, thrusting a finger towards her and twisting my head. "I was a soldier. I spent most of my adult life traversing the mountains, the forests, the plains of the heart of this nation, tracking down natives who raided farms or smoking out bandits that robbed trains and stagecoaches. Oh, sure, it's all romantic, the way they write about in dime novels like we're some badged heroes patrolling a lawless land and saving the day. But it wasn't like that. They were hard years of running and sweating, nights freezing in my coat in a tent half-way surrounded by snow or mud, far from society, far from any comfort, partitioned only by brief, intense periods of horrific violence and murder that I still see in my sleep! I still see the faces when I close my eyes! Every night! Do you know what's like!?"

Her stony stoicism, hardened by my verbal siege, shatters when she hears those words. Unsure of what to do and having nothing to say, she pivots away as if struck. Then she sidles down from me so as not to earn another helping. The cold realization of what I've done settles in, and I look away, pressing my hat down onto my head to hide my face. Her emerald eyes shoot back and forth as her rough exterior fractures.

And this is why I had to move far away, because people don't seem to understand that the reality isn't always as charming as the fiction. Like it's a game. And it is a game. One where every action has consequences. It's just, sometimes, those consequences are steep, steep and obscured when you play your hand. Lost in my own thoughts, something brushes against my hands, and I retract it reflexively. Gasping, I turn to find Rosaline with her hand held out. Her lips are parted.

"Look, uh, I'm—I'm real sorry," she stutters. "I didn't know, I just, when everyone I spoke to called you the Barghest, I just..."

Her voice trails off, and we're left with only the rattle of the wagon as it cuts along this trail aimed straight into the mountains and the distinct lack of playful banter from the drivers. A chill rushes down my spine as the thought that I've chased off the first person in almost two decades to take any interest in me. I force myself to stop biting my lip again.

"They called me that for my fur," I idly mention, my eyes staring out into the wilderness, at the birds. "And the fact that I moved through this world like a ghost. I was attached to a cavalry unit, sure, but I hardly fought with them. I was a Vanguard, a Ranger. I'd roam ahead of the armored unit, sniffing out traps, discerning tracks, herding our targets into a place where the fifty-beast strong regiment I led could massacre them. But that was a rare occurrence. Most of the time, I worked on my own, hunting down single targets. I was the Barghest because no one could shake my pursuit. Ever. Even the Indians couldn't hide in their own land from me. And for the fact that they'd be dead before they heard the rifle shot, leading to the belief I'd stolen their souls in their sleep, the very breath from their lips as they strode. My record distance kill is about a thousand yards, give or take. In over a decade of service, I've killed probably forty or fifty beasts single-handedly. The majority died peacefully, never knowing they were in any danger."

Out of the corner of my eye, I can see Rosaline perk, soothed by the story and the fact that I haven't shoved her away, literally or metaphorically. My stomach warms.

"Why'd you leave?" she asks. "After so long on the frontier? Decade and a half."

I turn my head and hold her gaze for a moment before quietly saying, "Wounded Knee. I never held no animosity toward the natives. Most of them respected me, and I them. I love this land and the people in it, and the work I did was just that, *work*. I killed beasts of all stripe, of all nationality, all background. The only commonality was they were all of them cruel and wicked, or soldiers like me, just with a different uniform. But I don't kill unless I have to, and I don't kill for fun. They gave out medals for that, killin' females and pups alike. When I read that in the paper, I walked away."

"Into killing for money?" Rosaline retorts, no edge to her words.

Somehow, her joviality catches me off guard, and I snort like a fool. "Naw, I hunted beasts who deserved it," I insist playfully. "And in the four years I did that, I only had to kill twelve of my bounties of over sixty I brought in. That's called being a professional."

Rosaline shakes her head. "You took most of them in alive?"

"Oh yeah," I say, returning to a relaxed lean. "Sometimes, they'd come without a fight, even. Those are the cheap bounties, though, $20 and not much more. Thievin', usually, and I made sure they didn't get punished but for a slap across the face."

"If I had the ability, I'd take a bounty on Davison and his crew. $250 for each of his gang, $2,500 for him, alive or dead,"

Rosaline muses.

The road dips to the right, and we take a small creek at full speed. Though I have to grip the bar around the driver's box to keep from being thrown, it crosses without a hitch. When the rear axle slaps into the water, a pack of turkey vultures take flight through the canopy of the thickening forest. We're nearing the mountains.

Buzzards are ugly creatures that prey upon the dead, beast and animal alike. Either some fish got itself killed or someone died out here, in the tall grass that lines the road. Don't smell anything, though, and my nose never lies. That's one of the reasons why beasts, native or otherwise, couldn't outrun me. Wolves don't lose their prey, canines rarely do. Most herbivores don't get that.

"Who is this fella, anyways?" I inquire offhandedly.

"Davison?" Rosaline asks, casting her gaze upon me. I nod, and she rubs the back of her neck as she thinks. "He's what we tell pups hides under their beds when they're naughty." She smacks her lips. "He used to be our forebeast, right? The beast that goes out 'n makes sure all the ore comes up safe 'n sound and all the miners don't get hurt. He's gotta be strong and responsible, which was up his alley. Gerald is a hulking rhino, built like a locomotive. And he spoke so nice, and everyone liked him at first. 'Cept, and we didn't know it when we hired him, but he liked hurtin' people. Miners started coming back with cuts, bruises, then broken bones. But no one would tell us why. They'd just say, uh, something like 'accident' or mumble something and walk off for a whiskey, smiles long put to bed. And Daddy and me couldn't be everywhere at once, the mine's huge. Davison was in charge of shafts C and D, but he never told us anything illuminatin'. He'd just shrug and say that's what happens when they don't follow his orders. So stupid. I shoulda seen it then.

"Took us near couple'a months to figure out he was hurtin'

folk. First, it was over gambling and drink. Then it was just because he could. But no one would say anything, we had no proof. So I started snoopin'. I followed them out to the C shaft up the mountainside and watched as Davison worked. Nuttin' outta line at first, and I almost went away until the shaft rocked when dynamite went off early. A whole gaggle'a miners come running out the smoke, covered in dirt. Davison snatched up this cat, this Chinese fella what didn't speak no English, and started yelling. Dumb cat yelled back, and they went at it. Davison didn't like insolence.

"He pulled his gun and shot 'round the cat to cow him and then beat him senseless with the handle. So much blood..." Rosaline looks away, brow knit, and raises a gloved hand to her lips. Then she swallows hard. "Anyways, I knew then he was gonna kill the cat for this. I bolted to stop it, but he was already dragging the poor fella into the mine. I was yellin', but everyone was deaf. Threw him down the shaft as I was pullin' my pistol, laughing, proud. Daddy took alla two shakes to decide what to do with him. We led him off the property at gunpoint and told him, if he came back, we'd kill him. We kept his severance for his cruelty and gave it to the cat's family. That lit a fire, I guess. He swore us out and marched off, and we thought that was the end of us, but apparently not."

"Apparently not," I repeat humorlessly and peer into the trees.

This Davison guy sounds like a lot of bounties I hunted. Strangely enough, a lot of the soldiers I worked with, too. They remind me of the vultures couched in the fields, the scavengers that live off of death and destruction, revolting and ugly, trailing in the wake of war and lawlessness, always hungry, always needing. And there's always a mob of them waiting for the right leader to come along. The problem, then, is fighting them.

"You said you killed two of them?" I ask, taking a peek at her from the corner of my eyes.

"That I can be sure of, I think," she proudly states. "That don't mean I didn't keep others away from me."

"So you're good with that pistol?" I continue to prod.

I indicate that shining iron at her hip. Without looking down, she draws it and turns it over in her hands.

"Oh yeah," she declares, beaming. "Gotta. I grew up on the frontier, same as my daddy. Have to keep your gun arm strong, 'less you wanna lose your head to Indians or bandits. I learned how to pack a musket, shoot a pistol, and skeet shoot before I was fourteen. Daddy never made no distinction between boys 'n me. I'm his only, so I gotta be his son, too."

I cock my head to the side and look off the road, into the underbrush and foliage. Then I stand up in the driver's box and turn 'round, to her initial confusion. The steamer trunk is right behind us, segregated from her things due to the sheer weight and magnitude of mine.

"Hey, what're you...?" Rosaline demands as I flip the locks up. Inside, she's able to get at least a cursory look at what I own. From within, I draw my favorite rifle, an old Sharps I used during my service. That and a bag full of ammo and spent shells. "Oh."

I slam shut the top and redo the locks. This rifle is my baby and, even after years unused, she still feels like an extension of my arm in my hands. With skilled fingers, I flex and loosen the tarnished rifle reverently, it clattering and creaking with my machinations. Once the tingle in my fingers has subsided, I rack front the lever and manually insert a cartridge size christened "The Big Fifty" by anyone who's shot it or been unlucky enough to be on its business end. And for good reason, too

"Then I need you to show me," I explain. "I'm gonna throw a handful of these shells into the underbrush, make those birds take flight. You need to kill them once they're up. Anything you miss, I'll kill. You got it, Rosaline?"

"Don't have'ta tell me twice, Captain Harrow," she quips. "I'm ready when you are. And stop callin' me Rosaline. Only my daddy calls me that, and that's 'cuz he's my daddy. Just 'Rose' will do."

Before I can stop myself, I chortle and shake my head. Course you are, *Rose*. I put both of my paws up onto the dashboard and recline into the seat to give her a wide berth. The last thing I need is to inhale gun smoke.

"Alright," I say. "One, two—"

I give the handful of spent casings a throw like a baseball pitcher. They tumble tip over tail, twirling, bright brass dancers that glitter in the evening sun, before disappearing into the underbrush. A loud, crashing rustle, then the flutter of birds taking flight. Tensing, I cover my ears. Two vultures appear over the trees, all feathers and fear. Rosaline-er-Rose, climbs to her paws and, while standing, opens fires. Her draw is like lightning, I couldn't even see her hand move or the hammer retract.

The first bullet clips one of the bird's tail, the second rips apart its wing. Screeching and squawking, it pirouettes to the earth about fifty feet out. In quick succession, the pistol empties itself in a vain attempt to kill the other, swinging wide. With my ears opened once more, I hear 'click,' 'click,' 'click.' She mutters something incomprehensible and starts to reload. The single remaining vulture is far off now, gliding away, becoming nothing more than a speck against the sky. It's well beyond pistol range.

"Well," she complains when I don't leap to shoot it down, "ain't'cha gonna kill it? It's getting away!"

"Just wait." The bird grows farther away with each second and, her pistol reloaded deftly, Rose returns to her seat. "You know, the stories you told me they said to you? Geronimo and such? They weren't all tall tales."

"Yeah?" Rose responds, expectantly.

I chuckle deeply. "I killed the Culver-Warp gang while they ate supper in a cabin in a remote part of Montana, near the Bozeman Pass and Fort Ellis," I describe and creakily rise to my paws. The old rifle, likely in need of a good oiling, takes up a familiar, comfortable position against my shoulder. The hammer recoils with a lazy groan. "I shot Henry through the head at three hundred yards, through a window as they sat at the table. Clipped Oliver on the other side and then shot *him* on the follow-up." The fore sight hovers over the black speck, and I begin to regulate my breath, shallow, shallower still. My ears lay back. "Nelson and Frederick rushed outside and met their death as they tried hitching up their pants." I take one last breath. "None of them even saw where I was."

The trigger squeezes effortlessly. The shot reverberates up and down the valley, the loud crack of a bullet that could tear the arm off a beast twice my size at point-blank range. Afterward, there's a moment where the sound retreats, the world standing still like the moment before someone's hanged. Then, in the distance, comes a soft 'thud,' and the bird splits in half, falling like so much debris in the wind. I rack the breech open and clear the spent shell. Smoke pours from both ends as I wearily return to my seat.

"You're worthy of your moniker, Captain Harrow," Rose mutters, awestruck as she returns to her seat.

I flash her a coy smile before saying, "Please, just call me Edward. No one's called me Edward since I left home."

Rose is a surprisingly quick learner, I discover, as I spend the rest of our journey teaching her what I know. Like most gunfighters in the mountains, Rose depends on speed and favors putting out as many shots as possible without consideration for accuracy. Conversely, I must rely on precision and patience, working with a gun that offers but a single shot at a time. So I offer to help her hone her skills, urging her to slow her draw and focus instead on hitting what she aims at. One shot, one kill.

Naturally, that isn't easy, nor is the outcome perfect, but, by the end of the day, I feel she at least catches my drift. We make basecamp near a stream not far down the hillside from her father's camp just before dark and eat a supper of canned food and preserved meats. The horses keep to themselves. By the way Rose acts, they aren't going to be taking up arms with us, and that is fine by me.

Before going to sleep, Rose gives me a rundown of her family's property, where the rail runs, where the permanent buildings are, the trails that go up the mountainside basecamp, where the shaft entrances have been cut, those sort of things. It's not a sprawling complex, thankfully, and, once we're clear of the trees, there's nowhere to hide for Davison and his crew but inside the company buildings or in the mines. Neither are appetizing possibilities.

As for how many there are of them, Rose doesn't know. She said it was like a plains raid back in the day, they swarmed in. Likely, I think that's hogwash and that there's a handful of them at most. Perhaps ten. And, if I'm correct, they're only fighting because they're getting paid. Paid beasts don't commit themselves to much of anything. I'm half shocked they didn't scatter once one or two were shot.

Rose hasn't many answers. She doesn't even know where her father would be held. The company office makes sense, what with permanent walls and all. Good cover, too. But that's right at the edge of the forest. A scout like me could sneak in, slit a throat, and be out like a ghost. Like the Barghest. My guess is he's up at the basecamp, being held at gunpoint by the bandits, or in the mine. Rose merely says she hopes not and goes to sleep. Come the morning, we have work to do. Once more unto the breach.

I rise with the sun out of habit, and Rose rouses not fifteen minutes later as if by clockwork to a cold morning, grass yet covered with dew, mist hugging the ground. Our breakfast is quick and dirty, but our preparations can't be. Rose dons the same clothes she had the previous day. Brown pants, sullied white shirt, that dark jacket with the frills around the cuffs, and that wide, cream hat she adores. But when it comes to her weapon, she has some surprises after all.

The package she bought in Keeling, she drags from the roof and opens. From within, she produces a brand new, deep brown gunbelt with twin holsters etched with intricate milling that, from a distance, seems very feminine, but, upon closer inspection, reveals the howling form of a wolf's head on one and the regal, vicious visage of a fourteen-point buck on the other. With it comes a mint Peacemaker, bringing her armory up to a respectable two.

I dress similarly. Heavy black pants, white shirt, black vest that's been torn near the pocket that holds my watch, and my old, wrinkled, ragged tan duster that has seen better places as much as it has better days. A bag of ammunition slung around my shoulder and a big Bowie knife shoved into my belt, Rose and I set out.

Rose hasn't uttered a word since waking, and her face is no longer alive with the abrasive personality she proudly displayed the day prior. In fact, her fur has all but turned snow white, even the blacks and grays that comprise her mask and cover her ears and neck. It's a familiar sight. Fear of battle, of the unknown. Fear of death, specifically her own or perhaps her father's.

Either way, I don't question it. And I can't offer up any sage advice. Not much to say except don't get shot. And she knows that, if we get seen, the bullets start flying, preferably from *our* guns first. I know beasts like Davison. They'd as soon kill you as spit on you, and there's no talking with that level of hatred, of cruelty. With beasts like Davison, it's eat or be eaten.

There's a rise just east of the train tracks upon which we pause. The sun has yet to truly crest the forest behind us, so the whole valley below is cast in shadow, ominous, transforming the collection of buildings, train cars, and mining equipment into fearsome monsters. Lifting my muzzle, I taste the air. The wind is dragging scents down the mountain that looms opposite us. Cold and bitter, it carries the metallic sting of rusting metal and freshly dug silver. Below that is a symphony of sweat, alcohol, and the lingering stink of stale tobacco and day-old food.

The company office is easy to spot, at two stories tall, and is the farthest building from us. Between us idles a black locomotive, cold from disuse, with seven cars attached to it and only half of them laden with goods. A large coal bunker stands adjacent the office and, rising above the locomotive at the head of the track, lies a water tower with its spout extended. Overturned carts of ore litter the loading docks nearer us. Beyond that, I can sense no movement. Maybe I'm just getting old.

"I smell smoke, Edward," Rose mutters and then raises her hand. "There."

She gestures toward the locomotive, and, after a moment of confusion, I notice a wisp of fog coming up from beyond that bunker. No, not fog, smoke. Dull light flickers there, and I nervously wipe my cheek and jaw. Still, I see no movement. But where there's smoke, there's fire. And where there's fire, there's a camp. Seems like the little lady was right after all.

"Well, what are we waiting for?" Rose tactfully whispers, her hands itching at her guns.

"For events to unfold," I explain. "Come on. And keep quiet. If your father is down there, it would be best if we could get to him without raising an alarm. Follow me. Carefully, now."

Though I can sense her frustration, Rose merely nods her head. I snicker through closed lips and press forward, the rifle adjusted in its cradle on my back. In the silence of early morning, over the chatter of birds and our paws crunching the crisp, dew-drenched grass, I hear whispers at the back of my mind. Whispers; whispers, and the whoop and cry of battle, growing and growing. My dreams are invading my waking hours.

The fog is a blessing in disguise. Yet to be burned off by the morning light, it conceals our approach from any eyes. Rose sticks to my back like a fly to tar, stepping how I do, where I do, and, together, we descend into the valley like ghosts. Once we reach the caboose on this lonely train, I throw my back to the frame and nose around the rear corner.

Rose was indeed right. Davison and his beasts have formed a camp here at the mouth of the company office. A squat fire smolders at the center of perhaps four prostrate beasts, merely shapes in the foggy distance. Tents have been erected, and a palisade wall of overturned mining wagons form an ad hoc fortress on the edges. Its close enough I could spit on it. Above that, soft light glows in the second floor window of the company office. No doubt that's Davison's little keep.

As my eyes glide over the camp, I catch movement. Something lights beneath the eve of the sole building, followed by the soft glow of a burning cigar. Sweet tobacco, fresh and warm, fills my nostrils but a moment later. The glow is enough to illuminate the face of a guard, rifle in hand, kicking his paws up on the porch railing. Beside him, another figure lingers. They're chatting, I'm guessing, though I can't make out a single word.

Then the standing one turns and drops into the yard and trots through it. The fog whirls around his waist, much like water would a boat's hull, leaving the camp's sleeping figures undisturbed. Up the line, he follows the train until it passes beneath the water spout running from between the tower and the locomotive's boiler, a shotgun adorning his back. A match is struck, and he lights a dogend of his own as he takes up a post at the train's catcher.

"What do you see?" whispers Rose.

I grumble. "There's gotta be at least six of 'em. Maybe more, I don't see Davison. Two guards are up and about. One's on the company office porch, another is going up the rails toward the engine and..."

My eyes suddenly focus upon something I can't believe I didn't notice first. A plank balanced upon two sawhorses stands back from the tracks, at the rear of the loading dock farther up the line, beneath what looks to be a cargo crane, isolated from everything else. Upon it, a beast kneels uncomfortably, a rope running from his body up to the apex of the crane's crossbeam. From here, I can't tell who it is, but, from the figure's obvious emaciation and the poor state of his clothes, I can easily put two and two together.

"It's your father, Rose."

Overexcited, Rose shoulders past me to catch a glimpse, and her once worried face transforms into unbridled joy. Her gloved hands leap to her muzzle as her tail waves like a puppy's. It actually brings a warm feeling to my stomach and catches me off guard enough that I'm not paying attention when her lips part and out slips, "Daddy!"

A painful chill stabs into my stomach, and I seize the girl by the upper arm and haul her back, throwing my other hand over her mouth. She grumbles something and then whines when I press her to my body and glance around the corner. The beast on the porch doesn't move, another puff of smoke rising from his lips. The one down the line, if he notices, he hides it well. He spits onto the ground and then stretches his arms skyward. I audibly sigh.

"What are you trying to do?" I hiss into her ear. "Trying to get us or your daddy killed?"

"No," she mumbles, and I take my hand away. "I'm sorry."

A pang of guilt permeates my heart and stomach, and I let her go. "It's alright," I tell her, "but we're vastly outnumbered. If we can get in and out with your father quietly, that would be ideal. But if we have to go loud, we have to make sure we're in a good position to do it, understand?"

Rose nods, and we both stick our noses around the corner. Now the only question is how do we do it? Obviously, going straight into the camp along the train would be utter suicide. And trying to slip around the camp office, what with those two guards, would leave us out in an open field with no cover. That only leaves a route up the other side of the train, which isn't exactly appealing, either. We'd be too close to the camp. But, at least, the fog and train can conceal us, and these wide, black hoppers grant us ample cover. It would also lead near to where he's shackled on the loading dock.

"I think going up the side of the train would be best," I suggest. "See if we can slip between the cars and nab him without being noticed. If not, I can cover you from between the carriages."

Rose nods enthusiastically and unhooks the straps restraining her guns. With a finger laid across my lips, I cock my head and begin up the side of the train, crouching low and making my steps light and slow. Two cars up, I'm able to discern the flickering of the smoldering fire, the snores of the beasts yet to rise for the day. The guard up on the porch yawns dramatically and shifts his legs, eliciting a forlorn squeak.

I force us both to a halt when pawsteps pass near us. Kneeling down, I spy the other guard wandering up the side of the train, bored. He has hooves; a mule, maybe. He coughs and then spits into the grass. Once he's gone, I wave Rose on, and we proceed cautiously. Only the tender remains before the locomotive when Rose comes to a sudden halt beside me.

I look to where she does and understand why. Her father is in plain view, now, fog swirling around the ground below his paws. He's not a big wolf by any measure, but he is a proud one. It's that pride that these animals tried to beat out of him. His face is dark, ringed with cuts and gauze. Once beautiful fur is matted by blackened blood, his clothes torn and ragged about his body. He hangs weakly on that tortuous prison of his, unable to lie down for his bonds.

"Daddy," Rose pleads, quietly this time. She bites her lip nervously and then turns towards me. "We need to get him out, Edward. If he stays like that—he's an old wolf, he can't tolerate much more."

"I know, Rose," I assure her. "But we need to do this right. If we don't, well, I don't want to think about the outcome of that." I eye up the coupling between the carriages and then splay a hand towards it. "Ladies first, Rose."

I half expect an acerbic response, but she just thins her lips and lays on, hopping over the coupling with one paw thrust upon it. Trailing after her a moment later, the cold steel needles into my pawpads as I step up and sidle into a narrow alcove at the rear of the coal tender which offers a modicum of metal protection. Rose hides in the shadow of the hopper, and I scout the space ahead.

That hooved guard has disappeared without a trace, causing my ears to flicker with concern. The one on the porch, however, remains. From here, he looks like a brown bear, the size of a house and the weight of one, too. A Winchester lazily slumps in his lap. The rest of the camp is graveyard quiet. No eyes or ears are trained upon us.

"Coast is clear," I whisper to her. Reaching over my shoulder, I gracefully withdraw my rifle from its cracked, aging sling and carefully retract the hammer. I nod. "When you're ready."

Rose returns the nod and then cycles a nervous, cleansing

breath. Sneaking one last look, she slips out and hurries across the open space and up onto the platform. The thing moans and whines something fierce as the wolfess toes across to the prisoner, to her father. Once there, she pricks her ears up and lifts his chin.

"Daddy?" she asks, just audibly.

The figure opens his eyes and recoils, but not with joy. What paints his face is distilled fear. His limp body becomes rigid, and he chokes back sobs, struggling with the shackles that restrain his arms.

"Rose, no!" he says, much louder than is wise. "What are you doing? I told you to go to your mother in San Francisco!"

"Shh!" she chastises. "I'm here to save you. I promised I would."

Rose stands up and circles him. Metal clatters as she desperately yanks and twists at the manacles behind him, to no obvious avail.

"It's no use. It's too late. He got the key from me, but he broke everything in me he could possibly find. There's only one thing he wants left," he cries. "And that's you! You have to get out of here. If you don't, I fear what he'll do to you, to me."

Rose comforts him, placing her hands onto his muzzle and then shushes him. "I ent in no danger, Daddy; you think I'd come back alone?" She says and then looks to me. Her father's eyes, one puffy, turn to me, and hope flits across them, if only for a moment. "See? He's a soldier, he's legend. We're gonna get you out, alright? He can't stop us."

"I fear this will only cause so much more pain."

Lord, miss, get on with it. You're kicking up a racket, and, sooner or later, someone's going to see us, or hear us. The bear has dived into a pleasant nap, and the other guard has yet to return, but the sun is cresting the forest over our shoulder, and the fog is thinning. We've not much time. I swallow hard and shift around in my seat. Something smells like cigarette ash.

It's only then when I hear the retraction of a hammer. And then another.

"Stick your hands up, or I'll blast 'em off!" a voice commands. "Turn this way; don't do nuttin' stupid, or you're meat!"

No. I swing my head around and meet the gleaming barrel of a brand new scattergun. Double barreled, it hovers a hand away from my face. At the other end, a donkey grips the stock and foregrip as if having never held it in his life. Self-assured, joyless eyes shine in a pitted face just out of puppyhood, shaded by a ragged bowler. As soon as he meets my gaze, he realizes he's not nearly as soldierly as he imagined himself.

The pitiless expression vanishes, and he inhales a sharp breath. The gun wavers, and that's all the window I need. My left hand darts out and snatches the end of the barrel and yanks it past me. All the while, my right abandons my rifle and strikes him square across the nose. Blood splatters, and his legs buckle beneath him. The thrill of combat begins to flow through me, but my exhilaration is wiped away mere moments later.

The donkey's fingers don't let free his gun, and the hammers fall.

A loud blast deafens me, and I stumble back against the wall of the coal bunker, gripping my ears, wracked with pain. Loud thuds pierce the din as the low-gauge load strikes a backstop of wood, dirt, and metal. It takes only a moment before the world returns, piecemeal, and I'm awakened to the nightmare we've accidentally wrought. The camp has sprung to life, beasts of all shapes and sizes racing to don their clothes and grab their guns. A monster awakens. Lanterns in the office blaze, casting a dark figure against the windows, formless and faceless.

On the porch beside his tipped chair, the bear recovers from being jerked from his rest and climbs to his paws. The rifle swiftly shouldered, he opens up on Rose. Idiotically, Rose continues yanking at her father's bonds, twisting and pulling and wrenching to no success. A bullet catches the floor, turning a board to splinters. It makes her jump.

"Rose!" her father screams. "Leave me! They won't kill me, not until they have you! Run, hide, before Davison comes down!"

Rose goes to argue, but another bullet lodging into the floorboards heads that off. Without hesitation, she kicks up onto her paws and streaks back toward me. She's sliding off the platform just as I retrieve my rifle again. The first thing I do with it is shoot into the leg of the donkey who snuck up on me. He haws and seizes his leg, effectively eliminating him.

Gunfire rings from the camp as four half-dressed males rush to their posts, ducking behind crates and barrels crudely thrown together to form a barricade or to the edges of the thin, wooden wagons. One, a raccoon, is actually holding up his drawers as he runs. At this distance, their fire isn't effective. We're just inside range, but, every so often, one will ricochet off of a hopper or buzz Rose close enough to make her sink below the platform and against the track.

It doesn't stop the wolfess from drawing her own pistols and opening up like a reservoir. Her aim is better than it once was. Splinters fly when the Colt bores holes through a makeshift wall, and loud voices cry out in surprise, fear, or for commands. It takes me a couple more seconds to reload before I close the breech and level my rifle.

Half-deaf, my ears filled with disembodied whispers, the fog whirling past us as day breaks, I shakily line up a shot. Emptying my lungs, I squeeze the trigger. The Sharps puts anything they can throw at us to shame. A barrel behind which a possum kneels explodes like dynamite, throwing shrapnel in the form of dried fruits in every direction. The possum screams something unintelligible, followed by something suspiciously like "Mother!" before falling into the mud.

Hot smoke billows from both ends of the gun when I rack open the breech once more. It brings back even more memories, more whispers. A fresh cartridge takes its place, and I close the gun. My head is starting to hurt from the stress. I'm too old to be doing this, and it's starting to become obvious. It doesn't, however, stop me from shouldering the rifle again and placing a bead over that hulking bear. The hammer retracts smoothly.

Just as I'm to pull the trigger, the door explodes inward, and a rhino marches out onto the porch, and I hesitate. The beast is monstrous in size and appearance. He towers over even the most impressive alpha and is equally as heavy. His arms are as thick around as my thighs, and his thighs are tree roots gifted movement. This beast, this Davison, could lift a smaller beast and pull him in twain merely for looking at him wrong. The gunfire ceases.

The Henry rifle in his hands is dwarfed by them, becoming merely a puppy's toy. And when he turns toward us, it catches the gleam of light, vainly displaying its intricate tooling. It stands in stark contrast to the rest of him, clean, pristine, and beloved where his clothes are threadbare and disheveled.

Davison's face is a war-torn battlefield of switchback scars and unhealed wounds. His horn, tall enough to be a deadly weapon, is chipped and worn, cracks running from base to peak. Even his hands weren't spared. Fingers are missing, large chunks of flesh, too. Even more knife wounds and scars run up into the cuffs of his clothes. His pants, jacket, and hat are midnight black. The only thing about him light is his shirt. And only by default.

He snorts and then calls out, "Rose McGinty!? That you?" When Rose refuses to answer, he snorts. "I know it's you, *girl!* You got some nerve comin' back like this! If you wanna see yer daddy alive, you will throw down your guns and gimme that key! I promise you, I will water this earth with your blood if you don't! Your family and whoever else's with you for good measure."

Rose stands up, stupidly, though I can't keep her from doing it.

"You let my father go, Davison, and I won't kill you where you stand!" she bellows, snarling.

"You hand that key over, and p'rhaps I'll think about lettin' you live, you jumped-up, puny cretin!" Davison threatens. He pauses, snorting, and then laughs. "And maybe I won't make good Papa Sean dance a gallows jig!"

He kneels down and snatches a rope from the floor near his feet. When he lifts it past his torso, it goes taut. It runs nearly seventy-five feet out, pulling up from where it was hidden with dirt, to the legs of the sawhorse on which Rose's father is kneeling. That's why he's tied up like that. That rope doesn't go around his hands, it goes around his neck.

The thick, wild smell of blood floods my nose, and my head becomes light. I actually have to lower the rifle and grip the train until my wits return. Sean McGinty lifts his head and, in the low light, I'm able to discern the noose that is wrapped below his neck. He then lowers his head, shamefully, fearfully, exhausted. I can empathize.

"Daddy?" Rose squeaks.

"I tried to warn you. Please. Please, just give up the key and run," he cries. "It's too late."

"It ent ever too late," she argues brashly. "And I don't bow to monsters like him! I'll see you dragged to Chicago to be drawn and quartered, or I will die trying, Davison! May you burn in the bed you made!"

Davison is quiet a moment before chuckling. It's soft at first, barely audible, but it grows to hawing, raucous laughter accompanied by melodramatic knee slapping. All the while, his hired guns look on at him with a bit of confusion. They look at him the same way a prisoner would their warden. That doesn't mean, however, their firearms are lowered. Quite the opposite, in fact.

"Well," Davison hollers, "we get that key whether or not yer dead or alive. And I figgur my patron in Denver'll find a clever way to make the signatures look genuine. So, boys, you heard the little lady! Oblige her!"

Davison yanks the rope clutched in his hands, and both sawhorses fall flat, the platform dropping like a stone. McGinty's paws stretch out under him, but they don't touch ground. The tips of his claws just barely scrape the ground below him. He swings and sways madly like a leaf upon the wind, gagging and sputtering.

"Daddy!" Rose cries and opens fire.

Our respite thoroughly spent, I put the rifle's foresight over Davison and pull the trigger. The bear beside him spins around as if kicked by a horse and falls to the ground. And I have the wind expertly knocked from within me. I slam back into the coal tender, gasping. My whole world spins, distorts, then disappears.

"... dying on the plains! They're coming down outta the rocks! We need to support the left flank! You said..."

"If you come back, honey. If you come back."

"...in your sleep, I swear to Jesus above, I'll—!"

"Edward, puppy? Edward?"

"Edward!"

My eyes peel open, and the cacophony of gunfire and terrified screams fill my ears. I sit up and peer around the wall, unsticking myself from it. Rose has returned to her hiding place below the lip of the platform. Her terror-ridden eyes gaze up at me, desperate, begging. Sean is gagging, kicking at the end of his rope, and what's been going on comes back to me.

"I can't get to him!" Rose calls. "And I can't shoot it! It's too small! Please! You need to save him!"

I don't think I can, though. My head feels empty, and my heart feels full. A violent tremor runs up both of my hands, and I can no longer taste my tongue. All I can smell is blood and gunpowder. And yet I snatch up the rifle and clear the spent shell. I reach across for my pouch of cartridges, and, when my hand comes back up, it's covered in blood. My blood.

Gasping, I turn and look down. My coat is soaked red on my side, and I search it. My claws discover two or three holes, and I press through them until I touch flesh. A loud yelp escapes my lips before I can stopper it, and I realize what happened. The shotgun blast didn't miss. Some of the shot caught the side of the tender and ricocheted into me. I didn't even notice it in the blast. Instinctively, I suck on my fingers, my breath rattling.

"Edward!" Rose cries from below. "Please!"

I meet her eyes and know she doesn't know I'm hurt. She doesn't need to. Not yet, anyway. Her father's dancing is becoming less lively, and I know I don't have much time left. The bullet enters the breech and disappears behind the falling block. With as much strength as I can muster, I cock the hammer and then lay the rifle across the bunker wall.

The foresight finds its mark, and I begin timing it as Sean swings to and fro like a macabre piñata. I inhale a deep, cleansing breath, and then let it out. I never was much for religion, even on the battlefield. But today, a silent prayer goes out, and I pull the trigger. Dust leaps up from the rope, and Sean plummets to the loading dock with a thud.

Rose howls with joy before ducking back down as a

fresh volley is fired. Davison screams bloody murder and fires wildly, shot after shot, most swinging wide of us both. Meanwhile, I can't collect enough strength to keep my fingers wrapped around the rifle. Still smoking from one end, it tumbles into the dirt beside her.

"Edward, what are you—?" Her eyes peer up at me, and it's only then when she realizes something's wrong. "Edward, what happened?"

"Hit," I rasp. "He's coming. You have to."

My fingers tug on my bag to give it to her, but all it does is spill the whole sack out into the dirt. Rose gasps and reluctantly holsters her own pistols. Then she crawls over and grabs my rifle as bullets drill into the dirt around her. Her hand snatches a fistful of bullets, and then she retreats. For a moment, she looks at the rifle as if she's never held a gun before. Reality soon sets in.

The breech opens, and the empty casing tumbles out. A new one is pushed in by her comparatively delicate fingers. It fights her to close, but, with a grunt, she forces it. Then she cocks the hammer and lays the rifle upon the platform. It's almost as tall as her and looks out of place in her hands.

"Hold it steady," I warn her as I slide my legs off the side so they can dangle. "Don't account for drop, the round's too big. Now breathe in and hold it." She does exactly what I tell her to. A smile tugs at the corners of my lips. "When you breathe out and your lungs are empty, pull the trigger."

Rose crouches silently, bullets showering around her. Davison yells, firing madly while edging forward to get a better angle, just outside his little fortress. She closes her eyes and gradually releases her breath. The world swims in my head, and I rock my head back to rest it against the metal behind me. It's good metal. Cold. When her breath runs out, her eyes open. Just as mine close.

In the darkness, I hear a solitary bang.

"Holmes stuck his feet up on the corner'a the mantelpiece," a sweet voice muses, the twitter of birds only audible in the background, "and, leanin' back with his hands in his pockets, began talking, rather to himself, as it seemed, than to us. The beast—"

Paper flutters as the page is turned, and my eyes weakly flutter open. Bright light blinds me, yet still I force them open. A formless figure huddles beside me. It draws a sharp breath and then puts something down. Rose leans in and runs her hand back my forehead, smoothing my fur and stimulating my ears. It's the only pleasant feeling in a symphony of agonizing aches and pain.

"R-Rose?" I mumble, expending the sum of the energy left within me.

As if I were donning glasses, the young wolfess comes into focus. Her clothes, previously prim and proper, are sullied and spattered with drying blood. Once pretty fur is matted, desperate for a bath and a comb. Yet her eyes are bright, and, for the first time since we spoke on the stagecoach, she grins brightly. It's reassuring.

"Shh," she coos, shaking her head, "it's alright. Yer safe; it's over."

After wetting my lips shakily, I ask, "What happened? Did we win?"

She covers her lips to stifle laughter, but, in my state, I cannot think why. "Yeah, we won. Thanks to you, my Daddy's alive, we're both alive. And Davison is dead."

An outstretched hand gestures across my form, and I roll my head to look. Down the porch in front of the office, just outside the door, a large, crimson-stained sheet conceals what must remain of Davison, the mountain of a beast. A solitary, limp arm hangs morosely over the edge and into the dirt. Seeing his scarred, gray skin brings flashes of memory back, and my eyes return to Rose.

"We killed him?" I ask.

Her face twists up, her brow knitting, concerned. "You don't remember?"

I shake my head as gently as I can. "It—it's a blur after Davison appeared. I think I shot someone. Or something. I don't remember. My head hurts too much."

She shushes me again, and I feel her fingers lace between mine. "It's alright. He was comin' across the yard when I got hold of your rifle. You gave it to me 'cause you were losin' so much blood. He was so confident that, even with the barrel pointed at him, he didn't give pause. Just kept on comin' like a thunderstorm. The bullet got'im just above the heart, and that was that."

"What—what about your father?"

She beams proudly and angles her body towards me. "Why don't you see for yourself?"

Her other hand digs below my back, and, with great effort, she helps hoist me into a sitting position. The yard spreads out before us, the dead dirt littered with the remnants of our battle, a battle that occurred only this morning. It feels like a thousand years ago to me. Across it, in his finest, ruined suit, Sean McGinty perches upon a stack of crates, perusing through a fistful of documents.

"No rest for the wicked, eh?" I aim for playfulness.

Despite my less-than-enthused tone, Rose chuckles and squeezes my hand. "No; not for us. We've got a lot of life to stitch back together. This is the west, after all. If you're aren't struggling, you're dying. And if it weren't for you, we'd both be dead. They tried hanging him, and you shot the rope clean in half."

I glance at her, half unbelieving, but nod in acceptance. "I've done crazier. What happened to his gang?"

"We locked 'em in the storage shed out back. Thankfully, they didn't destroy the telegraph or nothin', so the Marshal should be up tomorrow morning to fetch them. I had to patch up the raccoon and donkey we shot, but they'll go to trial in Cheyenne, sure as the sun shines. Only the bear perished."

Metallic, bitter, the scent of blood is still the only thing I can smell. It overwhelms everything else and compels me to touch my wound, though it pains me. The voices that pervaded my head have gone quiet, mollified. By my actions, by my wound, I'm not sure. But for the first time in memory, they're quiet. My jaw sets when I notice my book beside her paw. I stroke the hard cover.

"You were reading my book?"

She nods. "Had'ta. Daddy said you was gonna die, and I figured this was the least I could do. I was hopin' it would bring you back to the land of the livin'. Looks like I was right." She smiles at me and curls her knees into her chest. "You're gonna have to stay here overnight. We have places to sleep inside. If you really want to, you can ride back to Keeling with the Marshal. But..." Rose chews at her lip for a moment and then casts her gaze away. "You don't have to go. We could always use a good gun here, especially somebody of your talent. You could train me, even. And I'm sure Daddy wouldn't begrudge me that after all you've done."

"I—I don't know, Rose," I reply after a moment's thought. "I shouldn't have done all this in the first place. I was too old, too worn-"

"Didn't stop you from doing it, though," Rose cheerfully interjects. "And I'm glad you did. I made the right decision searchin' for the Barghest. But I'm glad I found you instead."

She leans over and noses into my cheek before standing up with a groan. My cheeks burn hot, and I'm unable to compose myself enough to even say something stupid in return. Standing above me, Rose grins and then delves into her coat. Her hand returns with a book, an old one. The spine is loose, the pages are bent, and it looks like something has been spilled on it.

"I know, I, uh, I promised I'd pay you whatever you wanted—and I will," she explains, stuttering. "But I want you to have this. As a small thank you from me." She hands me the book, which I silently take. Flipping it over to the cover, I read, 'The Memoirs of Sherlock Holmes.' "I, uh, I really love stories, too. And I know yours is a hard one, but, just because it's hard, doesn't mean it shouldn't be told or shared. If you stay, maybe you could write yer story so others ain't writing it for ya. Make 'em see Captain Edward and not the Barghest."

Rose turns and strides up the porch before I'm able to gather my wits about me.

"Rose, wait!" I call out. She stops and casts her eyes over her shoulder. "You think people would wanna read that tripe?"

"Of course, I would," Rose nods emphatically.

I gnaw on my lip. "I—I'll need help moving what little I own."

The wolfess beams brightly and shakes her tail, and I try to mirror her joy. Part of me thinks I'm stupid for even considering a change like this, of taking up the gun again. But, here, I'm being welcomed with open arms. Not hired reluctantly. When I look at Rose, I feel proud of myself, at home. Even though it's crazy and highly irresponsible, I feel more at peace now than I ever did in Keeling. There, the Barghest lurked around every corner. Here, he's been put to rest.

THE WOLF'S REIGN

Your ancestors knew me, my face, knew my strength, my
    cunning, and my grace.
Very much, I was feared, yet all the more revered.
Tribe members, who bore my name, once knew my high place
    in life's chain.
Many now disgrace me, but may they be no more displace me.
Great hope have I that the time is nigh.
The wolf will reign again.

—Sherayah Witcher

THE WOLVES OF ETERNAL RETURN: OF LUPINE COSMOLOGY AND TIME
Paulina Angela Szymonek

Throughout its storied existence, the wolf has fulfilled all kinds of roles—from a villainous beast and a more neutral trickster figure to a worshipped deity and a powerful, helping spirit. Steinhart aptly summarizes human attraction to the image of the wolf:

> Our interest in wolves expresses the hunger of our imagination. For many, science is too narrow a view, and wolves are as much spiritual as biological. They say that, to understand wolves, we must go beyond what we can see into realms of spirit. [...] A number of people suggest that, if we could regard the wolf as native Americans did, we would take it to our hearts, see it clearly, and recognize higher powers that stitch us to the cosmos.[1]

The wolf is woven into the narratives exactly because its presence is so deeply rooted in the collective unconscious, and because its symbolism evokes such strong emotions in both the storyteller and the recipient. Its dual nature is inscribed into its image, and so the wolf of one story represents the

1 Peter Steinhart, *The Company of Wolves* (New York: Vintage Books, 1996), 320.

collectivity of the wolves, both real and imagined.

The wolf is a figure that pervades the collective unconscious of humankind perhaps like no other animal. It presents itself as a benevolent and malevolent beast, a guardian and a destroyer, lurking in the deepest corners of the mind. Its representations undergo constant transformations, but the wolf itself remains a mythical figure, an expression of many archetypes. The trail the archetypal wolf leaves behind may be followed through time and history, for it is demonstrated in myths, rituals, dreams and creative acts. Its image is reenacted with its every occurrence, and its everlasting presence is but a proof of the potency of the symbol.

The Cosmological Wolves

"The whole mythology," Jung writes, "could be taken as a sort of projection of the collective unconscious." It is especially visible "if we look at the heavenly constellations, whose originally chaotic forms were organized through the projection of images."[2] Some celestial bodies, a star and a constellation in particular, have descended from chaos to be organized through projecting them into the images of cosmological wolves. These projections share an underlying myth of death and rebirth.

In regard to the rebirth stories, Mircea Eliade writes about the mythical connotations of the moon that appear to be universal across cultures:

> The moon is the first of creatures to die, but also the first to live again. We have [...] shown the importance of lunar myths in the organization of the first coherent theories concerning death and resurrection, fertility and regeneration, initiation; [...] if the moon in fact serves to "measure" time, if the moon's phases long before the solar year and far more concretely reveal a unit of time (the month), the moon at the same time reveals the "eternal

2 Carl Gustav Jung, *Structure & Dynamics of the Psyche*, eds. Herbert Read et al., trans. R. C. F. Hull, 2nd ed., Vol. 8 (Princeton: Princeton University Press, 1969), 152.

return."[3]

It is not only the moon that proves to be the archetypal representation of death and rebirth. The figure of the wolf—a lunar animal with aplenty associations with the moon itself—appears to be a recurring symbol with the same or similar connotations. Barry H. Lopez recounts a Pawnee story about Sirius, the Wolf Star. In this creation myth, Sirius was the only one who was not invited to the great creation of the world. In his fury, Skiritióhuts—the Wolf Star—decided to send a wolf to the newly created earth. Upon encountering the wolf, however, the first people chased it down and killed it. With this act, the first people "had brought death into the world."[4] For this death, a ritual had to be performed. The people were to skin the wolf and use its pelt to make a sacred bundle. The wolf would be reborn and become many, and the people would lose their immortality. From this point on, they were to be known as the Wolf People.[5]

The wolf that Skiritióhuts sends to the earth is as powerful as the gods and appears to have a significant role in the people's lives. Lightning, a god sent to earth by the Bright-Star, was the one who brought the people to the earth, with buffalo for them to hunt. He was also the one who was deceived by the wolf, witnessed its death, and commanded the people to commemorate it. "But Lightning was not satisfied. He was angry with the wolf: now death had entered the world and people would quarrel and would kill one another."[6] And so Lightning journeyed to find his brother Káuwaháru, Ready-

3 Mircea Eliade, *Cosmos and History: The Myth of the Eternal Return* (New York: Harper & Brothers, 1959), 86.
4 Barry Holstun Lopez, *Of Wolves and Men* (New York: Scribner, 1978), 133.
5 Lopez, *Of Wolves and Men*, 133.
6 George A. Dorsey, *Traditions of the Skidi Pawnee* (Boston: Houghton Mifflin, 1904), 19.

to-Give. Together, they were to choose another wolf to give to the people. "I want to give one to them," said Lightning, "I do not want them to fight and kill one another."[7]

The two brothers came to the earth again. Each pointed to a different wolf. Meanwhile, a little wolf heard them talking. "They are talking about a gray wolf, and I am gray," said the little wolf, "then they must be talking about me." Then the wolf addressed the brothers: "You people there, what are you talking about? Do you want to kill me? I am as powerful as you are."[8] Upon hearing this, Lightning and Ready-to-Give ran, and the wolf ran, too. He ran and ran until he died out of exhaustion. The wolf drove Lightning to the west, Ready-to-Give to the north, and he himself ran to the south, which would become the land of the dead.

> So in all ceremonies the old man recites the ritual to proclaim to the gods, to let them know that Lightning is now to control the earth, and that all bundles are to be turned toward the south. Although these two men ran, they never died, and thus they show that the gods in the heavens were never to die; but people, like wolves, were to grow sick and die.[9]

The time and history seem to have set their course once the first "sin" is committed. Just like the moon, the Wolf Star, or the archetypal cosmological wolf, serves as the measure of time for the Pawnee. For them, the hunting and agricultural tradition was essential—hence their rituals were centered around the crops regeneration and buffalo hunts. The cosmological wolf was identified with both activities, and the cyclical nature of the Wolf Star was revealed through its rising and setting on the sky each night. This death and rebirth of Sirius "was but a reflection of the wolf's coming and going from the spirit world, down the path of the Milky

---

7 Dorsey, *Traditions of the Skidi Pawnee*, 19.
8 Dorsey, *Traditions of the Skidi Pawnee*, 19.
9 Dorsey, *Traditions of the Skidi Pawnee*, 20.

Way [...] called the Wolf Road," or the Wolf Trail.[10] Lopez concludes:

> The wolf was a symbol of renewal, just as the willow, the sacred tree of the southeast, was a symbol of death and rebirth. When the willow was cut down it grew back quickly, just as the wolf who was the first to be killed became the first to return from the dead.[11]

It appears essential, after the loss of innocence in the Pawnee creation myth, to ensure a ceremonial renewal of the lost eternal present, in which crops and game animals are in abundance. In the words of Eliade, "the myths of many peoples allude to a very distant epoch when men knew neither death nor toil nor suffering and had a bountiful supply of food merely for the taking."[12] Once the cycle of the eternal rebirth is broken, however, men "are no longer immortal."[13]

In the Pawnee myth, Sirius the Wolf Star is both the bringer of death and the victim. The beast/victim duality of the celestial wolves is also evident in the names given to the Lupus constellation, called both the Wild Animal and The Victim. It was otherwise known as the Monster, or the Wild Beast:[14]

> The Assyrians called it the constellation of The Beast of Death, and its brightest star The Star of the Dead Fathers. It was incorporated by some into the constellation to the east, the Centaur, and regarded as a sacrificial offering [to the gods], so that it came to be known as The Victim.[15]

In a Slovenian story recounted by the ethnologist Monika Kropej, the wolf finds its way into the sky once more. Quite unexpectedly, the wolf appears alongside the bear in the creation of Ursa Major, the Great Bear constellation. As the

10 Lopez, *Of Wolves and Men*, 132.
11 Lopez, *Of Wolves and Men*, 132.
12 Eliade, *Cosmos and History*, 91.
13 Eliade, *Cosmos and History*, 91.
14 Richard H. Allen, *Star-Names and Their Meanings* (New York: Stechert & Co, 1899), 278-279.
15 Lopez, *Of Wolves and Men*, 277.

182

tale has it, the bear or the wolf encounters a traveler—usually
a saint—and eats the horses which pull his wagon. For this,
the bear or the wolf is harnessed to the wagon to replace the
horses. In different versions of the story, the wolf is either
harnessed with the ox or the bear, and, together, they pull the
wagon through the sky.[16]

According to a Wasco legend, a coyote and five wolves
are responsible for the creation of the Big Dipper, a pattern
of stars that lies within Ursa Major. The five Wolf brothers
hunted game, and, each day, they shared the meat with the
Coyote. Each time they ate together, the Wolves marveled
at the strange figures in the sky. The Coyote grew curious
and asked one of the Wolf brothers about it. The oldest
Wolf, however, did not tell. Over the next three nights, the
Coyote asked the other brothers; they did not share, either.
Eventually, the Wolves decided to tell him. They said they
see two animals high up the sky, but they cannot reach
them. The Coyote replied: "Then let us go and see them." The
Wolves still did not know how to get all the way up the sky,
so the Coyote said he would show them. He started shooting
arrows into the sky, one after another, until they created a
passage to the ground. The Coyote and the Wolves followed
this trail. Upon reaching the sky, however, they saw that the
two animals were Grizzly Bears. The Coyote warned them
against it, but the Wolf brothers, unafraid, approached the
bears, who did not attack. The Coyote liked what he saw and
decided it should stay like this—the Bears and the Wolves,
together up in the sky. He destroyed the arrow path as he
climbed down, and so the Wolves could not follow. This is
how the Big Dipper came to be.[17]

16 Monika Kropej, *Supernatural Beings from Slovenian Myth and Folktales* (Ljubljana: Scientific Research centre of the Slovenian Academy of Sciences and Arts, 2012), 121-123.
17 Ella Elizabeth Clark, *Indian Legends of the Pacific Northwest* (London: University of California Press, 1953), 152-155.

The Norse mythology has their cosmological wolves as well. Similar to the Wolf Star from the Pawnee creation myth, the wolf Fenris is the embodiment of chaos in the Scandinavian lore. It is, however, a more natural chaos: that of nature and wilderness. Because it was prophesized the wolf would bring death to the gods, they decided to bind him. Just as the people chased down the wolf to the edge of their village, "symbolically the edge of their world, which is the cosmos,"[18] the gods tricked the Fenris wolf and bound him to a rock, which was then thrown into the sea. The earth itself shook when the wolf howled. To stifle the earth-shaking sound, the gods drove a sword through his mouth, keeping the jaws wide open. Here, "[e]very image indicates that this myth positions the wolf's power at the foundation of the planet."[19]

Fenris is the bringer of death, but also of renewal—both the beast and the victim. He acts as an anchor, bound to the world until Ragnarok, the final battle, referred to as the "war with the Wolf,"[20] that precedes the death and rebirth of the world. Only then does Fenris run free, to stand against the gods. The wolf opens his jaws so wide they encompass the world, reaching from the earth to the sky, and swallows Odin alive—for which act his jaws are ripped apart by Odin's son Vidar.[21] Robisch refers to Fenris as "the World-Wolf," which calls back to both the Icelandic myth and *anima mundi*.

Fenris fathered other cosmological wolves, who would have a part in the twilight of the gods. Hati would chase the Moon, and Sköll would follow the Sun until the mythological death of the world. When it comes, Hati shall devour Mani, and Sköll shall squeeze the life out of Sol. When the world is

---

18 S. K. Robisch, *Wolves and the Wolf Myth in American Literature* (Reno: University of Nevada Press, 2009), 154.
19 Robisch, *Wolves and the Wolf Myth*, 137.
20 Joseph Campbell, *The Masks of God: Occidental Mythology* (London: Secker & Warburg, 1960), 485.
21 Lopez, *Of Wolves and Men*, 275-276.

reborn, a new sun and a new moon will shine. As noted by Eliade, a hero who finds himself in the jaws of an animal and is being swallowed by it, is about to experience resurrection.[22] The rebirth of the world is ensured by meeting its demise from the jaws of the cosmological wolf. This act would, presumably, bring back the paradisal conditions in which man and nature are one again.

The Wolf Gods and Goddesses

Faithful to their cosmological roles, the wolves cross the night sky, chasing the stars and leaving behind their mythological traces that fall into constellations. Following these traces, we find that their connection to the cosmic narratives expands beyond the sky above. Jolande Jacobi observes that:

> [t]he bilateral nature of fabulous animals is something characteristic of primordial times; [...] For they have their origins in the time when water was regarded as the beginning of the cosmos. [...] In their symbolic language, the animals belonging to this primordial world were also [...] representative [...] of the Great Mother as symbol of the deepest realm of the unconscious.[23]

Robert Graves, in *The White Goddess*, describes the Great Mother, or the Goddess, as a woman who can transform into a she-wolf, a vixen, or a tigress, among other animal forms. She is associated with the moon and its phases, as they represent the natural cycle of birth, death, and rebirth. The Goddess is an incarnation of fertility, Nature herself.

Graves links the wolf to the Goddess, as it is a nocturnal animal that is commonly believed to howl to the moon and feast on corpses. He writes about Artemis and Cerridwen, both called the moon goddesses. For Artemis, the goddess

22 Mircea Eliade, *Shamanism: Archaic Techniques of Ecstasy* (New York: Penguin, 1964), 94.
23 Jolande Jacobi, *Complex, Archetype, Symbol in the Psychology of C. G. Jung* (Princeton: Princeton University Press, 1971), 145-146.

of the hunt, the wolf is a sacred animal. Cerridwen, the sow goddess, is associated with the wolf as a corn spirit.[24] Morrigan of the Celtic folklore is a goddess of war and destruction, but also of earth and fertility. She appeared under the guise of a crow or a wolf to move through battlefields.[25]

The figure of the wolf appeared in the fertility rites throughout Brittany, France, Germany, Serbia, and other Slavic countries. In the French folklore, the corn wolf lives in the fields, and so, when the wind sweeps through them, it is said that the wolf is walking through. When a wolf is seen among the corn and its tail hanging down, it is the rye deity herself. During the harvest, the reapers follow the wolf, who is ahead of them in the fields.

> When they come to the last sheaf in the field, that is called the wolf sheaf and the person who cuts it (who kills the wolf in doing so) is called the wolf until spring. The sheaf is called the rye wolf or the wheat wolf or the corn wolf, accordingly. In some areas it is burned, in others taken home and destroyed in the spring. In the farm country around Bordeaux a wether, or castrated sheep, was led around the fields, its horns dressed with flowers and small harvest sheaves, its body wound with garlands and bright ribbons. Its sacrifice signaled the death of the wolf corn spirit.[26]

A similar tradition has been recorded in Brittany, where, during the midsummer bonfire rites, a new head of the Brotherhood of the Green Wolf is chosen. He is then chased around the fire by his brothers. When the Green Wolf is caught, he is carried to the bonfire, where they pretend to throw him into the flames. The Green Wolf holds his title for a whole year, until the next Wolf is chosen and symbolically

24 Robert Graves, *The White Goddess* (London: Faber & Faber Limited, 1952), 24-222.
25 Kathryn Hinds, *The Celts of Northern Europe* (New York: Benchmark Books, 1997), 36.
26 Lopez, *Of Wolves and Men*, 220.

sacrificed.[27] The rituals surrounding the rye wolf and the green wolf were to ensure fertility and bountiful harvest for the upcoming season. The Goddess often requires sacrifices—and the wolf of harvest becomes her sacred victim.

A union between a wolf and a goddess is also known in Japanese and Ainu mythology. Ainu believed their ancestors came from a coupling between a white wolf and a goddess. A version of this creation myth from Shizunai tells a story of a mountain god, Retaruseta Kamuy—White Wolf God—who could not find himself a mate that would befit him. Only when he looks across the seas does he see a woman whom he later takes as his wife. Parallel to this, in one story from Shizunai, a white she-wolf—clearly a goddess—transforms into a woman and marries an Ainu chief.[28]

For the Ainu, the wolf was known as a high-ranking god, Horkew Kamuy, which means "the howling god," while the Japanese called the wolf *kami* or "a divine messenger of the Daimyojin." Some Ainu communities even "sacrificed wolves, as they did bears and owls, in 'sending-away' ceremonies called *iomante.*"[29] In agrarian communities, wolves were worshipped at shrines, as they were believed to be protectors of the farmers' crops. Amulets with wolf images, which in the seventeenth and eighteenth centuries were paired with the images of the mountains and rivers, symbolized fertility in a broader sense. Wolf gods and goddesses roamed the mountains, and the mountains were a sacred landscape, home to the gods and spirits.[30]

A wolf god of Slavic tradition, called the Wolf Shepherd, is a chthonic deity. He is believed to be identical with the

27 James George Frazer, *The Golden Bough* (London: MacMillan, 1990), 628-629.
28 Brett Walker, *The Lost Wolves of Japan* (Washington: University of Washington Press, 2009), 83-84.
29 Walker, *The Lost Wolves of Japan*, 83.
30 Walker, *The Lost Wolves of Japan*, 57-60.

Serbian Dabog, a god of the underworld. According to Veselin Čajkanović, Dabog became St. Sava in the process of Christianization. In this way, the wolf god of the dead has become a saint. Čajkanović also links the Serbian Dabog with the Slavic Dažbog, a solar deity, suggesting his dual nature as a benevolent god of the Sun and malevolent god of the night and the underworld.[31] Often represented as old, lame, limping, or blind in one eye, the Wolf Shepherd rides or takes the form of a lame wolf.

> He usually appeared during the twelve nights (also known as "wolf nights") around Christmas, which are called the *kalikanderi* in the Balkans. He may also appear during the time of wolf holidays called the *martinci* (around the name day of St. Martin on November 11), including November 1 (All Saints' Day) and 2 (All Souls' Day), when, as they say, the dead return to this world.[32]

In Livonia, wolves were believed to be God's hounds. They would go to the underworld, where the devil dines with sorcerers, and steal cattle and grain. If the wolves were to be late, they would not be able to enter the realm of the devil and hence fail to steal the grain. In such a case, the harvest would not be bountiful in the upcoming season. The wolves' coming to the underworld was set for the night of Pentecost, Midsummer night, and the night of Saint Lucia (December 13).[33]

In ancient Rome, a wolf festival was held annually in gratitude for the she-wolf that suckled Romulus and Remus. Lupercalia was a ceremony that marked the end of winter and a beginning of the new year. Held on February 15, Lupercalia was supposed to purify and bring fertility. Traditionally,

---

31 Veselin Čajkanović, *Mit i religija u Srba* (Belgrade: Srpska knjizevna zadruga, 1973), 191-192.

32 Kropej, *Supernatural Beings from Slovenian Myth and Folktales*, 54.

33 Leszek Paweł Słupecki, *Wojownicy i Wilkołaki* (Warsaw: Wydawnictwo Naukowe PWN, 2011), 133-134.

188

Luperci—brotherhood of the wolf—sacrificed goats and young dogs at the altar. Presumably, in the absence of the wolf, the dog symbolized the original sacrifice.[34]

The Wolf Runs Among the Stars

The cosmological wolves have found their place not only in myths, but also in the twentieth century poetry. It seems fitting to conclude with fragments of poems by Vasko Popa and Ted Hughes, who invited the star-crossing wolves into their verse.

In Popa's "The Lame Wolf's Tracks,"

> The lame wolf walks the world
> One paw treads the sky
> The others earth.
> He walks backwards
> Wiping out each track in front of him
> He walks half blind
> With terrible bloodshot eyes
> Full of dead stars and living bugs
> [...]
> He walks with the twelve-faces sun
> On his tongue which lolls to the ground.[35]

In Hughes's "Seven Dungeon Songs," the wolf

> Gazed down at the babe.
> [...]
> The wolf was wounded in the jaw.
> The blood dripped

34 Słupecki, *Wojownicy i Wilkołaki*, 38-46.
35 Vasko Popa, "The Lame Wolf's Tracks," in: *Collected Poems*, trans. Anne Pennington, intr. Ted Hughes (New York: Persea Books, 1978), 145.

On to the babe's hands.
The babe reached towards the pretty creature,
Laughing a baby laugh,
A soft-brained laugh.
The wolf
Picked up the babe and ran among the stars.[36]

The wolf, as a symbol and a collective, mythical entity trespassed through the land and into the sky and cosmos, leaving lupine stars and constellations in its wake. It cannot be understood as a single symbol or archetype; it will snap and lunge among the patterns in the dark sky, its presence as ethereal as time itself.

---

36 Ted Hughes, "Seven Dungeon Songs," in: *Collected Poems*, ed. Paul Keegan (London: Faber & Faber, 2005), 1034.

WHY
Patricia Lehtola

WE WERE WARRIORS...

We were warriors
held aloft.
Elevated, revered, adored.
Fast forward through the years
and skip amidst the gathering storm
as man plunders the land.
We're now feared;
killed for fun
because they can
until now we are the hunted few,
falling prey every day
to the murderers of the howling clan,
surviving any way we can
where once we were gods.

—Sam Dutton

FROM DARKNESS, SHE ARISES
Hemal Rana

Sally ran. She ran blindly into the deep darkness of the night. She ran despite how much her feet were hurting. She ran despite how much her lungs were hurting. She ran despite the fact she didn't know where she was going. She ran despite the fact she was hearing growling in the night.

She ran because what really mattered was getting away. Getting away from her home. Getting away from her parents. Getting away from the fire. Getting away from the white hoods.

She remembered her mother opening a small, back window and ordering her to jump out and run away. Sally's mom then went to the other room to retrieve her weapon. Sally stood at the window and listened. She could hear her neighbors shouting and panicking. She could also hear the neighs of horses and the hollering of men in the far distance. They were getting closer.

She looked back to where her mother was just a few seconds ago. Her father passed the door, clutching the rifle he used to kill rebels during the war. When he saw his daughter still standing by the window, he shouted, "GIRL,

GET MOVING!" Sally, surprised by the sudden outburst of anger from her normally calm father, did what she was told and jumped out the window. When she got to her feet, she listened again and realized that the bad men were getting closer. She took off and ran in the opposite direction, into the black chasm of the forest.

Eventually, she fell down in exhaustion. She lay down on the ground and focused on catching her breath. She listened again and could hear the faint cackling of the fire, but, mostly, she could hear her heart ready to burst out of her chest. She supposed she was at a safe distance. She closed her eyes and tried to keep her mind off her utter exhaustion.

But something was out there. She could barely see a figure moving in the near darkness. Whatever it was, it was growling. Before she could think about hiding, something else was coming. Sally knew what this was. She could recognize the sound of horse hooves anywhere.

The horse came rushing in, carrying with it a hooded figure, Sally wanted to burst out crying over her unlucky fortune. She was too tired to run away again. The best she could do was to crawl into the bushes and to make herself as invisible as possible.

The hooded figure got off his horse and, from his satchel, took out a bottle, which was undoubtedly filled with liquor. The figure then walked away from his horse, closer to where Sally was hiding. Sally tried to make herself smaller, but the figure was right there. The figure took off his hand and let it drop to the ground. Sally could see the face of a man with pasty skin, red, trimmed hair, and freckles on his face. The man then took a large sip form his bottle.

As he was gulping down his liquor, the man started listening to something strange. The man's horse was, for some reason, neighing like it was upset over something, but he ignored it because he was hearing something else. He realized he was hearing breathing. Human breathing. Slowly, he turned towards the noise. Sally tried to quiet her heavy breathing, but her heart sank into her chest when she and the man were eye to eye.

The man smiled. He chuckled and said to her, "Damn girl. I barely saw you. You're almost as dark as the night sky." He moved closer to her. His horse was neighing even more, but he ignored it. "Come on now. I won't hurt you." His voice sounded comforting, but Sally didn't trust that smile. That smile wasn't comfortable at all. But Sally couldn't move.

The man only laughed even more and said, "Looks like I'm going to have to carry you. Just think of me as your knight in shining armor." His face was only inches away from hers, and he was about to touch her. But his horse got even louder, and the man didn't ignore it this time because he could hear what the horse was hearing. The man looked away from Sally and realized too late what was making the horse so worried.

The wolf jumped onto the man with such fierceness and speed, Sally only saw a dark blur bringing the man down. The man screamed in unholy terror, his smile gone. His horse ran away. Sally, too tired to scream herself, desperately tried to move herself away from the wolf and its prey. The wolf didn't take too long in ending the man's screaming.

The wolf got off the motionless man and proceeded to lick off the blood in annoyance. Sally saw the man and saw he was as still as the night sky. His outfit was no longer white. It was covered with dirt and, more noticeably, blood. Sally wanted to cry in pure relief, but she realized the wolf was looking right at her.

The wolf was looking at Sally without any real expression on its face. Sally instantly noticed how dark the wolf's fur was. Unlike her, the wolf blended in with the night perfectly. The man didn't see it until it was too late for him. But she also noticed the wolf's eyes. They contrasted greatly with its fur, for its eyes were as blue as the morning sky. "What a beautiful creature," said Sally, not realizing how loud she was.

The wolf and girl continued to stare at each other. Sally was about to thank the wolf for protecting her before it started running away into the forest. Before running out of sight, the wolf looked back at Sally to see if she was following her. After a few seconds, the wolf ran out of sight. Sally got up and realized where she needed to go. She looked back to where her home and her parents were. She quietly said to herself that she would go back when the time was right. When it was safe. But not now.

With renewed energy, Sally once again ran, but she knew where she was going. She followed the wolf into the darkness of the wilderness.

THE CORN WOLF'S TITHE
Shannon Barnsley

They say when the wind blows and the fields sway the corn wolf is on the prowl. Some say he steals children. Some say he eats them whole. Some say he sends the storm before we can reap the year's harvest. Either way, he steals our future, just as winter is about to descend.

These are old wives' tales, of course. Old threads worn bare but stitched and re-stitched over and over to mend something, to save something not yet beyond repair, to keep us warm on dark days when the world grows cold and the winds of change howl outside our door and clamor at the window to be heard. In times of uncertainty, we seek the comfort of the past. But in times of uncertainty, it is the discomfort with our past we sometimes most need to face.

Alena and Silvia Kerner knew many such stories. Like so many Kerners before them, they had grown up in these fields, growing alongside the rye, wheat, barley, and all other manner of corn. They had brought water to those working in the fields, played at hunting and hiding in them, and grown strong on the bread they yielded. When they were little, they used to watch their father out in the fields with his scythe.

Swath by swath, he'd shrink the swaying seas of wheat and rye until the corn wolf had nowhere to run. When the wolf was cornered in that last sheaf, he'd strike it down. The wolf vanquished, they'd feel safe. Yet every summer, there he'd be again, a sharp gale rippling over the amber fields, watching them with hungry eyes. Waiting. Laughing at them from his hiding place in the tall corn. Bristling at every change in the winds, haunting every corner of their little world. An invisible foe they'd learned to see in every shadow and stirring.

Until the night he wasn't invisible. The night Alena was late coming back from town, her basket laden with all the jams she hadn't managed to sell. The sun was dipping low, and the golden hue about the fields drained as darkness fell. The girl was in no hurry to get home, for she knew her grandmother would not be pleased.

Since Alena and Silvia's father had died, their grandmother had struggled to make ends meet. Nearly all of Alena and Silvia's clothes were long out of fashion hand-me-downs that had been patched and re-patched winter after winter. While girls in the cities ate jam cookies at Christmas, Alena and Silvia fed on only their grandmother's tales of the better days behind them. Times before the war had come, when their country had been great and their people respected.

Her weak voice would grow strong as she grew louder, her hands abandoning their work rolling little trinkets in spare bits of yarn to hang on the tree. Her eyes would glow with a fervency and a hunger the girls had never seen before in their grandmother. Her mouth, so oft pulled tight into a thin, disapproving line, seemed as though its stitches had been ripped free. The white bones of her teeth would shine in the dim candlelight, a wider smile or fiercer snarl on her face than either girl had ever witnessed.

Yet come Christmas dawn itself, their grandmother would

sleep away the winter's morning, her ancient joints throbbing, her will gone as the fire burned low and the house grew cold. No gifts to open, Alena and Silvia had only a few ancient corn dollies to play with, though, to them, they were precious as porcelain dolls dressed in the finest silk and lace. The kind of doll they knew they'd never see, made for tea parties with expensive teas from foreign lands and other exotic delights.

Alena made the mistake of longing aloud for such fine foods once and got such a lashing from her grandmother's tongue. Was not the bread and jam of their own labors good enough for her? Was she not proud of what their own land could produce? Of the recipes passed down by her mother's mother's mother? Alena never made such a mistake again.

Such thoughts swirled around Alena's mind as she made her well-worn way through the fields to their little farmhouse where her grandmother's angry tongue and Silvia's disappointed eyes waited for her. When she was broken from her reverie by a sudden shift in the winds. The fields swayed anxiously, like the troubled sea tossed back and forth between a coming storm and the jagged rocks of shore, unsure where to go. She thought she saw something move in the fields, but then it was gone. She convinced herself she'd merely imagined it.

Then she felt it. Something brushed against her hand. Alena dropped her basket, nearly jumping out of her skin. She whipped her head around, but still nothing was there. Just a stalk of grain, no doubt.

Still, she heard something in the fields. The dark sky growled a warning as its edges began to unravel into storm clouds. There was something different in the air. An eerie sort of calm building to some manic energy that made her hair stand up on the back of her neck. Alena picked up her basket and quickened her step.

"My dear girl," someone called, appearing out of the corn.

"You dropped this."

The man before her looked to be in the prime of youth, either his late teens or his twenties. He was handsome, but in an unkempt, wild kind of way. His clothes were humble and much out of fashion, and his brownish-red hair hung in his eyes. But his eyes were what caught her off guard. For they weren't brown or hazel, but a dark amber, like the fields on an autumn evening or a longed-for pint at the end of the day. He held out her old red kerchief, a hand-me-down from her mother's older sister's daughter, now a widowed washerwoman with dull eyes and no future.

"Keep it," said the young girl. "The girls in town mock me for it anyway."

"But it's such a good color," he said. "It suits you, my girl."

"Who are you, stranger?" Alena hesitated on the path, her way blocked by the mysterious field hand.

"You really don't know me?" he asked. "I've known your family for ages, just as I knew the people here before them. And the ones before them. You've called me by many names, but perhaps you'd know me by the Kornwolf?"

"Y-you're the Kornwolf?" she asked. "What do you want? You won't take me!"

"I didn't mean to startle you, dear girl," said the wolf in farm hand's clothing. "Have I given you any reason to fear me? You've known me all your life."

"Grandmother says you steal children," Alena said.

"My dear girl," the wolf entreated, "I haven't come to steal you. I've come to warn you. For there is much danger here for you."

"The only danger here is vagrants like you," Alena told him, clutching her basket.

"No, no, my dear," warned the wolf, his amber eyes sad. "There is far greater danger in this world than an old spirit like me. I fear you'll soon learn that, dear girl. Though I fear that lesson will still come too late."

"You speak in riddles, wolf," said Alena. "I'm going home to my grandmother. Now get out of my way."

The wolf sighed, his hand closing on the kerchief. He breathed on it, and, suddenly, a loaf of fresh bread appeared in its stead. It smelled heavenly, especially after a long day on an empty stomach.

"Here, little one," he said. "I beg you to remember my warning. But either way, take this. A hard winter is coming. A young girl like you shouldn't go hungry because of the mistakes of your elders."

"What sorcery is this?" Alena demanded. "What trickery will befall me if I eat your cursed fae bread?"

"It's just roggenmischbrot," he assured her, placing the brown loaf into her basket. She could feel the warmth radiating from it, as though it had just now been pulled from the oven. "A growing girl needs to eat. Lest her hunger turn on other things."

"Keep your bread." Alena threw the basket down on the ground, blood red jam oozing out of glass shards. "I don't need it."

"Little one, please-"

"I'm not little," she declared. "I'll be old enough to join the League next year."

"At least take the bread for your little sister," said the wolf, holding out the basket like an offering. "Or perhaps your dear friend, the one you used to play with in my fields. The eldest Baumann boy. Klaus, was it?"

"Klaus isn't my friend," said Alena. "And he can't play in your fields anymore." She looked around, nervous. "He's got leg braces now."

"True," said the Kornwolf. "But I saw you come through this field to visit him many times after he got sick. You'd pick wildflowers for him and bring him pumpernickel you and your grandmother made. But it's been a while."

"Grandmother says not to waste good bread," said Alena. "We need it more. To stay strong through the winter. Lord knows the Baumanns have enough mouths to feed as it is."

The Kornwolf frowned. "Your grandmother's shame doesn't have to be yours. That's something you choose whether or not you inherit."

"Keep your peasant rags and your pauper's bread." Alena's cheeks were red. "They're the only things I have to be ashamed of. That's why I didn't sell anything. Who would trust jam from someone in such a shabby state?"

"My dear, please," said the Kornwolf, offering her the basket one more time. "Just because your jams didn't sell doesn't mean you failed anyone. Times are hard these days. For everyone. I'm sure plenty who saw your jams are home tonight wishing they could have bought them and dreaming of toast and cookies."

"And what do you know?" Alena demanded. "What are you even? A man? A wolf? A ghost?"

"I may not be able to leave these fields, but crows are world travelers and great talkers, if you take the time to listen." The Kornwolf gently put the basket in her cold hands.

"Crows?" Alena echoed, her face skeptical.

"Money may have lost its value, but bread shared with good friends never will. We're all kin, the land and those who live on it. Those who give back to it." The Kornwolf plucked a crow feather from a nearby stalk of grain. "Feed the crows, tend the land, show your neighbors kindness." He twirled the feather in his hands, and it became a pair of beautiful mittens made of thick, warm yarn. "And they might be inclined to take care of you when you have need of a friend."

"Keep your tricks and your pity! I don't need them!"

Alena pushed the basket away and ran, her braids, loosed from her kerchief, whipped about in the growing gale. The wolf stood in the field, his eyes on the horizon and the storm he knew was coming but couldn't stop. The winter he feared above all that had come before it.

When Alena got home, she told her grandmother she'd been robbed by a no-good, layabout rover boy who'd taken her basket and all the money she'd made selling jam, as well as the fresh baked bread she'd bought for Silvia as a special treat for her birthday next week.

Her grandmother had words about that, and she tired herself out that night with them. Alena was relieved, but Silvia grew uneasy, her heart fluttering like a little bird in a dark cage. She hugged her corn dolly extra tight, unnerved in a way she couldn't put to words.

"Don't worry, child," her grandmother assured. "We'll make sure men like that can't hurt good girls like you anymore. Things are changing."

But it wasn't rovers Silvia feared. Outside, a storm was brewing.

The harvest came that year, and Alena was glad to see the last of the Kornwolf's hold loosed on their land. And the next year, she did indeed join the League of German Girls. Their grandmother put by every mark she had, and Alena did every odd job she could so she could look her best with the other girls. And it seemed worth it at first, as Alena made fast friends and grew into a confident and capable young lady.

But when one of the other girls came to pay the Kerners a visit and mocked her corn dolly, Alena lied and said it was Silvia's. The next day, she burned it. Silvia kept hers hidden after that, in fear Alena would do the same to it. The house grew cold and quiet as their grandmother mended less and complained more. It was a cold winter that year, indeed, and more followed in its icy footsteps.

Alena grew older and more beautiful. She beamed, radiant

as spring sunshine in her smart, perfectly prim uniform, but Silvia sensed a shadow growing in her heart. It had been a long time since she'd last played with Klaus Baumann and Annika Rosenfeld in the fields, but now she treated them as strangers, or worse, when she passed them on the street. Instead, Alena spent all her time with Berta Tritten and Heida Vogel from the League, trying to catch the eyes of the dashing Sieg Unterbrink and the handsome Johann Stroman.

And so it was that afternoon. The League had gone to a nearby lake for the day, and some of the local boys had turned up after a camping trip of their own, still in their HJ uniforms. Berta, Alena, and Heida had stretched out by the lake while the boys had made quite a show of jumping and splashing about, trying to impress them. Johann had smiled at Heida at one point, and all three girls had erupted into giggles and conspiratorial whispers. But when Johann and Heida both vanished while the remaining boys sang "Vorwärts! Vorwärts!" and the girls danced around a campfire, Berta soured. Alena later saw her whisper some secret of Heida's to Bianka and Meta, the firelight distorting her face into something ghoulish and making Bianka and Meta's grins seem wild.

Alena's thoughts were an uneasy jumble as she made her way home that night. The dark fields seemed to swallow her up as the grains were tall this time of year. They swayed in the summer air, whispering secrets of their own. Alena had wanted to leave for the last few hours, but, now that she had, she found herself longing for the campfire and the company. Even familiar things cast long shadows in the dark, and the summer night was beginning to lose its warmth. Gooseflesh sprouted over her skin.

Several times, she thought she heard something behind her, but no one was there when she'd turn. She was just imagining things, she told herself. Just like she'd surely imagined things with Berta. She must have been laughing about something else with Bianka and Meta. She and Heida were the dearest of friends and always had been.

Alena screamed as someone jumped out at her. Expecting the Kornwolf again, she felt both stupid and furious when she saw Sieg and another boy whose name she didn't know laughing at her. She scolded them with such a sharp tongue even her grandmother would have been impressed.

"Oh, come on, Alena," said Sieg. "We're just having a bit of fun. You don't need to be so serious all the time."

"We could have a bit more fun, you know," said the other boy. He tried to kiss her, and she pushed him away.

"Stop it!" Alena told him. "You're acting foolish. And I need to get home."

"Relax, Alena," said Sieg. "Heida didn't seem to mind. I thought you were fun like her."

"My grandmother's expecting me," said Alena. "Good night."

"Hey, don't be like that," said the other boy, grabbing her.

She tried to push him away, but he was too strong this time without the element of surprise on her side. She cried out and struggled loose, running full-tilt through the field. She could hear the boys behind her, closing in on her. One of them grabbed her braid. He cried out as something threw him to the ground. Alena turned to see the Kornwolf standing over the other boy and firmly between her and Sieg.

"You heard Fräulein Kerner," said the Kornwolf. "You two ought to be going now."

"Who are you?" demanded Sieg. "Only crows and thieves wander the countryside at this hour."

"A good point," said the Kornwolf.

A crow seemed to fly out of the very corn itself and straight at Sieg, who ran screaming without a thought for his fallen comrade.

"If you aren't a thief or a crow, get going," said the Kornwolf to the boy on the ground. "Never set foot in my fields again. Or I'll know. And I'll find you." His amber eyes fixed on the boy as fur rippled over his body. There in the fields before Alena and the boy stood a gaunt but ferocious wolf.

The boy screamed, scrambling to his feet. He tore through the fields after Sieg, who was already long gone. The wolf gave lighthearted chase for a few meters, nipping at the air behind the boy, and then trotted back to Alena. His wolfskin fell away like a shadow in lamplight. Alena got a good look at him and noted that neither his clothes nor his face had changed in the years since she'd first seen him. He hadn't aged a day.

"You alright, my dear?" he asked.

"What are you?" she asked.

"I'm the Kornwolf," he said simply. "I told you. These are my fields. They always have been. Since before, well, before."

"Why do you haunt me?"

"Haunt you?" the Kornwolf stared at her, puzzled. "My dear girl, I'm trying to save you."

"They were just boys making fools of themselves," said Alena. "It's just what boys do."

The Kornwolf's face darkened. "Those boys are hardly boys anymore. They've been playing at war for years now, and, pretty soon, it won't be a game."

"Then they'll serve their country," said Alena. "As they should. You're a feldgeist. A land spirit. Surely, you should respect their duty to the Fatherland."

"A land spirit," the Kornwolf corrected. "Not a Fatherland spirit."

"Are you not German?" Alena asked.

"This land is older than any nation dreamt up by old men," said the Kornwolf, the grain whispering around them. "I should know. I've lived longer on this land than any of you.

You're all newcomers and foreigners to me, somewhere along the line. And you're all my countrymen, too."

Alena eyed him warily.

"Times are hard, I know. But the people of this land have gotten through winters before. We can get through them again," assured the Kornwolf. "But not if we turn on each other. Not if we have boys like that pretending to protect us against the wolves while they hunt their own. They may serve something, but it's not this land, and it's definitely not you. And they'll protect neither."

"Grandmother says-"

"I really don't give a damn what your grandmother says, Alena," snapped the Kornwolf. "She's as deluded as those boys. And you're in as much danger from her."

"I am not!" Alena drew herself up to her full height, brushing the loose straw from her skirt. "And why should I trust you, some savage corn demon, over my own blood? Or the future heroes of Germany?"

The Kornwolf stepped back, incredulous. The wind hissed through the rye. "You mean those boys? Alena, my dear girl, they attacked you, chased you."

"It was nothing," Alena said. The wind was angry now and growing stronger. Her flaxen hair was still damp from swimming, and she tried to hide her shivering. "They were just boys being stupid. Summer always goes to their heads. That's why the HJ exists. To give them discipline and structure and keep them out of trouble."

The Kornwolf took a step towards her, but she recoiled. "Alena-"

"Begone, evil spirit," she ordered. "Trouble me no more."

"Call me a wolf or a spirit or a demon if you will, but your grandmother serves a darker and a hungrier idol than any sheaf or corn dolly," the Kornwolf growled. "And it will not rest until she has sacrificed everything to it. Mark my words, girl, and heed them well, for if she keeps to this path, she'll eagerly spill the blood of others. And her own. In time." The Kornwolf's face looked less human to her now, his entreaties sounding more like threats. "She'll doom her countrymen and let evil befall this land. And she'll sacrifice you, too, my dear. If you're not careful."

"Nonsense," said Alena. "My grandmother loves me and Silvia and our country above all else."

"Follow your grandmother and those like her, and you'll die for the dreams of old men and the nightmares of young men," he warned. "I cannot keep the darkness men call down from touching this land, from burning it and bombing it and spoiling it, but I can keep you from the path that leads only to your doom. And a shame you'll never wash out, branded on your very soul for all time."

"The only shame I have to worry about now is what people will think when Sieg tells everyone he saw me alone in the fields at night with some no-good, interloping rover boy," Alena barked.

"Interloping?" echoed the Kornwolf. "You have the nerve to call me interloper? On *my* land?"

The winds seemed almost mocking now as they whipped the stalks into a frenzy about them. Something shifted in the fields, making the land look sinister.

"Our land," said Alena. "It's ours. Those boys are Germany's future. I am Germany's future. Now move aside."

"I'm not even in your way," said the Kornwolf.

His wolfskin fell over him once more, and he vanished into the rye where the shadows held sway for now. Alena shivered in the field, alone.

Alena was gone more and more on trips with the League, though she'd have died rather than admit the price of her trips was subsidized. That winter, she was off on a ski trip with the

League, so there was nothing to distract their grandmother from her growing discontent. Much of that holiday season was spent berating Silvia for getting yet another hole in her already patched skirt and for pretending she wasn't hungry when the Trittens brought them Christmas pastries.

On Christmas Eve, she had only words as harsh as the wind outside. Silvia's eyes wandered past the frosty window to the empty fields beyond, which got her boxed about the ears for not paying attention. Her grandmother sighed, hoping that Silvia, too, would grow into a civilized sort of young lady now that she was in the Young Girls' League. She reminded Silvia again that she'd have to start hanging around "the right sort of people," like the Stromans' daughter or the younger Tritten sisters, if she wanted to be like Alena, not the wrong sort like the Rosenfeld girls.

"But Annika was Alena's best friend. Her family brought us food after father died. And Freya and I have always been like sisters," she added.

"That girl is not your sister," growled her grandmother. "Your sister is a good German girl."

"But Freya *is* German," said Silvia. "Her family has been here as long as ours."

"That doesn't matter," her grandmother hissed. "You're in the Young Girls' League, and, in a few years, you'll join the League of German Girls. The Rosenfeld girl won't. You'll make new friends, just like Alena."

Silvia leaped to her feet. "That isn't fair!"

"Hush, girl," her grandmother snapped. "Life isn't fair, so stop your childish whining or I'll give you something to whine about. Now go and make yourself useful."

The next time her grandmother sent her out on an errand, Silvia brought some of the Trittens' pastries to Klaus's family and then went to see the Rosenfelds. Even if they didn't celebrate Christmas, she figured everyone would be glad of company in the bleak of winter, when the fields lay bare and the nights were long and dark. But when she got there, the Rosenfelds were not glad of anything.

Someone had thrown a brick through their window, and Frau Rosenfeld was on edge. Her sister-in-law and her family had left the country and had urged them to also. But her husband insisted that this was their home, this their farm, and it would all blow over. They'd been here for generations. He'd fought in the war for Germany and lost two brothers in the process. Frau Rosenfeld was not convinced his medals were the shield he thought.

The oldest Rosenfeld girl, Annika, knit silently in the corner and kept her eyes down. Grete, a girl of three, cried into her mother's skirts, afraid without knowing what to fear. Freya was quiet. She and Silvia went out to walk the dead fields together. They spoke little, but their silences said much.

Even here in the country, where things changed slowly if at all, they knew things couldn't be the same anymore. The future hung heavy in the air between them. Silvia was in the Young Girls' League and would join the League proper soon enough. And girls in the League couldn't be friends with people like the Rosenfelds.

"I should go," said Freya, holding back tears.

"Freya-" The words caught in Silvia's throat. "Give your family our love."

"I'll give them *your* love," Freya promised.

Silvia reached out and took her friend's hand, squeezing it before Freya pulled away. She watched the girl disappear into the bleak horizon. Silvia had once feared walking the fields alone, lest monsters like the corn wolf dog her steps. But, as she gazed out across the dead land, she wished there was such a beast as a corn wolf, for, surely, they needed something watching them if breaking windows and terrorizing neighbors were the sort of things they got up to when they thought there were no witnesses.

When she got home, she threw the rest of the Trittens' pastries in the field. Let the corn wolf or the barleyman or the wheat bride or the birds or even the frost have them. Herr and Frau Tritten were little more than carrion birds themselves, feeding on opportunity and swooping in on the suffering of others. And Berta was just as cruel.

When her grandmother discovered the remains of her wasteful heathen tithe, she raged like never before, and it wasn't just her tongue that had a lashing for Silvia. The girl went without supper for a week. Klaus or one of the Rosenfelds must have returned her Midwinter offerings, though, as she found someone had left a basket on the doorstep one morning. Inside were jars of jam, still-warm loaves of weizenmischbrot and vollkornbrot, and a delightfully warm pair of red mittens decorated in an old-fashioned kind of pattern. A crow was already poking about the contents when she discovered it. It flew off with a defiant caw.

Silvia and Freya did stay friends in the years to come, meeting deep in the tall fields where no one else could see. And it was in those fields they shared their secrets and buried them, too. A corn dolly; a book no longer allowed; a pamphlet someone should have burned; a love letter no one could ever see, lest the Holzknechts find out that one of their boys fancied a Jewess or someone else turn them in for rassenschande. But a distance grew between them even as their secret acts of rebellion bound them closer together. Silvia's new full-fledged BDM uniform filled the uneasy silence that hung in the swaying wheat and rye.

The girls were fourteen now, and their little patch of earth seemed smaller and smaller by the day as the weight of the world pressed in around it. Frau Rosenfeld still wanted to leave, but it was getting harder and harder to do so. As well as more expensive and more illegal. And fewer and fewer places were taking Jewish emigrants.

But they couldn't stay. Not after the new laws. Laws that outlawed marriages like that of Freya's parents and meant Freya, born and raised on a farm a stone's throw from Silvia's and who had never known anything outside their quiet little corner of the country, wasn't a citizen anymore. Her vote, her German-ness, her future, all snatched away by politicians farther from their farms and fields than either girl had ever traveled.

Silvia wanted to say something, but Freya had turned away, her thoughts elsewhere as the waning sun and the breeze both danced in her brown curls.

"I'll miss you," said Freya. "When we go."

Once more, Silvia had no words but only held her friend's hand as they stared into the rye, two little boats adrift in the rough seas growing ever more uncertain about them. The storm would not blow over. That much, they knew, even if others still hadn't admitted it.

Suddenly, Freya looked around, wary, convinced she saw something in the tall corn.

"What are you doing?" a voice hissed as Alena burst into their sanctuary buried at the heart of the field.

Freya and Silvia jumped to their feet in alarm.

"Alena, leave us alone," said Silvia. "We weren't doing anything wrong."

"You know you can be kicked out of the League for being friends with *her*," Alena spat. "What will Grandmother think?"

"I don't care!" cried Silvia. "I don't care what that bitter old hag thinks. And I don't care what you think. I don't even want to be in the League." She tore the patch from her uniform and threw it at Alena. Her blue skirt and flaxen braids rustled in the wind. "Not if it'll turn me into a cold-hearted bitch like you and Berta. Or a self-important fool like Heida."

Freya's face went white as snow. Alena's reddened with rage, and she stepped forward as if to strike Silvia. She was grown now, the picture of blossoming German womanhood, and towered over her younger sister. But a rough, calloused hand caught hers. There, before them, stood the strange man who'd offered Alena bread all those years ago and driven off the boys a few years after that.

Freya and Silvia's mouths dropped open, and Alena drew back in fear.

"Enough, Alena," said the Kornwolf, overpowering her even after all her time in the League. "I warned you, but you did not heed me."

"Haunt me no more, Kornwolf," begged Alena. "Leave me be."

"It's not I who haunts you, dear girl," said the Kornwolf. "But if you continue on this path, you will be haunted by much worse."

"Stop it!" shrieked Alena. "Begone, demon!"

"I can save you," implored the stranger. "If you'd only listen."

He plucked the torn BDM patch from the earth and once more breathed his magic into it. This time, it became a white rose. He held it out to Alena, who stood straight-backed and stubborn, her dirndl and the grain whipping about her as if she were posing for a poster.

"A flower," the Kornwolf offered. "For a beautiful girl. You don't have to be what they want you to become, dear one. There is such cleverness and strength and will in you. Don't let them twist it into something ugly and evil. Do not let them make you into a monster."

Alena hesitated.

"Your grandmother has grown cruel. Your world has grown cruel. But it doesn't have to be." His amber eyes glistened like the fields after an unexpected icing. "The young do not have to be sacrifices to the whims of their elders. Stay on this road, and it is only the scythe you'll reap, only blood you'll taste, not the golden bounty you so crave."

"Lies!" cried Alena, pushing past the wolf. She grabbed Silvia, but the girl pulled away. "Silvia, stop it. You aren't a little girl anymore, and this isn't a game. You have to choose. Your country and your family. Or this Jew and feldgeist who'll temp you away from the true path."

"I choose this land," Silvia said. "I choose my friend."

"Don't say such things," said Alena, her voice low. She glanced about them nervously, as though someone else might be watching them from the corn.

"All your talk of our history and culture and people," Silvia continued, undaunted, "but you burned your corn dolly. You were too embarrassed to bring the quilt mother made you on your ski trip. You cheer when the papers show them burning more books than even the schoolmaster's ever seen in a lifetime. You spurn the kindnesses of others and spit on true friends like Klaus and Annika. You turn your back on neighbors who've farmed with us for generations, who were there when mother died and who helped us when father died. All to impress people like the Trittens and the Stromans who turned their noses up at us until you got your precious uniform. Until you were something they could use. People who are cruel and hateful and false."

"Silvia!"

"No, Alena. You call the Kornwolf a demon, but it's your heart that's grown wicked." Tears streamed down Silvia's face. "I don't know you anymore. I don't know any of you anymore. And I don't want to. I can't live among people as weak and cowardly and blind as you."

Alena took a step back, looking pale. "Fine." Her words were breathy and hollow. "Go. Rot here in the fields for all I care. You're no sister of mine."

"No," said Silvia. "No, I don't think I am."

Alena ran from the field. The Kornwolf sighed and turned to the two remaining girls. Silvia was crying, and Freya looked terrified.

"Silvia, what did you do?" asked Freya.

"What do you mean?" Silvia asked.

"You can't just say things like that," she said, looking over her shoulder. "What happens when Alena tells everyone? Do you know what they could do to you? Or to me?"

"I'm sorry," stammered Silvia. "I didn't think. But I just can't live like this. I can't bear it anymore."

"*You* can't bear it anymore?"

"I'm sorry, Freya. I didn't mean to put you in any danger." Silvia couldn't breathe. "But I hate her. I hate them. I hate them all."

"I do, too, but what are we going to do now?" Freya was still pale with terror. "You can never go back. Neither of us is safe here anymore."

"So, we run away," said Silvia.

"Run where?" demanded Freya. "We have no papers. No money. Nowhere to go. And no friends or connections or anything. Neither of us has ever been any further away than town."

"Perhaps I can help," said the Kornwolf.

"You can't magic up exit visas and travel papers, can you?" asked Freya.

"I'm afraid not." He shook his head. "I'm just an old field spirit. But I have some magic still. I can give you a way out, if you're desperate enough to take it."

"You can?" Silvia asked.

"We'll take it!" Freya said in a breathless rush, hardly daring to believe him.

The Kornwolf held out the white rose, though now there were two. Freya reached out and took one. Silvia followed after. The two put them in each other's hair. Freya smiled through her worry, and Silvia let out a wild laugh at her own boldness and the magic they'd beheld.

And for a moment, they were two young girls laughing in a field with flowers in their hair. Like so many before them and so many hopefully still to come. Timeless, untethered by the years and the cycles of war and politics, knowing only the earth, the seasons, the warmth of the sun, the fresh scent of the rain that had yet to fall, and the feel of the wind in their hair. But they could not escape their time, as it built a prison around them, an ever-shrinking net, where once the future had held only possibility.

"Silvia Kerner, Freya Rosenfeld," said the Kornwolf. "I can offer you my protection. I can take you away from all this. But we have to go now."

"But Grete," said Freya. "Annika. My family."

"I cannot help them all." Regret shone in the Kornwolf's amber eyes. "It's too late now. I cannot stop what will befall this land. My power wanes, for winter is on our heels. But I can spare you two now. For what it's worth."

Freya looked to Silvia, her brown curls flowing in the growing gust. Thunder cracked open the heavens somewhere beyond the fields. Silvia took Freya's hand. Freya held it tight.

The Kornwolf made a sort of swooping swish with his hand, and his body followed, fluid as the grain that flows with the wind. It was like a dancer. Or a scythe. A cape of great autumn leaves swept about him, collared in heather and tied about his neck with braided stalks of wheat and rye.

"Come away, O human child," he said, and the winds grew wild.

In another unearthly motion, he wrapped the cape about them, and they were gone. All that was left was an echo on the wind as it sent the amber waves rolling.

Alena never said what happened in the field, but the girls were not seen again. There were search parties for Silvia and tears for Freya, but people were disappearing more and more these days. More bricks came through the Rosenfelds' windows, and Frau Rosenfeld opened the door one night to find her husband standing there bloodied to a pulp, but, after summer died down, no one thought much of it. There were other things to occupy people's late-night thoughts and capacity for conspiracy. And, soon, there would be no one to worry over their sudden flight, for rye, wheat, and barley are hardly the only things reaped as German winters fall.

The Rosenfelds tried to flee. They bounced around from country to country, port to port, turned away again and again and finally sent back to Germany. Klaus's parents were pressured to sign him over. They refused at first, but, when they were told they might lose their other children, they relented. No one ever heard anything more of Klaus Baumann.

All of the young lads in town and the surrounding countryside were soon called away to war. As were Alena and Berta. Heida was called away to be a nurse. She watched other young lads from other towns suffer and die day in and day out.

And, like so many of those lads, Alena also never came home alive. Her grandmother's mantel was covered with BDM memorabilia and photographs of her beautiful Alena, but she died alone and bitter, grown lean on war rations. A neighbor found her one cold winter morning, and she was buried in a pauper's grave with no family left to grieve. The Trittens didn't even bother to pay their respects.

After the war, names of the disappeared began to be spoken again. Answers trickled in, though some fates were never known. Annika had died in the camps. Grete was in another camp but had survived. She returned years after the war, but her family's home—furniture, farm, and all—had been taken. And there were no warm welcomes.

She left after that, bound for some other country willing to take her. Her daughter, Shani, grew up in New York City but ran away to California with a boy her parents didn't approve of. Some others who had left or been taken came back after Grete. Some stayed, some didn't, some were driven away again. After the post-war revelations and unhappy returns, some wondered with renewed curiosity or rekindled guilt about Freya and Silvia's fate, but that riddle would remain a mystery, though local legends abounded, each more fantastical than the last.

That they'd run away with boys they'd loved. That they'd run away with each other. That they'd run off to join a band of Gypsies. That they'd been kidnapped by Gypsies. That Gypsies had robbed and killed them both. That Freya had killed Silvia. That Alena and Silvia had killed Freya. That Alena had killed her sister and Freya had witnessed it and ran away out of fear. That Freya and Silvia had loved the same boy and one had killed the other and ran away to escape justice or the boy's wrath and vengeance. That Freya and Silvia had killed themselves.

That the corn wolf or the oat man or the wild lady had taken them. That they'd been recruited as spies by either side, or both. That they were Communist sympathizers or black-market smugglers and had been caught. That Freya was a nurse living in Denmark. That Silvia was a painter in Boston or a factory worker in East Germany or a murderess in Paris.

Some locals still swore they heard a whisper here or a name called there when they walked through the fields in the years to come. A snatch of song on the winds or a hand brushing theirs. Others saw wolves in the corn. A reddish-brown one with amber eyes, one flaxen, one a rich brown.

When the wind howled, some swore they heard the wolves. Mourning, some said. Warning, said others. A remembrance of what had happened here. The sacrifices they'd made to gods far more insatiable and bloodthirsty than the ancient spirits in the fields, draped in altar cloths of red, forever stained by the blood of those they'd marked for death. And a reminder of what may yet come to pass if the people thought such false idols worth feeding again.

Two women sat on the porch of the summer home, looking out at the fields. It was a larger home than had previously stood here, and cars still laden with the trappings of a summer holiday sat in the driveway, but the fields were the same. Tall and eerie and ancient, no matter how much scythes or mows or pesticides tried to control them through the years.

"When's Reimund coming?" asked Klara.

Ritu set her phone aside, the spell of Instagram broken by her friend's voice. Her jet-black hair brushed her bare shoulders as it swayed in the summer breeze. "Tomorrow," she said. "He has a project to finish at work. And your wife?"

The woman shrugged, her honey-blonde hair aglow in the late evening sun. "You know Anelie. She said she'd be here three hours ago. So, she's probably leaving now."

"I hope she gets here before midnight," said Ritu, noting the sun getting awfully low on the horizon. It was cooling off, and she wished she'd worn a sweater. "I'm a light sleeper, and your room's next to mine."

"We'll be quiet," Klara teased. "It's not like we're in college anymore."

"Oh, don't remind me," Ritu laughed. "I still have those noise-canceling headphones somewhere."

Klara pretended to blush and took a sip of her beer. The two looked out on the fields where their three children played. They'd come here every summer since Ritu and Klara were in college. Two years ago, the children had found an old metal box buried in the field with a book, some old photographs and faded papers, and the shriveled remains of what might have been a doll made of wheat and rye inside. It was still in the attic somewhere.

"The corn wolf is on the prowl," said Klara, her eyes on the rippling fields.

"What?" asked Ritu.

"Nothing," said Klara. "Just something my grandfather used to say. When the wind blows through the fields like this. Like a storm's in the air."

"And what exactly is a corn wolf?" Ritu asked. "Is it a wolf made of corn? A wolf that eats corn? Corn that eats wolf?"

Klara laughed. The sun was all but gone now, but the children didn't seem to notice.

"Rea, come on, it's getting dark," Klara called to her daughter.

"Aw, Mom, five more minutes," the girl implored, her wheat-blonde hair and windbreaker bandied about by the gale.

"Yeah, please!" called a boy with a mop of brown curls and skin golden as the fields at sunset. "We won't be long."

"Please, Mom!" called the oldest girl. Her shiny black hair was plaited, though strands had come lose as the three ran wild in the tall corn. The wind blew them over her face like a veil.

"Please!" the wheat-blonde girl implored.

The boy suddenly jumped out at her, and the two toppled to the ground, laughing.

"Five minutes," said Klara, taking another sip of her beer.

"It's good to see them playing outside like children are

supposed to," said Ritu. "The rest of the time, I have to pry them away from their phones and video games."

Klara smiled to herself but said nothing. "It is nice."

Soon, the last golden drops of the summer day had been washed away by the cool night. Ritu shivered.

"Kamala! Rohit! Come on," she called. "Time to come in."

The oldest girl and her brother ran through the field like water in a brook.

"You, too, Rea," Klara called at the reluctant girl in the field.

"It's our turn to make dinner tonight. Time to break out some coveted Ackermann family secrets," Ritu said as her children filed up the porch steps.

Klara stood up, beer in hand. "Rea Gerst, I won't say it again."

"Coming," the girl groaned and made her way through the grain and the gathering dark.

She followed Ritu, Kamala, and Rohit into the house, the light from inside spilling onto the dark wood of the porch. Klara hesitated a moment behind them as she thought she heard something. The fields swayed ominously, as if they knew something was coming.

"What is it, Mom?" Rea asked, a shadow in the doorway.

"Nothing," said Klara. "Just the wind. I always forget what the country sounds like after our noisy apartment. It's so quiet here. Every noise makes me jump."

The women and their brood shut the door behind them and set about making dinner. Conversation and laughter rang like a merry song from within, but, outside, the corn shifted nervously in the coming storm. In the distance, thunder threatened, a low rumble, unheard by most, ignored by others. But the Kornwolf heard as he watched the house, amber eyes inscrutable. A bolt of blue lightning frayed the edge of the sky.

"Be safe," he whispered to the night.

"Be smart," said Silvia beside him.

"Be brave," said Freya.

"Be ready," came the Kornwolf's blessing. "For whatever is to come."

The girls each took his hand.

"Summer never lasts forever," he lamented, "and these fields have seen much. Much I couldn't see coming. Much I tried and failed to stop. And much I should have tried to stop sooner. And warned of louder."

"So, we try harder," said Freya.

"And we keep trying," Silvia agreed. "As long as we have any last bit of earth to hold out on, we make our stand. We protect those on it. We save those we can."

"If only they'd listen," the Kornwolf's voice echoed, lost on the wind.

Rea shuffled into the kitchen later that night, startled awake by a great peal of thunder, kept awake by the news alerts on her phone, and driven from her bed by thirst. She glanced out the window and could have sworn she saw three pairs of eyes watching her from the storm-tossed sea of grain. But when she looked again, there was only wheat and rye. Still, she shivered, uneasy as the corn before the scythe.

WISDOM KEEPERS
Virginia Romero

WOLF SPEAKS
Michael Bodin

I speak for Wolf.

There...I said it. In fact, I thrill at the very sound of that. Revel in the feel of that. Many of us say that—both because it is true and also because of how it makes us feel. We have a mission, a raison d'etre, a cause celebre. It unites us. We are empowered, emboldened.

But through the ages, Wolf has spoken quite eloquently for himself. In fact, he is the very one that is most important in this story. We are about him, after all and should fully immerse ourselves in all that entails. So we should listen.

But have we listened? Really listened? We love to watch him. We purchase books, photos, calendars, drawings, clothing, jewelry, even tattoos with his images. We study him. Write about him, prose and poetry. Fiction and non-fiction, popular and scientific. We imagine and are determined we pay him honor and respect in our awkward and peculiar (i.e., human) ways. We have also brought our noise and pollution to him, encroached on him, yet he mightily tolerates us, albeit from a respectful distance. And he is talking to us.

Are we listening?

I was recently struck by some thoughts on a trip to New England. Wolves are there—in Maine, New Hampshire, Vermont, and Massachusetts. Gray Wolves, Timber Wolves, and Eastern Wolves certainly are there, though few in number and only sporadically seen. They are elusive—and rightfully so.

Coywolves are also there, in greater and growing number. They are here in the Mid-Atlantic and have spread throughout the southeast. It seems that the official response of most of the authorities is, "No, don't worry, what you are seeing are coyotes and/or dogs." Therein lies the crux of the problem. The Red-Ridinghood public scares easily, so the powers that be would rather spin the yarn there are no Wolves. Period. It keeps the peace.

Plus, if you ignore their genetic background, you may also ignore that pesky Endangered Species Act—no harm, no foul, as long as you keep gerrymandering the goal posts. (Gerrymandering began in Massachusetts, after all, so it is a native construct—one that is still readily at hand and quite popular nationally.)

Wolf conservation, and wildlife conservation as a whole, is done a complete disservice when scientific truth is ignored or contorted for political expedience.

Yet, there are Wolves, and now Coywolves. The internet— social media, namely—will tell you scientists created a new creature called the Coywolf. But it was not an evil, mad government scientist responsible for this, after all—it was Wolf that did this.

An Eastern Wolf spoke. He propagated his kind by teaming up with an Eastern Coyote. Eastern Coyotes migrated from the west and blanketed the east. So Wolf spoke. His DNA cries out to the world. Why is no one listening?

The Coyote, also known as Brush Wolf, Little Wolf, and Prairie Wolf, has been around longer than man, as has Wolf.

What could Wolf possibly see in a future with Coyote?

The fact that there is a future?

Evolution does not happen overnight. Coyote is highly adaptable, and Wolf valued that enough to procreate with several—to maintain his legacy, to make a better world for his kind, to stay alive into the future.

To live, in the hope that he may have a future.

He has spoken and is speaking now. Why does no one hear him? Coywolves are not freaks of nature. Use the word Coywolf, and a ranger, warden, or other official will quickly correct you: "Coyote."

Because half of a Wolf may need respect and protection—but a Coyote certainly has none, will get none, and may be slaughtered at will.

If he is half Wolf, we need to protect him. Half-breed, Mud-blood—nicknames intended to belittle—ignore the fact that half a Wolf deserves our voice. Look at the double standard: when a Wolf breeds with Dog, it is a Wolfdog. The media will go out of its way to stress it is half Wolf and should be regarded as a Wolf.

Why is a Wolfcoyote a Coyote? Is that intended to minimize—delegitimize—its actual identity and genetic background?

We are watching history in the making.

Are we witnessing the genesis of a new species?

Or will this be a new subspecies?

We have seen this with breeds of other canids: the domestic Dog—himself a descendant of Wolf. A non-recognized breed slowly becomes recognized, legitimized, and a new breed is established.

Will our children see a new breed, or subspecies, of Wolf?

I not only want to sit at the feet of Wolf, to hear and observe—really listen—to what he has to say. I want my questions answered.

We need to figure out what this means for ecology, conservation, biology, and for law. Textbooks will need to be rewritten. High school and college courses will change. Biology majors will have their work cut out for them. Research papers are waiting to be written.

I gladly solicit the word of the Native American Indians. I believe their voice may be most potent and is always refreshingly honest. It certainly has been tragically long ignored. They speak for Wolf better than anyone, and I would welcome their opinions on Wolf, Coywolf, and Coyote.

Cannot Little Wolf be allowed into the circle and cherished for whom he is? Through the ages, Wolf has spoken. And he continues to speak. Will we not listen?

If he is speaking on a level that most do not understand, let us call in the translators.

If he is on a different frequency, then it is we who need to fine tune our own senses.

If we are simply making too much noise, we need to stop and listen.

Wolf's life is precious, vital. It must not languish and disappear.

We must listen first. Then we will speak. Together, we must all speak with Wolf.

WOLF WATCHER

890M, Junction Butte Pack, Lamar Valley, 2016

A crow unfolds into flight
when it sees me looking,
as if attention sharpened
my gaze into something
like an arrow, a bullet.

Then the mountain breathes,
clouds shifting. Pines edge
toward the ridge. People point
until I focus on a gray zigzag,
see the bolt-hole in the rocks.

Nearby, the beta lies on his belly
in the grass, a tree-shadow
with front legs stretched out,
head lifted, ears swiveling,
nose pointed at the crowd.

Former leader and go-to wolf,
he's mated with two grays,
both his successor's daughters.
Their unlikely den looks out
on Slough Creek, greening valley.

Mule deer pass, buffalo graze,
and people congregate below,
standing behind field scopes
like silver and black magpies,
heads turned toward the pack.

They shuffle, shiver, mutter
that he's not doing anything.
Oh, but he is. That wolf
is observing us. Smelling
cold metal and our interest.

Other packs avoid the roads,
so denning here may keep his
safe from them. But he knows
better than to look away—
black wolves like him exist

because our dogs got loose.
Who knows what he inherited
alongside the gene for darkness?
May he always watch so warily.
May he live till his coat goes gray.

—Dana Sonnenschein

THE WOLF OF ROMA

I was there when the two twins were abandoned.
I was there when they needed a mother.
I was there when they founded a city,
only to have one brother kill the other.

I stayed on as the Guardian of their city,
watching over every column and eave.
My kin were free to wonder the streets
with nary a harm headed their way.
Cults worshipped my kin in my honor,
extolling the virtues being a wolf might bring.
Alas, Rome was a city that saw many rulers and times,
times of prosperity but turbulence too.
Its invasion of others with armies so vast
expanded it thrice through gain of power and people.
The subjugation of others in the arena
fed the blood thirst inherent in the people I watched.

Its ideals questionable, I made good my leave,
the city I helped found now a shadow of its name.
Soon after came the city's decline,
a time for barbarians to make good their game.

I've seen it all, from dawn to dusk.
I've suffered it all, through feel and sight.
I've smelt it all, the good and bad.
Where, you then ask, would my legacy go?
With destruction comes renewal, centuries from then.
The glory of my people lives on, even now,
in language, architecture;
even college frat nomenclature.

But who knows what the future brings?
The dawn of an era's far too early to say.

—HJ Pang

THE RATCATCHERS
Chris Albert

1. Ellen and Mary

Nine-year-old Mary woke up from a recurrent nightmare memory she often had. In it, she had wandered too far away from the village, and a pack of wolves had appeared. She knew she would be torn limb from limb, but she woke up just in time, whimpering.

This time, Ellen, the village wise woman, was there on the edge of her bed to soothe her and wipe the sweaty, blond curls from her forehead.

"That's quite the nightmare you had, do you want to talk about it?" Ellen asked gently.

Mary shook her head no. She had often been chastised for wandering off and didn't want to spend one more minute thinking of the rangy wolves whose stare pierces your soul.

"As you wish," Ellen smiled, startling Mary in a good way. Mary had never experienced such kindness as she had this past fortnight when she had come to live with Ellen and be her apprentice.

It was spring, so Mary wore a simple shift of plain

homespun. Nights were cool, but Mary had her own bed and even her own blanket gently tucked around her. Mary hadn't had much tucking or other love from her beaten down mother or brutish father, and her siblings squabbled to survive. When Ellen had asked for Mary as her apprentice, her parents had agreed with a grunt and the comment, "One less mouth to feed." Mary knew she wouldn't be missed.

There was the daily glass of milk from the goat and a daily egg—almost unheard-of luxuries. Turnips, cabbage, and wild game meant that, for the first time in her life, Mary wasn't hungry.

In exchange, Mary happily milked the goat, saving Ellen from stooping. She gathered the eggs, cleaned the chicken house, tidied their quarters, and helped gather the wild plants that were the wise woman's stock in trade.

"What is this plant?" Ellen would say, and Mary would do her best to answer, forgetting some, but slowly remembering more. Then Ellen would teach her the uses of each plant, how and when to collect each, how to preserve each, how to dose them. It was a lot of information for a little peasant girl, but Mary was doing well.

Perhaps the greatest gift the old woman gave the young girl was encouraging her to notice connections: in their wanderings, Ellen gave Mary the time to watch the beetles, the rabbits, and occasionally the fox and even the rare wolf that lived in the deep forest. Mary started to notice the preferences and needs of the living beings in her world.

Mary's nightmare came from a time when she had wandered too far and stumbled upon a wolf family in a valley that the villagers superstitiously avoided, several miles away. They had been maybe ten feet away. Schooled in the tales of the villagers, she had been sure she would soon be torn apart and devoured. She had shut her eyes, crouched in utter terror, and awaited the inevitable.

The inevitable had not come. After minutes of shaking in terror, she had opened her eyes and witnessed a most amazing scene: wolf puppies clambering over their parents, parents playing with them, and the fierce predators catching and eating...rats! Mary didn't remember that part, so caught up was she in thinking she would be harmed....

2. The Journey

Winter in the village was always a difficult time. The villagers trusted Ellen to help with their burns and coughs and wounds, and she had obliged. Spring was one of several times she would need to go collecting to replenish her supplies. Today, she announced to Mary they would spend the day taking stock, checking the goat cart, and gathering food and baskets for the journey that would begin tomorrow. Mary was excited! They would leave at first light.

The day started auspicious, clear, and sunny. The cart had been packed with bread and empty bags for gathering and the last of the apples and potatoes and cabbage and turnips. There were knives and tools and even Ellen's six hens, for Ellen didn't quite trust the villagers to care for them and put them up every night. Ellen and Mary had a hearty breakfast, then set off for their gathering trip. The two goats pulled the cart.

On their way out of the village, a hunting party was coming home, hauling carcasses of fox and weasel; one even had a wolf. They were loud and boisterous and maybe even a little drunk. The villagers prided themselves on ridding the surrounding area of these vermin, not knowing that the "vermin" just might be helpful, even essential in their own way.

Ellen sighed. Ellen knew the value of the fox and stoat, wolf and weasel. She had lived through many plagues and was a keen observer. When the "vermin" around a village were mostly killed off, the rats thrived, and when the rats thrived, the plagues came....

It was a great sadness and frustration of Ellen's life she had never been able to convince the villagers to leave the creatures alone and just make sure their own livestock were locked up at night.

As the two journeyed away from the village, their attention was drawn to a minstrel coming towards the village. Wandering minstrels and troubadours were not such an unusual sight, and the village welcomed hearing of news of the outside world and fresh entertainment. But Ellen was disturbed by this one. He didn't look well. He was just a little bit puffy, and his eyes were glazed as if he had a fever. Ellen gave him a bit wider berth than usual as they passed.

Much to Ellen's delight, Mary had noticed something off about the minstrel also and was brave enough to say so.

"He didn't look well," Mary offered.

"Indeed, little wise woman. Can you tell me WHAT looked wrong?" Ellen asked.

"Well," Mary thought out loud, "he was puffy...and he seemed hot..."

"Like a fever, perhaps?" Ellen encouraged.

"Yes! Like that."

"Well noted, Mary. You are becoming a fine observer," Ellen smiled, and Mary basked in the praise.

"Perhaps he will bring more than music to our village," Ellen added cryptically.

Ellen fell into a thoughtful silence. Mary stole glimpses at the old woman's face, and the usual cheeriness looked grim. Something was shifting.

A rat scampered across the path, bringing Ellen out of her reverie.

She laughed out loud. "What a blessing! Here we are, all

prepared for a journey with everything we need. We will go a little further and for a little longer Without the ratcatchers, I cannot stop what will surely come"

At the time, Mary had no idea what she meant.

3. The house in the woods

Mary did not know the earth was that big! They had travelled for days and were in wild country, uninhabited by humans.

Ellen veered off the track, looking like she would fall in a ravine, but the path just kept curving around. At this point, it was barely visible, clearly unused. After another half a mile, the most amazing sight appeared: a little stone house with a rounded thatch roof that blended into the landscape. It was a little bit bigger than the village cottages, like it might hold a large family comfortably. Attached to the house was another structure—perhaps a barn. Mary was enchanted.

Ellen unlatched the big oak door, and, though the house was cobwebby and had clearly not been used in a while, it still felt welcoming. Directly in front of them was a stone hearth, and, as Mary's eyes adjusted to the dimness, she noted sleeping areas along the walls, a table to the right of the hearth with rough, hewn chairs beside it. The stone in the inside was not smooth, but irregular, leaving nooks where all manner of things were tucked: a big nook by the hearth had a pot nestled in it. Smaller ones nearby held mugs and carved wooden spoons.

Attached to the side of the house was the barn, with half-doors to keep the animals on their side. They unloaded the goats in the barn and put the chickens in the chicken house, also in the barn.

She motioned Mary out the other door down a short corridor to the left of the hearth, saying cheerfully, "I believe we shall just SIT for a moment."

Outside the door was a spectacular view of green and wild and rolling hills, copses of trees and some areas of craggy rocks. Just beside the stone house was a brook, where Mary rinsed and filled the mugs with clear fresh water. Then the two sat in chairs made of bound saplings in companionable silence. The birds and animals returned to their chatter as the people dozed.

After a while, Ellen announced, "We will go cut grass and leaves for the goats while the light lasts." "Plenty of ratcatchers here, but they will catch goats and chickens also. We need to be careful"

That reference to ratcatchers again....

They bolted the animals in the barn side of the hut and proceeded to collect a huge mound of fodder for the goats and water for themselves. Ellen had a sack for collecting wild greens and mushrooms also.

They spent the rest of the day sweeping and tidying, putting up their provisions and cleaning the cobwebs. It was a solid little house, and Mary felt safe and snug.

Late that night, the wolves howled, throwing Mary into a screaming terror fit. This time, Ellen gathered Mary in her arms, soothing her, and finally saying, "I think it's time for me to hear your story."

"There are WOLVES!" Mary blubbered.

"Yes, pet, but why are you so frightened?"

Mary looked at Ellen like she was insane. Everyone was frightened of wolves.

"Tell me your story," Ellen gently insisted.

For the first time ever, Mary spilled the memory that so terrified her. Last year, her brothers were bothering her, and she was just tired of it. She left the crowded hut early one morning and just started to walk away from the village. After a while, she got thirsty and veered off the path to find a stream. She was further than she had ever been, and, when she drank, she sat by a tree and realized how tired she was. She must have dozed off.

Suddenly, a whole family of wolves had materialized from the brush. They were so close she could have touched them. Mary's breathing came fast as she relived her terror. The wolves looked at her with their intense eyes, and she was sure she would die and curled up in a ball. Suddenly, there was a squeak behind her, and a wolf pounced just inches away...on a rat. The whole pack was then distracted, and Mary was able to get up and run away.

Ellen hugged Mary close. She had an entirely different view of wolves but knew just telling Mary wouldn't convince her. Mary would have to see for herself the nature of wolves. For now, she just soothed the frightened girl.

4. The Nature of Wolves

The next morning, Mary woke up feeling good. No one had ever comforted her before. The chickens had delivered two eggs during the night, and, after a night of rest, even the goat had some milk. Ellen and Mary had breakfast.

So many tasks! Fetching water, cleaning the rain barrels so they would have water when it rained, fetching greens for the goats, beginning the repair of the outside pen for the goats. The latter was made of saplings woven together and even had a roof of woven saplings. They worked on housekeeping chores in the mornings, and, afternoons, they gathered food, started a garden, and collected herbs.

At night, the wolves howled back and forth. Ellen always smiled and narrated a different kind of story.

"Father wolf has been away hunting for his children. He is saying, 'I am home!' Now you can hear mother wolf answer and the high-pitched yipping of the young ones. Father has carried food in his stomach, and the family that has been home will tug at his lips and ask him to deliver the food."

Mary grew a little more comfortable with Ellen's narrations, but there came a day when they were foraging in the afternoon and her nightmare almost came true again: suddenly, a wolf appeared out of the brush and was coming towards her. Mary would have screamed and ran, but Ellen clamped her hand over Mary's mouth and held her tight.

"Don't scream," Ellen commanded. "And don't run Watch."

A big rat scurried across the clearing, and the wolf was on it in a flash. There were other rats, and the wolf pups also appeared and pounced on them. Pups were learning to hunt! Rats! They were hunting rats! Mama wolf then looked them in the eye and melted into the woods again.

"What did they hunt?" Ellen asked before Mary could give in to her fears.

"Rats...just like the last time..." Mary was starting to see for herself.

"Two things are happening here," Ellen explained. "The pups need to learn to hunt, and they start with small game like rats and squirrels, even fish and birds. The other is that, as summer goes on, the big game like deer grow healthy and fleet and hard to catch. Sometimes, all they can catch is rats."

"The wolves won't bother us," Ellen announced further. "I don't know why, and there are exceptions. If you ran screaming and acted like a wounded deer, they would treat you like a wounded deer." Mary shuddered.

"And we must be very careful of our goats and chickens— the wolves will gladly take those if we slip up. But it is our job to keep them safe."

5. The Role of the Ratcatchers

"How can there be so many rats?" Mary asked Ellen when they came upon the wolves hunting. The pups were growing, and Mary had even named them.

Ellen looked carefully at Mary. It was time, she thought, to explain the whole truth.

"Do you remember before we left the village, how the men ranged farther and farther to kill the animals they called varmints—the wild cat and weasel, fox, stoat, and wolf? "

Mary nodded.

"All of those catch rats. So, what will happen when those are gone?"

"Oh!" Mary said. "More rats!" She understood now. "Even here? Far from the village?"

"Everywhere," Ellen said. "Too many rats," she added emphatically.

Mary got up to go, but Ellen patted the ground beside her.

"There's more to tell. Do you remember when we left, there was a troubadour..."

"The puffy one with a fever," Mary offered.

"Yes, that one."

"Twice in my long life, I have seen the signs before. First, the men of the village proudly kill all the 'vermin' for miles around. They think they are protecting the chickens and pigs and horses and goats and all the other livestock. But what they don't know is they are killing ratcatchers—all of those are ratcatchers.

"When the rat numbers go up, when you start seeing them scurrying across the paths and by the privies, and everywhere you go, something terrible happens: Black death."

Mary's eyes widened. Everyone had heard of Black Death. It took whole villages, coming seemingly from nowhere and ravaging the whole countryside.

"The rats have something to do with black death?" she asked.

Ellen nodded. "The rats have everything to do with black death. And the first signs of it are puffiness in the neck and a fever."

"Like the troubadour?"

Ellen nodded again, waiting for Mary to make more connections.

"Our village..." Mary began, wide-eyed.

"Likely, everyone is dead," Ellen confirmed gently. "But it is not safe for us to even go check. The black death is likely raging right now."

"There are no other people but us?" Mary looked stricken.

"There are some. We will find them in time. The Black Death doesn't kill everyone. We will have to stay here for a time, but, eventually, we will venture forth."

"What about us? Will WE get the Black Death?"

"Not likely," Ellen smiled. "For we are surrounded by ratcatchers!"

That night, a wolf howled, and, for the first time, Mary felt safer at hearing the song.

Author's note: In the 14th century, half the population of Europe died from the Bubonic plague, or "Black Death." The disease was carried by rat fleas. Historical accounts have frequently pinpointed the initial cases of an area, but none address the population of rats (and their fleas). Could it be that humans, in their drive to rid the world of predators, had eliminated the ratcatchers and tipped the scale towards their own destruction?

There is even a modern equivalent: one of the faster spreading diseases in America is Lyme disease, spread by ticks. One of the predictors of Lyme incidence is the population of mice. Meanwhile, we humans wage war against coyotes and other predators who consume mice.

EMBRACE
SL Westerfield

MOONLIGHT HOWL

(A Hymn to Moon, god of Moon)

Oh, Moon, shine down
your sorrow-beams
of silver light.
Bright and blue.
A luminous hue.
A silver gleam on land.
A glittering sparkle
on clear water.

Your children adore you,
we wolves of the night,
howling to you,
our father and maker.

Sing of home. Sing of hearth.
Sing of bygone days,
when we wolves roamed
across the lands.

No trees unturned,
Nor mountains nor bergs.
Our spirit was freedom.
We howled for joy.

Now, we are lost.
Now, we are withered,
torn down asunder
by the furless ones.

But you, oh, Moon!
Oh, Baldor Moon!

Your luminous light
lifts up our hearts,
casts sorrows away.
We howl to you
at the sparkling lake,
singing of family,
singing of home.

—Travis Kane

REMEMBERING THE FORGOTTEN
HJ Pang

The square and its surrounding streets were as bustling as ever. The better part of a thousand years hadn't changed that. Tourists came and gawked at the pillars and marble facades, much the same expressions today as they were last week. So many faces; so many places. Yet the mystique remains.

Lupa lounged on the roof of the Pantheon, viewing it all with half-lidded eyes, her tail flat against the warm marble. It amazed her how an Empire that had fallen so many years back could still be revered. Sure, much of its legacy remained in the stone and marble landmarks that dotted this country, along with the marble likenesses of figures mortal and god. If Lupa cared to interfere, she would have pointed out much of the gods' features were exaggerated. She had known a couple of them first-paw, not that she could have avoided it, having been a National Being of an Empire that spanned all the way to the Eastern reaches.

Has been...that was how she felt like these months. When one was around for over two millennia, time was counted not in minutes, hours, or days, but segments of a year.

Though she was a great fan of the sun's constant gaze,

Lupa was no stranger to walking the streets of the city. For, after all, wasn't it there where things of note took place? A true wolf didn't sit idle; they went wherever they pleased. Lupa remembered a time when feral wolves could roam the city without fear or resentment, where they were seen as descendants of the divinity she was. There was even a cult dedicated to lupine worship. More in acknowledgement to her worshipper's intentions than its entertainment value, Lupa had even partaken in viewing the festivals put up in her honor. Too many animal sacrifices for her liking, but, at least, she got to eat them afterward. National Beings didn't need sustenance like mortals did, but, when one's existence was repetitive to the point of being mundane, a good snack was always welcome.

Which brought Lupa back to the present. These streets, so familiar and yet not. She had walked down it far more times than she could count, in different times and eras. She had seen paving slabs give way to cobblestones, cobblestones to tarmac and concrete. She had seen bakeries, potters, and amphora makers replaced by cottage industries. And, only a few centuries back, this city was the heart of a nation. Craftsmen of all specialties set up their workshops of glass, metalwork, and finery. It was even the center of religious fervor, with the great walled compound in the center of city the epitome of everything spiritual. Lupa had wandered within its walls a couple of times. Though the Roman gods of old were absent, the saints of more recent times always frowned upon her whenever she took a walk through the hallowed halls. Only Saint Christopher and Saint Francis seemed to be more welcoming to her presence, though Lupa had never figured why. But countless mortals thronged these halls, such that, often, Lupa felt she couldn't be alone with her thoughts.

But now, all the craftsmen and their storefronts were gone,

having either packed up, switched trades, or died out. For a Being that could live forever, change was painful. When one got to know the details of each family, along with each and every member's hopes and aspirations, each passing was a dull hurt within. And all that pain gradually built up, such that Lupa had to sever all mental bonds to the people and live the rest of her life in solitude. Not that Lupa would waste the rest of her life—however long—sleeping on a roof. She continued to prowl the street once in a while, if only to check out what's new in her old domain. A reenactor dressed as a centurion might be replaced by one resembling an Egyptian mummy, for reasons Lupa couldn't hope to fathom. And, when she thought she'd seen everything, another oddity would present itself, such as a sidewalk performance in which some guy sat upon a pole held by another, either seemingly asleep or in a trance. Why would anyone throw money at someone who did nothing but sit? Each era had their own oddities and quirks, but modern mortals never failed to surprise.

Which led back to the fact there's nothing left for her here.

These thoughts sought only to tire Lupa; so she did what she always had for times like this. Reaching for her amphora across a sizable crack in the marble, the she-wolf unstopped the jug and took a long draught. The sharp sourness of long-fermented grapes stung first across her tongue, then throat, copious amounts running down the matted fur of her once fluffy chest. Once, the beverage used to calm her and let her relax for a month or more, but the contents of her amphora, though ever-full, now tasted worse by the day. At the height of her domain's power, the wine always tasted tangy and sweet, as well fermented in the finest mortal winery. It used to be something she partook in moderation, something to savor whenever she felt proud of her people. But then the Empire of her esteemed people fell, quickly sacked by the very people they had invaded. And Lupa's last link to the people had died with the fall of the Senate.

But National Beings couldn't die. And so here she was, a washed-up, old wolf reminiscing about times long forgotten. To think she'd raised the very founders of the people, with her own teats, no less. For all the good it had done, she mightn't have bothered. She closed her eyes and slept, plagued by the countless events her people were a part of. Dreams that had repeated itself for over a thousand-and-half years. The toppling of many an unpopular ruler. The endless march of the Legions through countless forests and deserts. The battle cries of the barbarians as they laid waste to the city. Screams of men and legionaries, women and children. Screams that died out into an uncomfortable silence, only to be broken by the settling of strange people in her lands. Changes that happened so quickly it registered as a blur compared to the centuries of her people's existence.

She knew there were preparations for some festival or other going-on at the moment, but she didn't see the need to bother herself with the details. There was a time when Lupa would prowl the streets to see what's happening, to walk among the people as she once had. But that time is long past, for she had already seen every festival and event the mortals of this era held, made deafening on the ears by overloud contraptions that broadcasted every song and shout. Hardly any cause for excitement when one had seen (and heard) it all.

Lupa didn't need to open her eyes to know whether it's dawn or dusk, afternoon or night. She felt it not by the absence of the sun on her pelt, but by the tingle in her bones. But there was an unnatural tingle that had nothing to do with the rise and fall of the sun, but a presence near her.

Her eyes opened, just a crack. She could have been looking at a reflection of her own muzzle, complete with amber eyes, were it not for the fact National Beings exhibited no reflection of any kind, save the image of humans they took the guise of.

"Happy Birthday, Ma," said the "reflection," and, for the second time during her existence, Lupa jumped, fur fluffed up and fangs bared. The newcomer did none of that, however, confirming he was no optical illusion.

"What was that?" Lupa asked. Her voice was coarse, a consequence of not having spoken for far too long. Who would she speak to, anyway? The Roman gods were long dead, and the saints weren't exactly welcoming. She racked her throat hard, to better clear out the remnants of wine, and repeated her question.

"I said 'Happy Birthday,'" confirmed the newcomer with a grimace, waving the air before his nose. He was a wolf just like her, except that he was perhaps smaller in stature. One was never sure with National Beings; their sizes occasionally changed on account of their ego or their people's fervor. His fur was smooth and immaculate, almost giving off a soft glow in the fading evening light. His bright eyes and upright ears also carried an energy that would have Lupa up and prancing if it wasn't for the strangeness of the encounter.

Lupa only stared, so the newcomer continued, "I would have thought it calls for celebration, not fear." He smiled, reaching beside himself. Lifting a cloth off a basket, his paw rummaged through it. Lupa caught the whiff of fresh bread, cheese, and cured meat before a green bottle of red liquid presented itself, its bottom encased within a basket. Glass? That stuff was rare in Lupa's time...

The she-wolf shook herself. "I think you've mistaken me for someone else. You're better off looking elsewhere." Lupa gestured to the side with her muzzle.

The newcomer looked reproachful, his whiskers skewing. "How can one mistake you for the founder of this country? Besides, is it not the anniversary of Roma's birth? Your birth?"

Lupa laughed, a harsh staccato of barks that carried across the planes. Mortals looked around, wondering if they had imagined it, while feral dogs whimpered in their homes. The young wolf before her merely lowered an ear in questioning, his muzzle tilted.

"Founder!" laughed Lupa, gesturing at herself with a wine-streaked paw. The newcomer's ears flicked. "A washed up Being, you mean! For all the good I'd done, I might as well not have achieved anything!" She gestured at the cracked buildings across the expanse of the city. "My people are long gone, wiped out. And you still think what I've done matters?" The wolf crossed her paws, eyes half-lidded.

The younger wolf smiled once more. "There exists a saying that Roma wasn't built in a day. Neither so was Italia."

Lupa cocked her head to her side. "Who are you, exactly?"

"Your son."

Lupa sat back down. "Goodness. To think I can't remember who I'd lain with." she breathed.

"It was through no fault of yours, Madre," laughed the young wolf. "The people of Italia had called for a symbol. I was birthed forth from their belief." He spread out his paws. "Just as you were by the people of Roma."

"Good for you. But what has all that got to do with me?" Lupa's eyes narrowed.

"Everything and nothing," said the wolf, waving his paw around him. Already, the red hues of dawn were visible, bringing highlights to his sleek pelt. "Without your guidance of the ancient people of Roma, the forefathers of my people wouldn't have existed. Without the Roman Empire, the knowledge that came with the Renaissance wouldn't have happened, giving rise to the people's enlightenment. In fact," here, a twinkle appeared in his eyes, "many domains benefited from your influence, even if they don't care to admit it."

"Like the many roads that lead from them to us." stated

Lupa.

"Among other things, yes," said the young wolf. "Your domain may have forgotten you, but not your accomplishments. Did you see the fair down below? The festivities taking place all around the city?" The wolf stood, pointing in the direction of a street. Lupa looked, blinking her eyes hard. Reenactors, dressed in the togas and caligae of her people, the arms and armor of her legions. Performances featuring many popular Roman plays, both comedies and tragedies. Even from up high, the she-wolf recognized one that highlighted Jupiter's earthly escapades. It was then Lupa realized it was not through her own eyes she saw it all, but through that of the people. So long has it been since her people drew their last breath. Though her people are gone, forgotten were they not.

"On this day, the people celebrate the founding of Roma, a city in which your people's legacy still live," exclaimed the young wolf. "So how about you partake in this food and wine, Madre, and remember that no Being's ever a failure?" With that, the young wolf pushed forth the bottle with one paw, the basket with the other.

Lupa licked her lips. Uncorking the bottle, she brought it up to her muzzle, a weight far less than that of her amphora. Visually, it told her nothing about what to expect. Scent-wise, it carried myriads of distinctive flavors, flavors that she recognized not just that of Roma, but would later know as those from the many states of Italia. Where Roma was but one domain, such was a united Italia, all under one flag, one guardian.

She had to admit, this wine tasted damn good.

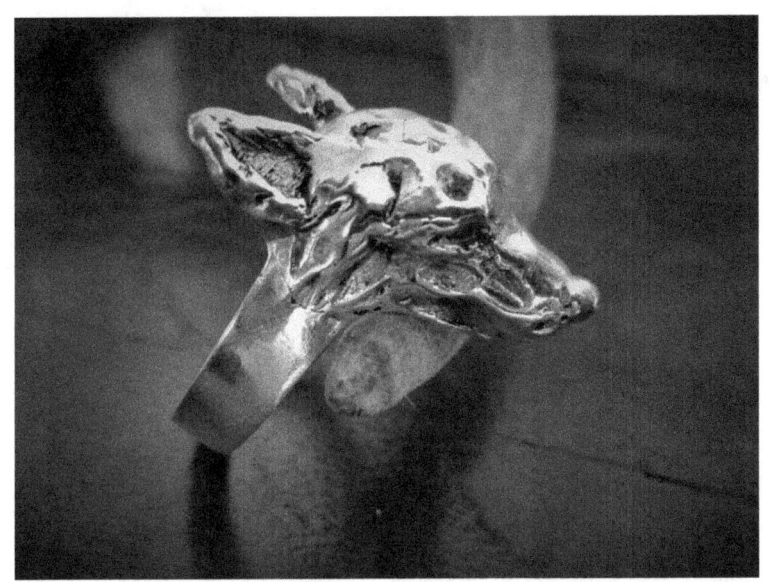

WOLF RING
Monique Box

THE RED COVENANT
Dana Sonnenschein

Based on "Story of the Lost Wife," collected by Marie McLaughlin in Myths and Legends of the Sioux *(1916).*

The Dakota move across the high plains, following the buffalo. The men on their hunting ponies, the women and children following with packs and pack ponies loaded with tipis and poles, robes and baskets. One woman lags behind, ribs aching, lip swollen. Her man promised to treat her kindly before she married him, but, if he meant his words, he's forgotten them. Everything she does is wrong, he says. He could just kill her, he says, and she believes him. So, she walks more and more slowly and lets herself drift off in the tall grass.

Hours later, when she's tired, she lies down. When she wakes in the early evening, there's someone beside her, sitting on his haunches, watching her face. He has thick, brushy hair and yellow eyes, but she isn't frightened; he could have killed her while she slept, and she's no longer scared of anything else.

He looks away and gets up. He licks his lips then glances at her and away again in the same direction. Come to my village, and my people will feed you. She rises to follow.

When she gets there, she sees what looks like all the wolves in the world: prairie wolves and timber wolves and crowds of coyotes. Her guide and his wife are the chief wolves, with a den dug into a hillside, where she is welcomed by their children who lick her face and whine. The she-wolf is a beautiful golden color that shines nearly white in the sun, and the pups are tawny or streaked gray like their father. They bite and paw at the woman's braids until she laughs. But she is hungry, and her stomach rumbles.

The wolves offer her a bloody piece of buffalo shoulder. She draws flint and steel from the pouch at her waist and wanders away to gather tinder. She keeps her fire small so no flames frighten the wolves and no smoke smudges the sky.

She stays with the family, sprawling in the sun until her ribs are healed, watching over the new pups in the spring, playing tug-of-war with sticks and bones, trotting after the she-wolf until her legs are stronger than ever. She learns to hear mice in the grass and snatch them up and to distract the buffalo so the wolves can dash in and tear at their ankles and loins. She watches how the young respect their elders, crouching and glancing away. Sometimes, she stares, but then she rolls and shows her belly, and no harm comes to her. At dawn or dusk, they drink at rivers twisting back and forth like snakes or at seeps and hollows not muddied by hooves.

The buffalo move like cloud shadows and thunder over the land, and the wolves follow them. In a year and a day, they arrive back at the Dakota hunting grounds. When the wolves smell the encampment, they bark in alarm and dash back and forth. The young ones cringe, and the older ones' hackles rise.

Later, when she lies down to rest during the hottest part of the afternoon, the chief wolf noses her side. He paws at her legs, growling, and drops something on them. She reaches down and takes up a broken arrow. Sun-warmed, chewed off at one end. He catches her eye and stares off toward the camp. Growls again. Surely, her people do not need to kill the wolves; there is enough buffalo for all of them.

In the cool of the evening, she howls with the pack, and, in the morning, she leaves. The wolves follow her until she reaches the top of a knoll above the hunting camp. Then the chief wolves turn back, the others follow, and she stands, looking down. She can smell people on the wind, and they do not smell like grass and fur and dirt and sunlight, or even like buffalo dung or blood. She feels sick and sits down. And that is where she is when they find her.

When they bring her to her husband, she growls. She tells him the wolves have been kinder to her than he was. Her father and the other men agree.

"When you have hunted," she tells them, "you must make peace with the wolves. You must bring me the tongues and other choice parts of tomorrow's kill, and I will offer them to the pack who treated me as a sister."

And the hunting party does. So the lost wife has some boys bring the ponies to a swale between two hills and unload the packs, piling the meat so high it seems to bridge the hilltops. After they lead the ponies away, she plants a stick on top of the heap and ties a strip of red cloth to the tip. Then she begins to howl.

The wolves come from far and wild, the chief wolves and their family and all the other prairie wolves and the timber wolves and the coyotes. They eat the meat, every last scrap, and lick their paws and muzzles and loll about with their bellies taut as the sun sinks and the light grows longer. At last, they sing and then fade into the dark, leaving her alone. But the chief wolf has brought her a gift, and she holds the broken arrow at her side when she rises and turns toward the faint sound of human voices. If her husband ever raises his paw to her again, she will snarl and let him feel the arrow's tooth.

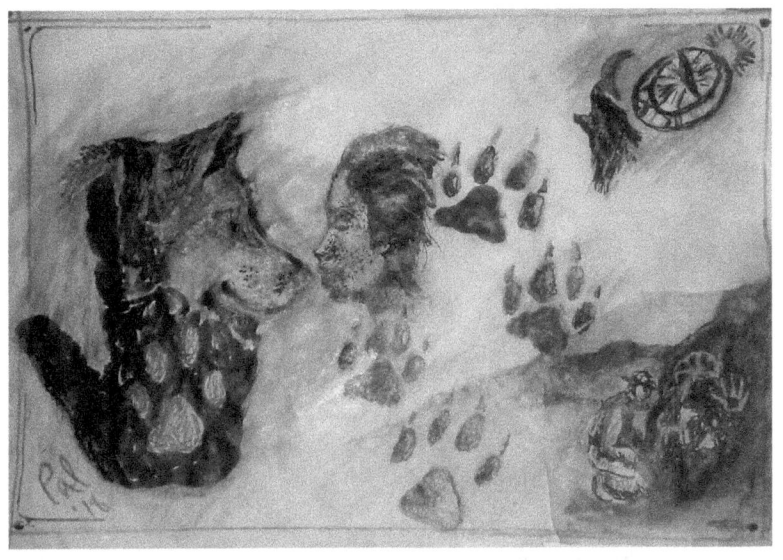

COMPANIONS ACROSS THE TIMELINE
Patricia Lehtola

CEREN
Sorren Redpelt

His name was Ceren. He wasn't sure when he was born, but, at first, there was nothing, then there was him. He opened his eyes to a snow-draped forest, a soft, warm glow in the distance; the great star was leaving. There was something else, a gathering of creatures; weak, feeble minded souls that knew not of the spirits. The moment the white wolf stood up, he felt it in his gut; a twisting feeling that brought feelings of ruination and despair. The shadows were approaching, and they were headed for the town.

The light was trailing toward the soft glow of the great star, and, in its departure, the shadows followed; they sought only death and malice, to claim the souls of the innocent and weak and add to their ranks. It was in this epiphany that Ceren knew why he had been made. He had been made to serve as guardian of this land, to follow the setting of the great star and keep peace between shadow and man.

In a burst of speed and agility, Ceren rushed forward, meeting pace with the last of the great star's light, the shadows now taking visible form. In a burst of primal instinct, Ceren leapt onto one of them, a massive boar three times his size, and bit down with jaws of pure retribution. The creature let out a bone chilling howl as it fell to the ground. Ceren, now filled with a purpose and a desire, leapt onto the massive back of the nearest shadow, a bear taller than the trees themselves. In one swift strike, he plunged, claws first, into the beast. The bear erupted into a nova of light, causing the nearby aberrations to fade like ice in boiling water.

Within the village, the men started to take notice of the commotion going on outside of the gates. The shadows, appearing as simple fauna of the local environment, and Ceren as a beautiful arctic wolf, keeping the creatures from entering their domain.

Ceren continued to combat the creatures long into the night, tearing through the shadows like a wildfire through a forest. As day came, the shadows retreated to their hellish domain from which they came. The villagers, seeing that Ceren was no ordinary wolf, built a statue that would remain in the land for eons to come.

The sun set on the small town. Ceren paced his statue as he watched men in business suits enter their homes and apartments; the children with Walkmans in hand and the young man with a polaroid who lived right by his statue. Everyone thought he was crazy, going to the statue to "pet the nice wolf." Most thought he was simply paying respects in an odd fashion; others thought he may actually believe in the legend of the white wolf.

The man gave Ceren a gentle pat on the head before heading home, the great star, or "sun" as they've come to call it, drawing close to its final minutes upon this land. As they did, the shadows approached once more.

Ceren prepared himself, having grown accustomed to the nightly duels with darkness itself. No one ever saw the creatures anymore except the man, the man with the polaroid. As Ceren leapt onto a shadowy condor, toppling it midair, the man would watch in awe, knowing the wolf was protecting the land he had been born unto.

Once more, Ceren fought well into the night, toppling shadow after shadow until the rising of the great star deterred them from his home. Upon sunrise, the man would leave his home and greet and congratulate Ceren with a piece of cooked meat; the two grew into close friends.

The sun began to set amidst the skyscrapers; kids on their smartphones texting as they entered buildings near them. In an old park to the side of the massive city lay an old wolf statue, Ceren resting under it. No one knew of his presence now save a few children whom he happily greeted with playful licks and even rides while their parents were engrossed in technology. These children brought him great joy.

As with every night, the shadows crept out of their hellscape to hunt the city's inhabitants, Ceren being the lone wolf to defend every last man, woman, and child. Even if they were unaware of his being.

Ceren sunk his teeth into the neck of a leopard and watched as it dissipated. The nights had only gotten more challenging as more people broke from tradition; staying out past sunrise meant there were people more vulnerable to the shadows. Twice, a man had nearly been swallowed whole by a lion and a tiger, both of which became victims to Ceren's holy claws.

Ceren bit through the hide of a rhino as the great star began to emerge, once again causing the creatures of the night to flee.

Time would pass, and customs would change, yet Ceren and his statue would remain upon the land, protecting the innocent and dispensing justice to the creatures of the eternal void. As time went on, the shadows would attempt to attack people through their dreams. Ceren, too, would grow more powerful, splitting his body and sending a portion of himself into the minds of those who needed him, combatting the darkness and comforting the scared citizens. Word of this white wolf entering people's dreams spread, and he became known as the Dreamwalker.

So, should you ever see a white wolf in your dreams, let it be known that you live in Ceren's territory, and no harm shall befall you.

You probably wonder how I could possibly know about all this, don't you? Well, wasn't it obvious from when I started? Perhaps I need to tell my story again, or maybe you'll see it in a dream...

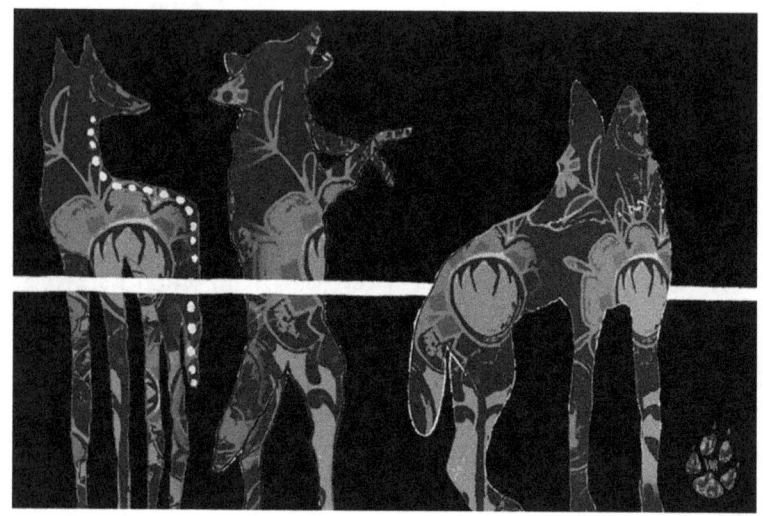

CROSSING THE LINE
Virginia Romero

LEGENDS

Life was easy back then,
or so I've heard.
Those were glory years.
The good old days.
How things have changed.
From open fields
to honey pot prisons,
with trees as our fences,
bullets our cages.
We lay low
awaiting the next blow.
Our plight clearer each day
as we howl,
communicate
with a quieting voice
on either end of the exchange.
When we are gone,
our silence will roar
through the ages,
and we will be legends once more.

—T.F. Webb

Biographies

SHANNON BARNSLEY'S work has appeared in Wolf Warriors, vol. I-IV; The Cost of Paper: Volume Three; Fabulously Feminist; The Concord Monitor; Redhead Magazine; and The Climax. My first book, Beneath Blair Mountain, was published by 1888 in Fall 2015. Shannon is a graduate of the Hampshire College Writing Program.

ROSE LACROIX—I have BA in social science from Portland State University. I have published four novels with Furplanet Productions and short stories in various publications. My first novel, "Basecraft Cirrostratus," was nominated for an Ursa Major Award. My short story "St. John's Bridge" was included in THP's Coyotl award-winning anthology "Arcana." My historical research has been published on Britannica.com.

HJ PANG has been published in several anthologies under the pseudonym of MikasiWolf, and won Third Prize for the Weasel Press' Poetry contest in Feb 2018.

J.D. PHILLIPS— I am a Pennsylvania-based writer of primarily westerns, noir, and crime/police thrillers in novella and novel lengths. My first work, titled 'Folly,' will debut in 'A Sword Master's Tale,' published by Armoured Fox Press and edited by Tarl Hoch.

DANA SONNENSCHEIN—I've had the pleasure of having poems in several previous Wolf Warriors anthologies as well as in online and print journals; I'm currently working on a manuscript mixing flash fiction and poetry about wolves, which I hope will make a good follow-up for my other books, Corvus, Natural Forms, and Bear Country. Visiting the Wolf Conservation Center in South Salem, New York, is my main source of inspiration ... though I've also camped in Yellowstone twice in the last five years and have become an avid wolf-webcam watcher.

IVIC WULFE is a long-standing member of the South African fandom, attempting to ensure that our own group grows, to some extent, in its capacity to levels of familiarity that many other communities across the world enjoy. He runs a, mostly weekly, podcast in conjunction with furry.fm (a Swiss-run furry radio station based in Europe) and is con-chair to the, now completed its second year, "South African Furry Convention" (SAFC). His passion lies in the idea that "furries can and will be furries wherever they are."